# Culture and Customs
## of the Netherlands

Map of Netherlands. Cartography by Bookcomp, Inc.

# Culture and Customs
# of the Netherlands

## JOHN B. RONEY

Culture and Customs of Europe

**GREENWOOD PRESS**
*An Imprint of ABC-CLIO, LLC*

A B C ☰ C L I O

Santa Barbara, California • Denver, Colorado • Oxford, England

**Library of Congress Cataloging-in-Publication Data**

Roney, John B.
    Culture and customs of the Netherlands / John B. Roney.
        p. cm. — (Culture and customs of Europe)
    Includes bibliographical references and index.
    ISBN 978-0-313-34808-2 (hardcopy : alk. paper) — ISBN 978-0-313-34809-9 (ebook)   1. Netherlands—Civilization.   2. Netherlands—Social life and customs. I. Title.
    DJ71.R67   2009
    949.2—dc22        2009024195

13   12   11   10   09      1   2   3   4   5

This book is also available on the World Wide Web as an eBook.
Visit www.abc-clio.com for details.

ABC-CLIO, LLC
130 Cremona Drive, P.O. Box 1911
Santa Barbara, California 93116-1911

This book is printed on acid-free paper ∞

Manufactured in the United States of America

# Contents

# Series Foreword

THE OLD WORLD and the New World have maintained a fluid exchange of people, ideas, innovations, and styles. Even though the United States became the defacto world leader and economic superpower in the wake of a devastated Europe in World War II, Europe has remained for many the standard bearer of Western culture.

Millions of Americans can trace their ancestors to Europe. The United States as we know it was built on waves of European immigration, starting with the English, who braved the seas to found the Jamestown Colony in 1607. Bosnian and Albanian immigrants are some of the latest new Americans. In the Gilded Age of one of our great expatriates, the novelist Henry James, the Grand Tour of Europe was de rigueur for young American men of means to prepare them for a life of refinement and taste. In the more recent democratic age, scores of American college students have Eurorailed their way across Great Britain and the Continent, sampling the fabled capitals and bergs in a mad, great adventure, or have benefited from a semester abroad. For other American vacationers and culture vultures, Europe is the prime destination. What is the new post–Cold War, post–Berlin Wall Europe in the new millennium? Even with the different languages, rhythms, and rituals, Europeans have much in common: They are largely well-educated, prosperous, and worldly. They also have similar goals, face common threats, and form alliances. With the advent of the European Union, the open borders, and the Euro, and considering globalization and the prospect of a homogenized Europe, an updated survey of the region is warranted.

*Culture and Customs of Europe* features individual volumes on the countries most studied for which fresh information is in demand from students and other readers. The Series casts a wide net, including not only the expected countries, such as Spain, France, England, and Germany, but also countries such as Poland and Greece that lie outside Western Europe proper. Each volume is written by a country specialist with intimate knowledge of the contemporary dynamics of a people and culture. Sustained narrative chapters cover the land, the people, and offer a brief history; they also discuss religion, social customs, gender roles, family, marriage, literature and media, performing arts and cinema, and art and architecture. The national character and ongoing popular traditions of each country are framed in a historical context and celebrated along with the latest trends and major cultural figures. A country map, chronology, glossary, and evocative photos enhance the text.

The storied and enlightened Europeans will continue to fascinate Americans. Our futures are strongly linked politically, economically, and culturally.

# Introduction

ALTHOUGH THE NETHERLANDS is a small state in the world, being small in number and even smaller in geographical size, its influence and importance in the growth of modern institutions is a good reason to learn something about its history and character. Its role in medieval Europe was insignificant since it had no agricultural benefits; its low-lying land kept shifting with the wind and water of the sea or the constantly changing patterns and floods from its major rivers. By the High Middle Ages, however, it became a key trade route between the British Isles and the continent. Its rivers became key transportation routes to central Europe; a large volume of goods passed through or were stored in its numerous depots. The cities of the Low Countries developed technical abilities that created extensive textile industries, the printing trade, wind-powered mills and pumps, and later, in the Renaissance, a thriving artistic business. Despite this increased economic activity, however, the many cities and regions of the early Netherlands, which were divided into 17 provinces, remained independent, and a variety of ethnic, cultural, political, and religious groups developed separate from one another.

Because of its central position on the new trade routes of northern Europe, the Renaissance cities and regions of the Low Countries became the battle ground for dynastic European families and kingdoms. Out of this struggle for independence from their Habsburg overlords in Spain emerged one of the most modern states, which developed almost all of the institutions that would later come to characterize the West. Born amid a diversity of political, economic, and religious groups, the Dutch Republic became one of the most pragmatic new states of Europe. Early capitalism, with banks and stock markets, and multiple levels of government that would later develop into democracy, laid the foundations of the modern state very early. A unique Christian piety without strong European institutional affiliation kept the Roman Catholic and Protestant churches divided equally, even though the Reformed Church offered a more pragmatic solution for the new republic.

Today, the Kingdom of the Netherlands is part of the European Union, and as such, has an affinity with its nearby neighbors in terms of history, culture, and identity. Still, there remain several characteristics that maintain its unique national identity and character. The following characteristics are embedded in the history and experience of the Netherlands.

## GEOGRAPHY, CREATION, AND TRANSFORMATION

Geography has played an extremely important role in forming the Netherlands, and the intricate balance between land and water cannot be underestimated. As the people struggled with the storms of the sea and the floods of the great rivers, they learned to control the water, turning it into their greatest resource. Well-known windmills drained the swamps and low-lying lands, and a constant vigilance from these same mills kept the land dry. When attacked by their enemies, the Dutch could reverse the process and re-flood their own space to prevent the attackers from coming any closer to their fortified cities. This necessary struggle forced cooperation far beyond normal. The Dutch also took to the sea, and soon ships sailed to all parts of the world, creating one of the first global economies. Life on the water and traveling across great distances, like life on dike-covered land, made technological inventions a great necessity. Beyond windmills, a variety of efficient boats were developed, and Dutch scientists invented optical equipment for vision both near and far.

## CONSENSUS AND COOPERATION

Beyond its harnessing, the struggle with water had far-reaching consequences. Local dike and flood committees had to work out their differences and maintain control of the dry land. Within their geographical borders, the reality of many small and regionally loyal groups created a long-lasting character for consensus thinking and cooperation. Rather than forming a kingdom or any other variety of lesser dynastic houses in the 16th century, the seven provinces, born in adversity to monarchical power, chose a much looser political arrangement. In their unique republic, coalitions eventually determined policy and executive powers. Although 19th-century Netherlands decided to begin a monarchy, it soon gravitated toward a vibrant constitutional state recognizing many diverse constituencies and its extensive cooperation has been labeled a "consociational democracy." While the clearly defined "pillars" that organized society from the late 19th century until the 1960s did not last, diversity is still officially recognized by the government in its policies toward education, religion, regional interests, and culture.

## CHRISTIANITY, PLURALITY, AND DIVERSITY

A strong sense of religion has always played an important role in the history of the Netherlands, yet it has been one of the states least concerned about large institutional churches. In the High Middle Ages, the independence and personal spirituality of the Modern Devotion, with its mix of mysticism, reform of practices and rituals, education, and ecumenism, became some of the most fruitful ground for Renaissance Humanism and the Protestant and Catholic Reformations. With little ecclesiastical oversight for most of the medieval period and a bitter struggle during the Spanish Inquisition, these experiences ensured that no single religious group would become a state church in the early modern period. Long after the reformations of the 16th century, many new religious movements would be nurtured in the Low Countries, and a diversity of Protestant denominations, Catholic movements, Jews, and, despite some problems, Muslims would find a greater degree of toleration than in most other countries, even today. The history of tolerance and diversity has certainly not been without its problems, but a clear pragmatism in religious matters has been a key characteristic of Dutch society.

When almost every other state in early modern Europe had strict guidelines on printed material, the Netherlandic presses continued to offer a great diversity of opinion in religious, social, and political ideas. The Netherlands has gained a reputation as one of the most tolerant states in the world—indeed, it has been criticized for too much toleration in the 20th century on many social matters, including soft drugs, prostitution, gay and lesbian issues, euthanasia, and radical literature and film. The 21st century has somewhat altered international opinion on many issues, yet Dutch society has also experienced some great shocks as front-page murders of politicians and artists who reacted in more intolerant manners found themselves in open conflict in the culture wars.

## CAPITALISM AND PRAGMATISM

With a lack of traditional natural resources that often supported many other rapidly expanding states, such as large tracts of agricultural land, timber, or minerals, most of what the Netherlands used for their economic growth had to be reclaimed or imported. In time, the Netherlands became one of the first modern economies where early capitalistic institutions and practices flourished. Rivers became highly organized routes for transporting goods from central Europe to the sea, and to organize the flow of goods, its rapidly increasing urban centers became some of the most important harbors and entrepôts in Europe. Amsterdam overtook Antwerp in the early modern period, and today, Rotterdam still ranks as one of the world's largest and busiest ports. In this world of business, where no centralized monarchy controlled the economy, banking, stock companies and stock exchanges, and investment capital all thrived. Without competing with the large grain-producing states of France and central Europe, the Netherlands created a niche market with highly efficient dairy, flower, and vegetable businesses that produced exports for its neighbors. In addition to transforming its own resources into products, its extensive colonies supplied luxury items and spices that greatly increased its wealth. The development of this economy was driven by very pragmatic values and led to greater tolerance. The Jewish community, for example, found a home in the Netherlands and created a thriving diamond and jewelry trade. Other immigrants, when needed in the ship building or sailing industries, could more easily find work there than in many other places.

## COOPERATION AND INTERNATIONALISM

The Netherlands has been at the forefront of international cooperation. As one of the most densely populated areas of Europe, and with little land of its own, the Dutch economy has been more dependent on international cooperation than almost any other state. Hugo Grotius demonstrated this spirit in the 17th century in his book *The Free Sea,* where he explained the necessity of international law that could regulate the seas. After a turbulent 18th century, when it lost most of its colonies to the emerging powers of England and France, a position of neutrality in the 19th century allowed it to operate in a variety of shared international ventures. Larger than but similar to the city and canton of Geneva, some of the first international organizations found their homes within its borders. The Hague has a long reputation for its international courts of law. After the great devastation that World War II wrought on the economy and land, the Netherlands eagerly supported more official international cooperation in business, trade, and politics. The Dutch were one of the original supporters of the League of Nations, NATO, and the United Nations. The BENELUX trade pact between Belgium, the Netherlands, and Luxembourg became the predecessor of the European Economic Community and later, the European Union. In more recent times, the Netherlands has sent key advisors and a small force of soldiers to war-torn areas of the world, and they have been involved in the most recent conflicts in Iraq and Afghanistan.

Given the themes that characterize the Netherlands, one can see that a unique combination of factors has facilitated the rise of a modern state. Constant pressure to regulate wind and water, trade and travel, and ideas and investments has created a culture that has adapted to an ever-changing world. Because of its unique geography and diversity, the Netherlands has often been first to experiment with new institutional organizations and social programs. Today, it plays an important role through its international corporations and economic interests, diplomacy and legal institutions, philanthropy, and not only physical but social engineering. With increasing population throughout the world, and the possible decrease of land due to rising sea levels, the Netherlands will continue to provide an example of how to deal with these problems long before many other states face the same dilemmas.

# Chronology

## Medieval Netherlands

692        Anglo-Saxon missionary to the Frisians Willibrord, Bishop of Utrecht 695–739, and established the Abbey at Echternoch, Luxembourg.

862        County of Flanders formally established as a feudal fief by Charles the Bald, king of Western Francia.

922        Dirk I, first Count of Holland, established rule.

1300s      Modern Devotion reform of Christianity, with lay piety built on mysticism, tertiary monastic movements, and humanism.

1312      *Blijde Inkomst/ joyeuse entrée*: urban elite formed Council of Kortenberg. Subjects free to disregard dukes who transgressed the law.

## Burgundian Netherlands (1384–1477)

1387      Geert Groot founded the Brethren of the Common Life; a new Augustinian monastery was founded in Windesheim by Florens Radewyns.

1404      50,000 people perish in the Flanders and Zeeland floods.

1418      *Imitation of Christ* by Thomas á Kempis is published.

1421      St. Elizabeth's Flood in which 100,000 people perish.

## Habsburg Netherlands (1477–1556)

| | |
|---|---|
| 1477 | Mary of Burgundy forced to grant *Grand Privilège* to Flanders, Holland, and Zeeland. |
| 1530 | St. Felix's Flood in which 400,000 people perish. |
| 1548 | Burgundian *Kries*: formal tie of 17 Provinces to Holy Roman Empire. |
| 1549 | Charles V introduced the Pragmatic Sanction, a unified dynastic law of succession, declaring the Netherlands "forever one and indivisible." |

## Spanish Netherlands (1556–1581)

| | |
|---|---|
| 1561–1564 | Spanish Inquisition in the Low Countries. |
| 1568 | William of Orange invades Brabant and rejects the King of Spain. |
| 1568–1648 | Eighty Years War and the Dutch Revolt against Habsburg Spain. |
| 1569 | Spanish General Alva assembled States General and imposed higher taxes. |
| 1570 | All Saints' Day Flood; a "hyper-storm" over 16 feet (five meters). |
| 1573–1574 | Spanish Siege of Leiden. |
| 1575 | Union of Holland and Zeeland. |
| 1576 | (Nov. 8) Pacification of Ghent. |
| 1577 | Treaty of *Satisfactie*. William of Orange grants religious peace between Protestants and Catholics. |
| 1579 | Division of the Low Countries: 10 southern provinces remain with Spain under the Union of Arras; seven northern provinces join the Protestant Union of Utrecht. |
| 1580 | Act of Adjuration repudiated the sovereignty of Philip II. The Oath of Adjuration signed July 26, 1581. |

## Republic of the Seven United Netherlands/Dutch Republic (1581–1795)

| | |
|---|---|
| 1584 | Murder of William of Orange. Spanish conquered Ghent, Brussels, Antwerp; 200,000 people fled. |
| 1584–1702 | The "Golden Age" of science (Huygens, van Leeuwenhoek, Leeghwater); art (Rembrandt, Vermeer, Hals); and trade and wealth. |
| 1602 | VOC: *Verenigde Oostindische Compagnie* (United East India Company) founded with trade monopoly for Asia. |

| | |
|---|---|
| 1609 | Peace between the Dutch rebels and Spain (Twelve Year Truce); Amsterdam Exchange Bank founded. |
| 1618 | National synod at Dordrecht and "States Bible" established. |
| 1621 | GWIC or WIC: *Geoctroyeerde Westindische Compagnie* (West India Company) founded with trade monopoly for West Africa and the Americas. |
| 1648 | Peace of Westphalia grants the United Provinces full independence. |
| 1650–1672 | First stadholderless period. |
| 1652–1654 | First Anglo-Dutch War. |
| 1665–1667 | Second Anglo-Dutch War. |
| 1672 | *Rampjaar* (disaster year): England, France, Münster, and Cologne attacked the United Provinces. The Grand Pensionary Johan de Witt lynched. William III restored to stadholder. Third Anglo-Dutch War, 1672–1674. |
| 1674 | (Feb. 19) Netherlands and England signed the Peace of Westminster. New Amsterdam became the English New York. |
| 1677 | (Nov. 4) William III of Orange married Mary Stuart and became King of England, Ireland, and Scotland, and remained stadholder until his death in 1702. |
| 1689–1697 | War of the League of Augsburg/*Negenjarige Oorlog* (Nine Years War) with France. Peace of Rijswijk in 1697. |
| 1702–1747 | Second stadholderless period. |
| 1780–1784 | Fourth Anglo-Dutch War. |
| 1791 | GWIC or WIC and VOC liquidated. VOC renamed Council of Asian Possessions. |
| 1793 | (Feb. 1) France declared war on Britain and the Netherlands. |

## Batavian Republic (1795–1806)

| | |
|---|---|
| 1795 | (May 16) The Hague Agreement created Batavian Republic. |
| 1795–1806 | William V, last stadholder, led the Government of the Dutch Republic in Exile in London. |
| 1795–1802 | Fifth Anglo Dutch War; Peace of Amiens. |

## Kingdom of Holland (1806–1810)

| | |
|---|---|
| 1806 | King Louis (Lodewijk) Bonaparte becomes king of Holland. |

## First French Empire (1810–1813)

1813        (Dec. 2) William VI Prince of Orange–Nassau declared sovereign of
            the Netherlands after liberation by Prussian and Russian troops.

## United Kingdom of the Netherlands (1815–Present)

1815        United Kingdom of the Netherlands created by the Congress of
            Vienna, and Prince William VI declared himself William I King of
            the Netherlands and Duke of Luxembourg.

1831        (Aug. 2–12) The Dutch army invaded Belgium in the "Ten Days
            Campaign" and defeated Belgian forces near Hasselt and Leuven.

1834        *Afscheiding*: Hendrick de Cock succeeded from the state church,
            forming the Christian Reformed Church.

1838        William I signed the Partition of Belgium.

1839        (April 19) The Treaty of London recognized the independence of
            Belgium, and placed the Duchy of Limburg and Grand Duchy of
            Luxembourg in personal union under William I.

1840        (Oct. 8) King William I of Holland abdicated to his son William II.

1848        New Constitution headed by Johan Rudolf Thorbecke.

1849        William II abdicated to his son William III.

1853        Pope Pius IX created an Archbishoporic in Utrecht, with subordinate
            bishops in Haarlem, 's-Hertogenbosch, Breda, and Roermond.

1857        Van der Brugghen Law on Education of 1857 continued the prin-
            ciples of the 1806 law, with no government support for private
            schools. The *Schoolstrijd* began.

1860        Railways Act of 1860 created a state railway system.

1864        "Confessional Union" established under Guillaume Groen van Prin-
            sterer.

1874        Labor Act banned children under 12 and limited women to 11-hour
            days.

1879        Anti-Revolutionary Party (ARP) founded by Abraham Kuyper.

1886        *Doleantie* split the Dutch Reformed Church. In 1892, the Reformed
            Churches in the Netherlands were founded, merging with many *Af-
            scheiding* churches.

1890        William III died, and his wife Emma became Queen-Regent until
            their daughter Wilhelmina reached the age of 18 in 1898, becoming

the first queen of the Netherlands. Grand Duchy of Luxembourg separated from the Netherlands.

1890    The Royal Dutch Petroleum Company was founded.

1891    (May 15) Gerard and Anton Philips began their Philips & Co. in Eindhoven.

1899    First International Peace Conference in The Hague. Andrew Carnegie funded the construction of the Palace of Peace.

1900    Compulsory Education Act. 1901 law allowed state to take neglected children.

1917    New constitution. 1922: universal suffrage.

1920    Netherlands joined the League of Nations.

1920    KLM Royal Dutch Airlines established.

1930    British Lever Bros. merged with Dutch Margarine Union to form Unilever.

1932    *Afsluitdijk* dam completed.

1940    (May 10) German *blitzkrieg* of the Netherlands, Belgium, and Luxembourg.

1941    (Aug. 18) The concentration camp at Amersfoort opened.

1941    (Nov. 25) German Jews in Netherlands were declared stateless.

1942    (June 9) 3 million Dutch were sent to Eastern Europe.

1942    (July 9) Anne Frank and her family in hiding.

1944    (Aug. 4) Nazi police arrested eight people, including 15-year-old Anne Frank. She died at the Bergen-Belsen concentration camp in the spring of 1945.

1944    (Sept. 5) "Mad Tuesday": 65,000 Dutch Nazi collaborators fled to Germany.

1945    (May 5) Netherlands and Denmark were liberated from Nazi control.

        (Dec. 27) The Dutch formally relinquished sovereignty to Indonesia.

1948    (April 18) International Court of Justice opened at The Hague.

1948    (Sept. 4) Queen Wilhelmina abdicated to her daughter Juliana.

1949    (Dec. 27) Queen Juliana granted sovereignty to the United States Indonesia.

1950    The first Delta Works dam was completed in Brielsegatdam; the last was finished in 1997.

1951    Treaty of Paris created the European Coal and Steel Community

1953    (Jan.) A powerful storm breached sea dikes in the south of the Netherlands, killing more than 1,800 people.

1957    Eastern Flevoland polder completed.

1968    Southern Flevoland polder completed.

1980    Queen Juliana abdicated the throne to her daughter Beatrix (1938–).

1992    (Feb. 7) Maastricht Treaty formed the European Union.

1997    Maaslandkering and the Hartelkering dikes completed (one of the seven engineering wonders of the world).

1999    (Jan. 1) The new Euro monetary system began.

2002    Brothels and euthanasia "legalized," with strict guidelines, and can still lead to criminal offense. Amsterdam cut brothels by half.

        (May 6) Pim Fortuyn shot to death in Hilversum.

2003    Marijuana legal at Dutch pharmacies for medicinal purposes.

2003    *Protestantse Kerk Nederland* (PKN) union of Protestant churches established.

2003    (Sept. 30) Air France purchased KLM airlines.

2004    (Nov. 2) Filmmaker Theo van Gogh is murdered.

2007    Royal Bank of Scotland Group (with Fortis and Santander) purchased ABN-AMRO bank; then in 2008 it was purchased by Deutsche Bank.

2007    Royal Philips Electronics purchase Genlyte Group, Kentucky, making Philips the biggest lighting firm in the American market.

2008    Geert Wilders (parliamentarian) released his film *Fitna* (linking violence with the Qur'an).

2009    400th anniversary celebration of Henry Hudson and the founding of New Amsterdam ("400 Jaar Nieuw Amsterdam"); 400th anniversary of trade with Japan ("400 Jaar Handel").

        Royal Dutch Shell paid the family of a slain Nigerian environmental activist $15.5 million.

# 1

# Land, People, and History

## GEOGRAPHY AND LAND

### Geography

"God created the world and the Dutch created the Netherlands" is a common saying used to describe the Netherlands. Approximately 24 percent of this northwestern European country's dry land is below sea level, including a significant portion of the land devoted to agricultural and urban sites. Due to this low elevation, the modern-day Netherlands and Belgium, as well as Luxembourg, which has a historic connection with these two countries, have been collectively termed the "Low Countries." Any land that has been permanently reclaimed from either swamp or open water is called *polder* or *koog* in Dutch. Another 25 percent of the Netherlands's land is just above sea level, but is vulnerable to floods from either ocean inundation or overflow from the major European rivers that pass through the land, bound for the ocean. In the late ancient world and during the Middle Ages, the few inhabitants of these low-lying areas survived by building small raised mounds (4–25 feet high, [1.2–7.6 meters]) called "terps" (*terpen*). Despite periodic inundation from the sea or rising rivers, inhabitants, homes, and animals could be protected from the water, as some 900 terps dotted the landscape. Useable land was further diminished, however, by the extensive use of peat as fuel and, to some extent, the extraction of salt; over time, the inland lakes actually grew larger. It is important to point out that around the year 1000 AD, more than half of today's *polder* regions simply did not exist, and much of the land that existed to the west of the Low Countries was uninhabitable.

By 1200, parts of the western delta area had begun to naturally silt up from North Sea storms, and blowing sand increased the protective dunes that formed along the coast. Local inhabitants organized and began to co-operate to build dikes, dams, and, in many cases, connecting terps to try to control the forces of nature. In regions characterized by population increases, councils were formed to control the flow of water. By the late Middle Ages, these councils were led by dike barons. The English word "landscape" is de-rived from the Dutch *landschap* that combines "land" with the suffix *schap,* meaning "ship" in English, in the sense of human creativity and skill, such as "craftsmanship." This is significant because the Dutch viewed their relation-ship with water and land as a delicate balance wherein they needed to be extremely diligent to ensure enough dry land, while recognizing that their very livelihood depended on access to the sea and the cultivation of water-logged regions. Later, the term "landscape" was used to describe nature paint-ing or nature that had been maintained by human hands and highlighted by the vision of the artist, who told the story of that creation.

By the 16th century, much larger systems were organized throughout the Low Countries to control the great rivers: the Rhine (Rijn), with its distribu-tary rivers Lek, Waal, and IJssel, which branch off, the Meuse (Maas), and the Schedlt, which generally flow north and then west through the lower portions of the Netherlands. But what the great rivers may have taken away in flooding, they gave back in land over time. Originating in the Alps and central Europe, the sand, silt, and gravel washed down to the coastal deltas of the Low Countries, creating alluvial plains. One vast new area became known as Zeeland, literally "sea-land," for its shifting islands and coastal duns, which created a rich environment for fish and shellfish in the estuaries. Grasses, plants, and arable land were established here, as well.

The entire region can be geographically divided into the low Netherlands and the high Netherlands. The actual height above sea level is not extreme but it is different enough to distinguish the permanent land and vegetation in the higher elevations from the changing land and water in the lower elevations. The country's higher elevations are found predominantly in the eastern and southern regions. The highest elevation of 322 meters (1,059 feet) is evident in Vaalserberg, which is located in the province of Limburg at the southern-most tip on the border with Belgium and Germany. By contrast, the low Netherlands is comprised of either polder or land merely a meter above sea level. However, the coastal dunes rise from 10 meters (33 feet) to as high as 50 meters (165 feet), protecting the Rhine-Meuse Delta and western regions. The lowest point in the Delta region, Prins Alexander

Provinces of the Netherlands. Cartography by Bookcomp, Inc.

Polder, just west of Rotterdam, is actually 6.7 meters (22 feet) below sea level, and only constant drainage keeps this area somewhat dry. Today, the Netherlands measures 193 kilometers (120 miles) from east to west, and 306 kilometers (190 miles) from north to south.

The Netherlands is often referred to as Holland since the province of Holland has been the heart of political, economic, and religious developments, and the modern Dutch language is largely based on the dialect *Hollandse,* which has been common to this region since the Middle Ages. The origin of the term "Holland" is somewhat disputed, but all of the possible origins tend to describe the land in some way. This term can easily be linked to the English word "hol," meaning low or hollow and is used in the region of East Anglia, England where similar conditions exist. In another tradition, the Viking word *Halland,* a region in Sweden, may have been assigned to an area the Vikings raided. But a better case can be made for its derivation from the ancient Saxon word *holtland,* meaning woodland and referring to the more permanent locations of the higher elevations. In this case, the high Netherlands is comprised of low pine forests and scrub-brushed plains that are quite unsuitable for agriculture on the scale for which Medieval nobility searched in extending their feudal manor estates from central and southern Europe. Clay soil needs extensive fertilizers for higher production, and this was not possible until the Renaissance.[1] Some of the oldest European terms refer simply to the "lands over there," or *landen van herwaarts over* in low German or Dutch and *pays par deça* in French, because they had very little agricultural value.

### Early Land Reclamation

Until the 16th century, land reclamation was limited by the available technology. Early dike construction consisted of building low fences out of twigs and sticks harvested from young shoots and branches extracted from fast-growing trees and bushes, with wooden poles used to provide some stability. Any available rocks and gravel were then mounded next to the fences, and covered with sand, clay, and soil. These earliest dikes were hardly reliable, however, and periodic flooding kept farming to a minimum; constant rebuilding was necessary. A series of sluices—called *sluis* in Dutch, from which the English word stems—functioned as locks allowing various water levels and flows to be regulated. The sluices carried off water when the tides were low, and closed when the tides came in. This created the first newly claimed land, yet the area remained small. Lake Flavo was the largest natural inland lake in the north, but in 1170, a great North Sea storm, known as the All Saints Flood, broke through the narrow strip of land at one point and opened it up to the salty ocean environment, forming the Zuider Zee.

Substantial land reclamation and protection could not be sustained until more modern technology was adapted. Although windmills (*molen*) are today synonymous with the Netherlands, they were used for milling grains in the ancient Mediterranean world. The Dutch began to employ them for pumping water, and given the steady North Sea winds and flat lands, it was possible to begin to drain vast areas of waterlogged deltas. Another innovation was the construction of lighter, hollow wooden mills, rather than the heavier solid stone of the south. This enabled the mills to be constructed on newly formed dikes that did not have a stable land mass. Windmills for drainage first appeared in the southern Low Countries (Belgium) in the 1300s, but moved north to Holland by 1400 and became far more extensive. But the technology and funds required to construct a sufficient number of mills to drain large areas of land did not come until the 16th century. Jan Adriaenszoon Leeghwater is the famous hydraulic engineer who designed systems of drainage and land reclamation on a massive scale, particularly in north Holland, where he used 43 windmills to lift water four feet, with dikes reclaiming 17,500 acres of land. In 1999, UNESCO named the Beemster Polder a World Heritage Site.[2]

Windmills were also used in the new industries, including wind-powered sawmills, grain, oilseed, or plants for dyes, all of which fed the shipbuilding and textile industries that thrived in Holland. The refinement of windmills for draining water became far more effective by the 1650s when the Archimedean screw was employed. During the third century BC, Archimedes had designed a cylinder with a revolving screw to lift water, and this was fitted to the redesigned windmills. The number of windmills steadily increased, and by 1800, there were more than 9,000 windmills, but shortly thereafter, the steam-powered pumps became far more efficient and powerful for any future land drainage.

Modern Archimedean screw pumps in *Kinderdijk* continue to drain an enormous amount of water. Courtesy of the author.

Once windmills could be employed to drain larger areas of land, a series of dikes were constructed on a massive scale. Within the largest dikes, smaller dikes surrounded areas with canals, which further drained water from the lowest lying areas, forming honeycombed patterns. A newly claimed piece of land required constant draining, however, since water percolation continued. When the water level of the new land was finally manageable, this land became known as a *polder*. In the years 1200–1400, only about 135 square miles (350 square kilometers) of land were reclaimed in each century. The next century increased this reclamation to 164 square miles (425 square kilometers), and the 16th century nearly doubled it to 274 square miles (710 square kilometers). But when both technology and wealth increased from 1600–1700, more than 432 square miles (1,120 square kilometers) became polders.

In 1505, the house in Delft of the chairman of the polder board (Gemeenlandhuis), Jan de Huyter, was decorated with the coat of arms of the most powerful members. Courtesy of the author.

## History of Floods

The Netherlands has been called a "diluvial culture" since the struggle against the sea and the floodwaters of the great European rivers that flow through its heartland has made land reclamation and protection a significant aspect of its history and culture. Rather than merely creating barriers of protection against water, the Dutch have embraced the water for transportation, irrigation, pleasure, and even for moral lessons. According to Simon Schama, "They may be said to have lived in a Christianized diluvian culture in the sense that the behavior of the waters acted as the arbiter of their safety and freedom. From whether the flood came as a benediction or malediction, victory or nemesis, friend or foe, harbinger or destroyer, they might learn whether they continued to enjoy the protection of the Almighty."[3] Cooperation in community, prayer, and vigilance, and the constant work to maintain dikes, became the routine of daily life.

Prior to the 16th century, the human toll from floods was devastating. In 1212, a flood killed approximately 60,000 people, and seven years later, another 36,000 were killed in the St. Marcellus' Flood in the Zuider Zee region. While the Bubonic plagues of the 14th century claimed more than a third of the population, severe floods returned in the early 15th century. In 1404, 50,000 were killed in Flanders and Zeeland, and in 1421, the worst recorded flood, known as the St. Elizabeth's Flood due to its occurrence on the saint's day, swallowed up more than 100,000 people and 73 villages in the center of one of the most prosperous areas of Holland. A popular legend surrounding this event claimed that a cradle containing a baby with a cat perched on top miraculously washed ashore, and the two were saved. The phrase "cat in a cradle" was coined as a result, while the new system of dikes became known as *Kinderdijk,* or children's dikes. But despite the newer technology, in 1530, an unprecedented storm known as the St. Felix's Flood claimed the lives of 400,000. The highest recorded level of floodwater came in a hyper-storm of 1570, the All Saints' Day Flood, which rose to over 16 feet (5 meters), or well over the average sea level. In 1997, *Kinderdijk* was placed on the UNESCO list of World Heritage sites, as it contains 19 windmills that were built around 1740.

The struggle that the Dutch constantly faced with water could be transformed into a line of defense. When the Spanish tried to capture the northern provinces that had declared themselves independent of their Habsburg overlords, the greatest Dutch defense was to open the dikes and flood their own land. When the Duke of Alva, King Philip's northern governor and military general, sent 86,000 troops to conquer the important city of Leiden, the newly inundated land kept the Spanish troops at bay, while at the same

*Kinderdijk* windmills sit atop a dike that drains one of the largest poldered areas in the south of Holland. Today, it represents the largest collection of older structures and is a UNESCO World Heritage site. Courtesy of the author.

time allowing some small Dutch ships to support the tired Leideners with new firepower and supplies. This tactic also worked against the French in 1672, and during World War II against the Germans, who were unable to move their heavy tanks and artillery through the flooded polder regions of Holland.

### Modern Land Management and Reclamation

With the advent of steam engines in the early 19th century, it became possible to dig extensive canals throughout the Netherlands. One of the primary goals of Willem I, the first Dutch monarch of the newly formed Kingdom of the Netherlands in 1814, was to modernize and renovate the economy. Although some funds were spent on the construction of roads, which demanded extensive bridge building, Willem I concentrated on inland waterways and canals that had the advantage of connecting existing rivers together for far more efficient transportation. In the north, the Dutch needed to solve the problem of Amsterdam trade with a new waterway. The older routes through the Zuider Zee had silted up, and this stifled trade. From 1820–1824, a 47 mile

(75 kilometers) canal, the Great North-Holland Canal, was dug in order to connect Amsterdam to the North Sea. In the south, another transportation problem was solved by digging a 76 mile (123-kilometer) canal in order to shorten the distance from Maastricht and 's-Hertogenbosch, bypassing the much longer Maas River, with its shallow shoals and uneven widths. Finally, the most important central European river, the Rhine, required additional and better transportation. In 1824, the Cologne Passage canal was excavated, and in 1826, the *Zederik Kanaal* covered the final 53 miles (85 kilometers), connecting Amsterdam with the Rhine. Finally, in 1830, the *Voornsche Kanaal* was excavated, but the project was not completed until 1866 when the North Sea Canal began to be dug, making it a very efficient means to sail larger ships directly from the North Sea to Amsterdam. By 1876, the basic canal was dug and a series of locks allowed a proper flow of water and ease of transport. Today, there are more than 2,244 miles (3,611 kilometers) of canals through the Netherlands, which is double the total length of the 1,511 miles (2,432 kilometers) devoted to the railway lines. In addition to creating more efficient and direct inland water routes, in 1823, the country founded the Netherlands Steamboat Company in Rotterdam, and steam-powered barges, too, could travel much faster and more efficiently.

Steam engines increased the effectiveness of pumping, and soon the windmill was replaced by large steam-pumping stations. One of the first large projects to be completed was the construction of the large inland Haarlemmermeer (lake), where the extensive Schiphol airport is now located, just south of Amsterdam. Although plans had been drawn up much earlier to drain the lake, no permanent solution was found until 1836. Plans were proposed by Leeghwater in 1643, by Nicolaus Samuel Cruquius in 1742, and by Baron van Lijnden van Hemmen in 1820, but it took a violent storm in 1836 to finally convince Willem I that land reclamation and a series of dikes was needed as a permanent solution to the problem. By 1839, a canal encircling the lake, the Ringvaart, allowed for the disposal of lake water, and this canal later served as a means of transportation. In the years 1848–52, the Haarlemmermeer was pumped dry by means of three steam-powered pumping stations called *gemaal* and named Cruquius, Leegwater, and Lijnden in honor of these earlier engineers. Today, there is a Museum De Cruquius in place of the old De Cruquius pumping station, not far from Schiphol airport, which was part of the extensive line of forts and canals that surround the Amsterdam region, called the Defense Line of Amsterdam. This includes 84 miles (135 kilometers) of canals with 42 forts, a design that allows the region to be flooded during an invasion.[4] UNESCO has designated two pumping stations as World Heritage Sites, including the De Cruquius pumping station and the Ir. D. F. Woudagemaal (D.F. Wouda

Steam Pumping Station) in Friesland—currently the largest steam-powered pumping station in the world.

Despite the successful construction of inland waterways and land reclamation, the Netherlands continued to exhibit some vulnerability to storms from the North Sea. Disastrous storms devastated the country's coastal defenses in 1894 and 1916. Two areas were in need of massive projects that only the newest 20th-century technology could now accomplish: the northern Zuider Zee region and the southern Rhine-Meuse Delta region. In the north, the Zuider Zee needed to be controlled by a massive dike dividing the North Sea from the once inland Lake Flavo, now the Zuider Zee. Construction on the *Afsluitdijk* closure dike of 32 kilometers (20 miles) began in 1927 and was completed in 1932, forming the inland freshwater IJsselmeer. Once this was accomplished, engineers began to build more dikes to create several new polder areas within the vast new lake.

The Dutch have created the most amount of new polder in the 20th century with more than 734 square miles (1,900 square kilometers) of new land. The newest polder was the Wieringermeer, completed in 1930, and it created more land in the northern part of Holland. Once the water is pumped from within the largest polder, the land is still quite wet, and therefore smaller ditches are constructed to constantly drain water into larger canals that eventually pumped water out of the polder by the *gemaal* stations. To create a fail-safe system of pumps, Dutch engineers have purposefully used different means of power; some stations use diesel, while others use electricity. Despite these very modern means of power, which have replaced the windmill, the most effective means of pumping water today is still the ancient Archimedes' screw.

The next polder in the Zuider Zee region, the Noordoostpolder, connects the small islands of Urk and Schokland with the Frisian land for the first time in 1942. In 1995 UNESCO designated Schokland and the surrounding polder as a World Heritage Site. After World War II, work began on the Flevoland polders, and in 1957 Eastern Flevoland was completed, and the Southern Flevoland in 1968. In order to plan for another polder in the future, the Houtribdijk was constructed in 1975 to divide the remainder of the IJsselmeer in half, creating the Maarkermeer to the south. Plans had been designed to construct the Maarkerwaard *polder,* but with changing demographics and land use, this has been put on hold.

The second important area to control was the Rhine-Meuse Delta region.[5] While work had already started in 1950 with a dam in Brielsegatdam, the most devastating modern flood came on January 31, 1953, along the Rhine-Meuse Delta, when floodwaters from a raging North Sea storm covered vast areas of south Holland with well over 10 feet (3 meters) of salty water. This devastating storm killed more than 1,800 people, and across the English Channel it killed 307 people in Eastern England. The massive storm also killed 200,000 farm animals , 50,000 buildings were demolished, and flooded 500,000 acres (200,000 hectares). The Hoek van Holland on the North Sea area of Rotterdam reached 12 feet (3.80 meters). The project to construct dikes and dams differed from the Zuider Zee construction. Whereas the Zuider Zee project had a protective element to it, extensive poldering of vast new land was an important component; the Delta works had a primary interest in protecting the vast estuaries that were prime fishing reserves, and secondarily recreational areas. The important goal was to allow the Rhine and Maas Rivers and their connecting rivers to flow freely and safely to the North Sea, and to regulate the effect of the storms that periodically inundated Zeeland. Unlike the wide mouth of the Zuider Zee, which opened to the North Sea, Zeeland had a series of islands separated by far closer alluvial plains.

A series of dams were constructed at the far end of the islands, creating protective estuaries. The real challenge was to then create a series of openings to the sea to allow for ships and fishing boats, and to allow the natural

The Delta Works (Deltawerken) are designed to protect the important estuaries in the southern Netherlands, where the fishing and shell-fish industries thrive. When the North Sea is storming, massive gates are lowered, keeping the rising seas at bay. Courtesy of Hans Grootveld.

exchange of water, as well as to release river floodwaters. From 1958 to 1987, seven dams successfully closed of all inland waters to the North Sea. At the same time, a series of sluices carried off some water and, in addition, the important storm surge barriers (*kering*) were also necessary where the main shipping lanes met the open sea. The Eastern Scheldt (River) Storm Surge Barrier was constructed in 1986, resulting in one of the engineering wonders of the world, with 63 hydraulic-powered sluice gates, each 20 feet (6 meters) tall. The final project, the massive Maaslandkering was completed in 1997, further protecting one of the world's largest harbors, Rotterdam, from dangerous North Sea surges. The Delta Works has now successfully completed 10,250 miles (16,000 kilometers) of dikes and 300 water control structures for one of the largest water protection systems in the world.

Floods continue to challenge the Dutch landscape, and in recent times, new techniques for flood control have actually returned some flood plains back to their natural habitat as marshland and low-lying areas. In 1990, the government approved a plan to return approximately 600,000 acres (242,000 hectacres) of current farmland, or about one-tenth, to wetlands, lakes, and some forest. With the new threat of global warming and the rise of sea levels, the Dutch are continually raising the level of the major dikes and studying new ways to live with the surrounding water. Today, the Dutch government spends approximately $400 million (286 million euros) a year to maintain the polders.[6]

The 1953 massive flood in South Holland and Zeeland inundated the polder, as shown here with flooded green houses. Courtesy of Hans Grootveld.

## THE DUTCH PEOPLE

### Indigenous People

Any discussion that attempts to define the Dutch people must address several issues. On the one hand, the oldest concepts of ethnicity (ethnos) and "nation" help define a group of people with a similar or unique combination of genetics and a common culture comprised of several elements, such as language, customs and laws, and religion. In the modern world, the "state" is defined as a group of people who are citizens with officially recognized nationality, regardless of ethnicity, and are granted citizenship, which is a political term alone. With far greater ability to travel and migrate, we are far more aware of ethnic diversity within the modern state. The modern notion of citizen, including all permanent residents, could not be applied until the 19th century.

During the Roman Empire, the Roman historian Tacitus, in his book *Germania,* recognized several different tribes inhabiting the area of the Low Countries. The area below the Rhine-Meuse Delta was originally inhabited by many Celtic tribes, and the Romans called this area Gaul. Once Julius Caesar, as described in his *De Bello Gallico,* had been successful in defeating many uprisings, he incorporated many of the Celts into the greater Empire. When the Roman hegemony had come to an end, the Sallic Franks, one of many Germans tribes, began to move in. Two particular northern peoples have become famous for their efforts to remain independent of the Romans and other outside powers. The Belgae were Celtic people with approximately 16 tribes, and were located to the north of the Loire, as well as in a settlement in southern Britain; in both locations, the Romans always described them as fierce warriors. Another group of people, the Batavians, originally from central Germany, settled in the land between the Rhine and Waal Rivers. Today, this is called the Betuwe area, and the central city, the former capital of the Batavians, is Nijmegen. The cities of Utrecht and Leiden, which were important Roman border fortress cities on the old Rhine River that passed to the North Sea, are a lasting reminder of the extent of the early Roman settlements in the north.

To the north of the Rhine-Meuse Delta, from Zeeland along the western coastal areas as far north as the southern reaches of Denmark, were the Frisian (Frisii) peoples. They had a maritime culture of fishing and trade, and their language was a distinctive departure from the German dialects developing in the High Middle Ages. One can see some resemblances with old English since Frisian is halfway between High German and English. The Frisians signed a treaty with the Romans in order to remain unoccupied. By the High Middle Ages, the lower Frisians distinguished themselves as

Hollanders, partially due to the changing land masses that separated them from the northern groups. Along the north east border, the German Saxons spread their culture and language, and as late as the 16th century, many cities on both sides of the Ems River, such as Emden, were vibrant centers for northern Netherlands trade and culture. When the Reformation came to the Low Countries in the mid-16th century, this area of western Saxony was an important place of refuge from Spanish oppression.

When the Low Countries entered the early Renaissance period, the Franks inhabiting the southern Low Countries distinguished themselves as a common Flemish people opposed to the growing power of French nobility centered in Paris. In 1302, the Flemish defeated the French in the Battle of the Golden Spurs (named for the many spurs collected from defeated cavalry) and rejected any formal ties and direct control by an outside power. Throughout the early Renaissance, the Flemish, the Hollanders, and the Frisian counts furthered consolidated their power and created a sense of common ethnicity within each group.

This new identity in the Renaissance derived from three factors: (1) a distinctive Flemish-Dutch dialect that had been used in the Low Countries, (2) the highly urbanized society that created a rich culture and customs, and (3) their sustained battle to retain their ancient agreements and laws against centralized states to the south who wanted to subjugate them. Like the hundreds of ancient Greek poleis who organized themselves in sovereign city-states until they had to fight their common enemy Persia, the 17 provinces that had developed found themselves united against Habsburg Spain in the 16th century. No doubt the nobility of the Low Countries understood the story of the ancient Greeks since they claimed that their own Knights of the Golden Fleece had roots in the Trojan warriors of Jason and the Argonauts.

### 16th-Century Immigration and Refugees

The battle between the forces of the Spanish Inquisition and the people of the Netherlands further cemented their feelings of national identity, and so the Inquisition was not merely a religious struggle. While Philip II of Spain believed he was being faithful to the Roman Catholic Church, the Spanish oppression symbolized an outside power trying to ignore ancient customs and local leadership. Very few people from the Low Countries supported the harsh methods used to enforce centralization and increased taxation. The Reformation added another dimension to the struggle, and meant that vast numbers of Flemish people, as well as French-speaking people from either France or the French-speaking provinces of the Low Countries, fled north, carrying with them local customs and skills. The refugees from the Walloon, Flemish, and Brabant provinces of the Southern Netherlands also brought much more refined manners, clothing, and culture to the north, where the indigenous people had not developed the higher European culture. The city of Leiden, for example, benefited greatly from their knowledge of weaving, and French-language churches (Walloon) were established to accommodate the immigrants. In time, many intermarried, but a significant number of French names have become a recognized part of contemporary surnames in the Netherlands today. Some Hollanders complained that more than 50 percent of the residents of Leiden were foreigners. Even after the Dutch Republic was able to establish itself as a sovereign state in 1580, its residents included almost an equal number of Roman Catholics and Protestants; neither group became a state church. Despite the great efforts to proselytize, neither of these dominant forms of Christianity could claim complete participation by all citizens since the strength of localized and pious, yet humanistic, forms of Christianity prevalent prior to the 16th-century divisions were still present, pointing to the great diversity within the Low Countries.

By the beginning of the 17th century, the Dutch continued to offer a far more tolerant environment than many other regions of Europe, and they opened their doors to increasing numbers of Jews fleeing from persecution in Portugal and Spain. Some Jews converted to Christianity, and in time, Portuguese names were at times seen in important figures, such as Isaac da Costa, a well-known poet in the early 19th century. As the Dutch expanded their overseas colonies, eventual intermarriage with South East Asians, Africans, and Caribbeans added further ethnic diversity to the Dutch population.

Until the French Revolution, the concept of universal citizenship and nationality throughout Europe was limited in most cases to the elites. Oligarchies ruled and had their unique identity, and royal families continued to underline the importance of birth into a limited number of households. But early modern concepts of citizenship limited to cities and provinces did exist. Members of guilds and merchant companies had bonds as a community of burghers. Their status could be passed on to their offspring. Some others, such as Jews, had no hereditary rights, but could purchase citizenship for a price. French occupation of the Netherlands in 1795 created the Batavian Republic; Jews were given citizenship, all aristocratic titles were denounced, and democratic forces began to transform the older notions of national identity. Napoleon annexed the Low Countries to France, but even after its emancipation in 1813, elements of the Napoleonic Code has continued to offer some important articulations in Dutch law to recognize individual rights and citizenship.

### Modern Immigration

As the modern Kingdom of the Netherlands developed, it established a succession of laws throughout the 19th century that attempted to steer a course between the rights of bloodline (*jus sanguinis*) and the rights of birthplace (*jus soli*) to determine citizenship. While the development in the German lands was heavily weighted toward bloodline, with the Romantic notion of *volk* and later the Aryan race, the French had underlined a new nation of citizens based solely on birthplace. The Netherlands, together with the United States of America, although it discussed a mixture of the two, was essentially assuming bloodline. However, the concept of nationality had important qualifications. The *Burgerlijk Wetboek* (law) of 1838 denied a woman nationality if she married a non-Dutchman, and even those who qualified as Dutch nationals did not have access to public rights. Some of these problems were dealt with in the Nationality Act of 1892, which relied much more on the concept of bloodline, and was extended to all residents until that time. This law was not amended until 1985.

Until World War II, the Netherlands was a country of emigration. Directly after World War II, 560,000 Dutch citizens migrated to the United States, Canada, South Africa, Australia, and New Zealand. The U.S. Census Bureau reports that over five million Americans have full or partial Dutch heritage.[7] Until the 1950s, the Netherlands more or less assumed that to be Dutch was an ethnic category, based on the myth perpetuated since the Golden Age that they had been a unique people of the Low Countries. In the 1950s and 60s, much of the immigration to the Netherlands was from asylum seekers and former colonies. With great economic success, the Netherlands needed laborers in industry, following the *gastarbeiter* model. Many Italians and Spaniards came first, followed by Moroccans and Turks. In time, most Italians and Spaniards returned to their place of birth, but the Moroccans and Turks remained. In an atmosphere of decolonization, residents of former colonies had a limited chance to seek Dutch citizenship, and many from Indonesia, Surinam, and the Antilles came, as well. By the 1970s, the Netherlands embarked on a conscious effort to promote multiculturalism to help integrate new immigrants and highlight their long-standing policy of tolerance. Today, the designation "indigenous" is given to persons who are minimally descendents of third-generation births in the Netherlands. Despite these efforts, a clear distinction has been made between citizens who are ethnic (*jus sanguinis*) Dutch and those considered *allochtoon*. *Allochtoon* is derived from the Greek word meaning an "other land," denoting that one of the parents was born in a foreign land, despite the person's place of birth. A further distinction is denoted by *niet-westerse allochtonen*, which means "non-western places of origin" (including Turkey, Africa, Asia, and Latin America), although this excludes the westernized countries of Japan and the former colony of Indonesia. After three generations of birth in the Netherlands, one can be considered Dutch. Those who are born outside the

Netherlands, but have two Dutch parents, are considered *autochtonen*.[8] In 2007, the population reached 16.4 million, and the number of non-Western minorities rapidly increased from only 1–2 percent of the population in 1967 to 7.3 percent in 1995, and 10.6 percent in 2007. Two-thirds of non-Western immigrants come from Turkey, Morocco, and Suriname (each 2%) and Netherlands Antilles and Aruba (1% total).[9]

Multiculturalism began to break down in the 1990s as the increased numbers of asylum seekers and immigrants amplified the social problems associated with a dramatic increase in new residents. Some protest against any increase in immigration had occurred already in the 1980s, for example by the Central Party of Hans Janmaat, but the more elite Netherlanders found multiculturalism consistent with their liberal social attitudes. An underlying resentment was growing among many others, however, as the limited resources available in a socialists society that had prided itself on generosity began to disappear. Large cities like Amsterdam, Utrecht, and Rotterdam began to be transformed and new ghettos developed. In 2005, the *Centrum voor Onderzoek and Statistiek,* Rotterdam, recorded the numbers of indigenous residents and the numbers of foreign-born immigrants: Rotterdam had 47 percent immigrants, Amsterdam 50 percent, The Hague 45 percent, and Utrecht 31 percent.[10]

In 2006, the Dutch government passed a new immigration law that requires prospective persons to be examined in some fundamental elements of Dutch society. Those seeking a residency visa must pass both a civic integration and a Dutch language examination before they arrive in the Netherlands. An additional exam determines their compatibility with Dutch liberal values, which they are exposed to by being shown a video with a scene from a nude beach and homosexual activities. Critics say that all of this is carefully orchestrated to offend fundamentalist Muslims and their religious values.[11] But Immigration Minister Rita Verdonk defended her position by stating that there were more than 600,000 unemployed immigrants, most of whom are Muslims and do not really understand Dutch. Certainly the Netherlands is not alone in facing these problems when comparing very similar issues in Britain, France, and Germany.

Today, the government of the Netherlands recognizes several languages and dialects in addition to Dutch in conformity to the European Charter for Regional or Minority Languages.[12] In the provinces of Groningen, Drenthe, Overijssel, and Gelderland "Lower Saxon," a western Low German dialect is spoken; Frisian is spoken in Friesland, and in Dutch and Belgium Limburg, the dialect of the western Maas and Rhineland, Limburger, is spoken. In addition, many speak English because of their long interaction with the United Kingdom and the fact that there are a limited number of people in the world who speak Dutch. In 2007, the Central Bureau of Statistics reported that 46 percent were fluent in English, with another 20 percent able to have simple conversations in English.

## HISTORY

### The Medieval Low Countries

Until the Late Middle Ages, the Low Countries were on no major trade routes, and hence were of little importance to the rest of Europe. Certainly the Rhine-Meuse-Scheldt delta regions proved difficult to travel and farm, and periodic floods created an ever-changing environment. In the Rhine-Meuse delta region, the current provinces of Zeeland and Holland had developed under Count Dirk III, who founded Dordrecht in or around 1015 and made it his residence. At the time, his title was Count of West Friesland since much earlier, the shifting coastal areas had connected the Frisian northern areas with the southwestern areas. By establishing a stronghold in Utrecht, Count Dirk could control much of the river trade necessary for the German princes to reach the North Sea via the Rhine and Meuse Rivers. But his most important fortress was in the very south of Zeeland in Vlaardingen, where he could also control the Scheldt river trade coming from Flanders and northern France. When the German emperor sent an imperial army to quell the Count's power, they were solidly defeated in the Battle of Vlaardingen (1018), giving him further control of the area. Later attempts by the German emperors to reestablish control were met with resistance from both Frisian and Flemish counts.

Despite the feudal laws that began to rule the Low Countries, overlords knew they could only maintain their rule with the support of the local nobility. In 1312, a historic charter was signed by Duke John I of Brabant, instituting a council of estates that shared power and creating perhaps the first quasi-democratic government in Europe, similar to the English *Magna Carta* of 1215. The Charter of Kortenberg, so named from the Abbey where they met, was supported by 16 lords, the Church, and the cities of Brabant. This fundamental law became so important to the developing regions that by 1354, Duke John III was forced to offer further powers to the lords in order to gain their support for the marriage of his daughter Jeanne to Wenceslaus of Luxembourg, which changed the dynastic house. His new charter became known as the "*Blijde Inkomst*" or "*joyeuse entrée*" (joyful entry); the image of the arrival of the overlord—who was not a resident—was celebrated because the agreement to consult the local nobility on matters of taxation, diplomacy, and war forged a happy rendezvous. The Charter of Kortenberg became the model for all subsequent agreements in the other provinces. In 1464, the

States General, the earliest parliament, met for the first time in Bruges and later Brussels, and represented the provincial states.

By the early Renaissance, Flemish cities established a thriving textile industry. In 1400, Ghent had more than 60,000 inhabitants, Brugge 40,000, and Antwerp 45,000. Together with Zutphen, Deventer, Zwolle, and Kampen on the northern Ijssel River (each with approximately 10,000 inhabitants), these cities became internationally linked with other important centers through the Hanse system. This trading alliance of guilds and cities, with Lübeck, Brunswick, Danzig, and Dortmund as the chief cities of the Baltic trade, and London and the Flemish cities as their depots, created powerful economic ties. The Baltic supplied fur, timber, metals, wheat, rye, and flax, the North Seas provided herring, and London and Flanders produced textiles and other manufactured goods.

In addition to the growing conflict between the counts of Flanders and Holland against French or German powers, the Burgundians entered the contest to control the rising wealth of the Low Countries. When Louis de Male, Count of Artois and Flanders, died in 1384, his son-in-law Duke Philip the Good of Burgundy inherited his feudal lands. Over the next 60 years, the dukes of Burgundy, under the house of Valois, acquired Brabant, Limburg, Namur, Holland, Zeeland, Hainaut, and Luxembourg. The Burgundians established a capital in Brussels, a parliament in Mechelen, and a university in Leuven. They also established the Order of the Golden Fleece to unite the nobles; initially, the Order was limited to 24, but by the 16th century, it increased to 50. While this increased their centralized power, it was achieved by sharing power and granting local autonomy.[13] However, the last great duke, Charles the Bold, died in battle in 1477 after constant wars to aggressively aggrandize his lands even further. His daughter Mary married Maximilian I, Archduke of Austria and the son of the Emperor Frederick III, and this collection of 10 provinces passed onto the Habsburg family. Like the dukes of Burgundy, the Habsburgs increased their territorial area, and by 1500, there were 17 autonomous provinces regarded as the Low Countries, or the Netherlands.[14]

The centralization of European states became the trend by the early 16th century, and strategic marriages allotted the key royalty increasing territories. The Habsburgs were masters of strategic marriages. When the Habsburg Philip I married Joanna, the daughter of the Spanish throne of Ferdinand and Isabella, the lands were passed onto him. Their son Charles of Ghent, named after the Flemish city where he was raised, ruled over a vast territory in Europe and the Americas. His titles reveal the breath of his power: ruler of the Netherlands and Burgundy (1506–1555); Charles I, King of Spain (1516–1556), which included Sicily, Naples, the duchy of Milan, and the colonies in the Americas and the Philippines that had been conquered by Spain; and Charles V, the Holy Roman Emperor (1519–1556), which extended his powers throughout central and southern Europe, although he had to rely on the seven Electors who wielded local power. In 1521, however, he assigned the Austrian lands to his brother Ferdinand I, and from this time forward, the Habsburgs officially split into the Spanish and Austrian branches. The Low Countries became known as the Spanish Netherlands.

Since Charles had been raised in Ghent, his native languages were French and Flemish/Dutch, and while he later learned Spanish and German, he had a deep understanding of the culture and politics of his native land. He also understood the strategic importance of the Flemish cities as a source of wealth and trade. He enlarged his territory in the Spanish Netherlands by repudiating the temporal powers of the bishops of Tournai/Doornik (1521) and Utrecht (1528), and extended the territory in Groningen, Friesland, Drenthe, and Gelderland. Prior to Charles' rule, the Low Countries were nominally fiefs either of the French or Holy Roman Empire, but he worked over time to unite them, culminating in the 1549 Pragmatic Sanction that declared the 17 provinces of the Netherlands "forever one and indivisible."

### The Renaissance and the Reformation

Charles V's vast territories brought great wealth and power, but also many expensive wars with the Ottoman Empire. He also fought on the side of the Pope and England against the French and the Venetians. But the tide turned when the Pope, France, and England formed a new alliance. The rising debt financing remained, and because of the wealth of the Low Countries, taxes rose to more than three times their 15th-century levels, and the growing conflict became inevitable. Cities and trade guilds began to revolt regularly over this new problem.

But economic problems did not account for the great revolt that was soon to come. Beginning in 1517, the Saxon monk Martin Luther had begun to protest the economic gain that the Dominicans and Rome had enjoyed through the imposed sale of indulgences. Soon, widespread calls for major reform in the practices and beliefs of the Church caused bitter battles throughout Europe. The Reformation came to the Low Countries due to their merchant trade, printing houses, and communication with the rest of Europe. No doubt the long-standing reforms already accomplished by the Augustinians and the Brethren of the Common Life created an interest in new forms of piety and devotion. While Lutheranism did not spread in the Low Countries, the non-institutional Anabaptist movement among the lower orders became very popular, especially in Friesland. Menno Simonszoon became the leader of a local manifestation of Anabaptism, and soon this grassroots Christianity became the origin of the Mennonite churches throughout Europe. Although Anabaptism appealed to many peasants and lesser burghers, it did not have an impact on the politics of the region. It was the introduction of Reformed Calvinism that would transform the landscape.

Flanders saw the first great wave of support for this new Reformed Christianity, and it appealed greatly to both the merchant elites and the common population. At first, the actual numbers who rejected Roman Catholicism for the new Reformed churches were not great, but there was a huge "broad middle group" who flocked to hear Reformed preachers or buy the new literature available from the many local publishers.[15] The Humanist movement had paved the way for a new discussion of the origins of Christianity and the importance of personal piety, and their fierce independence and desire to learn fueled this popularity.

In 1555, Charles V abdicated in favor of his son Philip II, who became King of Spain and the Americas and ruler of the Habsburg Netherlands until 1598. Unlike his father Charles, Philip was raised outside of the Low Countries in the courts of Spain, and therefore he spoke neither Dutch nor French, nor did he understand the local culture and politics. In 1559, Philip II appointed Margaret of Parma regent of the Habsburg Netherlands, and she attempted to reverse the long-standing policy of working with the local nobility. She appointed Antoine Cardinal Granvelle, archbishop of Mechelen, as the first Councilor of State, and he proceeded to dominate local politics through a Secret Council effectively denying many nobles of the Golden Fleece their due. The 1560s were therefore filled with social and economic unrest due to rising taxes, less collaboration between nobility and overlords, and the call for religious reforms. The political-religious unrest directly affected the economy when most of the English cloth departed from the lucrative Antwerp markets by 1563. Natural forces also increased the unrest in 1564–1565 through severe winters and very poor harvests.

Rather than listen to these local concerns, Philip II answered with a radical solution, one he inherited from Spain: Inquisition. Not only was the Inquisition ineffective in the rest of Europe, it was especially strange in a region that had a history of very little direct ecclesiastical control. In the years 1561–1564, there was an average of 264 convictions of heresy a year. In 1565, a League of Compromise, composed of Protestants and crypto-Protestants and led by Henrik Brederode and the Sea Beggers [*Gueux*], presented a petition to Margaret of Parma in Brussels. Essentially, they pledged support for the King and the established Church if Margaret would dismantle the Inquisition and end religious persecution, reopening the States General (the early parliament). A year later, an "Oath of the Nobles" urged the governor-general to soften the Inquisition. The entire future of the Spanish Netherlands hung in the balance at this point. But Margret was neither empowered nor will-ing to risk any compromise with the local opposition to Philip's centralizing directions. In August 1566, a fiery sermon in Steenvoorde, Brabant, called for an end to the "papist idolatry." This anger was far more political than re-ligious, and centered on Philip as the offensive hand of the papacy. Spreading quickly from town to town, local inhabitants expressed their fears and hatred by breaking all symbols of centralized and Inquisitorial oppression in what became known as the Iconoclastic Fury. Statues and stain-glassed windows fell to the iconoclastic fury, which lasted for weeks. The local militias (*Schut-ters*) were both unable and unwilling to stop this anticlerical and institutional hatred. Politics and religion were inextricably intertwined; by the end of 1566, many prominent nobles switched their support from the King and the Church to Reformed Calvinism; this became known as the "*wonderyear!*"

This clash in cultures (Low Countries versus Spanish) might have found some common ground, but conditions worsened when Fernando Alvarez de Toledo, Duke of Alva, was appointed Governor in 1567. He quickly gained a reputation as the "iron duke" among many Protestants due to his harsh rule in quelling any protest. With an army of 10,000, Alva fought all religious and political opponents to his centralized rule, and some records suggest that in the years 1567–1573, approximately 100,000 Protestants died in the struggle. Alva instituted his iron hand in 1567 through his secret "Council of Troubles" (known as the Council of Blood because of the many deaths), and his worst offense to local rule was the imprisoning of important knights of the Golden Fleece—Lamoral, Count of Egmont, and Philip de Montmorency, Count of Hoorn—even though they were opposed to the spread of Protantism. Alva also attempted to raise taxes even further. On September 9, 1567, Egmont and Hoorn were beheaded, after which another 18 "rebel" nobles were also executed. In the years 1567–1568, more than 1,000 people were executed and over 60,000 Netherlanders left the Low Countries for the cities of Emden, Cleves, or other areas of the Rhineland, or crossed the channel to England.

With great hubris, the Spanish had overstepped their ability to control the Low Countries. In 1568, William of Orange-Nassau (known as William the Silent), the greatest Knight of the Golden Fleece, decided to support the opposition.[16] This started what was to become the Eighty Years War, which was fought from 1568–1648. William descended from the German province of Nassau, which had been linked to the Low Countries through marriage, and hence held the barony of Breda. He had inherited the title of Orange from the principality in Burgundy that was a fief of the Holy Roman Empire. Hendrik III of Nassau-Breda had become stadholder of Holland, Zeeland, and Utrecht under Charles V. The role of the stadholder (*Stadhouder*), literally

William of Orange-Nassau (1533–1584). Key,
Adriaan William I, Prince of Orange, called William
the Silent, c. 1579, Rijksmuseum, Amsterdam.

"place holder," was a lieutenant or provincial governor for the crown. Later,
under the Dutch Republic, the Princes of Orange-Nassau would become de
facto hereditary stadholders.

   In 1569, Alva assembled the States General and declared yet higher
taxes.[17] In July 1572, the States of Holland assembled in Dordrecht, not The
Hague. William of Orange was reaffirmed as Stadholder of Holland, Zeeland,
and Utrecht (26 major city councils backed him). But however oppressive
the new taxation was, in August 1572, the St. Bartholomew's Day Massacre claimed the lives of 2,000 French Protestants and perhaps 5–10,000
throughout France, raising the stakes. By the end of the year, Alva extended
his power with massacres in Mechelen, Zutphen, and Naarden, but a famous
victory for the Dutch came in Leiden. Alva attempted to take Leiden in 1573
with 86,000 troops, only to be thwarted. Leiden was an important symbol of
power for both sides: its weaving and textile industries; printing and publishing houses; population of 150,000; and strategic position made it desirable.
In classic fashion, the Dutch employed their greatest weapon against foreign

invaders; they opened the dikes and re-flooded the land. While the Spanish could not manage a large-scale army, the Dutch navigated the low-lying areas, re-supplying Leiden with food and soldiers. By October 1574, the Spanish gave up, and this event has become a national holiday. William of Orange rewarded the city with the founding of the University of Leiden, first in the northern provinces. The university's official Latin name was *Academia Lugduno Batava,* which connected it to the ancient Celts and Germanic tribes who inhabited this area (*Lug* was a Celtic god, *dun* is a fortress, and the Batavians a tribe recognized by the Roman historian Tacitus).

Things looked grim indeed for the Spanish. In 1575, the government was bankrupt, and as a result it continued to lose support. In addition, the States of Holland conferred sovereignty on William of Orange. Alva now concentrated on the south, and in 1576, the Spanish Fury was unleashed in Antwerp; some 8,000 citizens who had revolted lay dead as a result. Gaining widespread support in the north, Holland and Brabant proclaimed the Pacification of Ghent and formed a new States General as the official governing body representing northern interests against Spain. Ghent declared itself the Calvinist Republic of Ghent in 1577, and the guilds from Ghent, Brussels, and Antwerp formed revolutionary committees to support a more formal resistance. In an effort to unify all Netherlanders against outside Spanish oppression, William of Orange was instrumental in designing the Treaty of *Satisfactie,* which brokered religious peace between Protestants and Catholics, and setting up a government in Brussels and Antwerp.

By 1579, however, any unity between the north and south provinces appeared impossible for both sides. The 17 provinces formed two different unions. Ten provinces of the south remained with Spain, under Parma, establishing the "Union of Arras" (January 6, 1579), and seven northern provinces joined together in the Protestant Union of Utrecht under William of Orange in the "United Provinces" (January 23, 1579). In a summary of the political and religious reasons for a break with Spain, the northern United Provinces signed the "Act of Adjuration" in 1580, repudiating the sovereignty of Philip II for several reasons: (1) He ruled over the law, which included the constitutional tradition of Great Privilege and *Blijde Inkomst*; and (2) ruled over conscience, meaning he denied religious freedom practiced in the Low Countries. The Oath of Adjuration was signed on July 26, 1581. Loyalty to an overlord had clear limits:

> As it is apparent to all that a prince is constituted by God to be ruler of a people, to defend them from oppression and violence as the shepherd his sheep; . . . And when he does not behave thus, but, on the contrary, oppresses them . . . then he is no longer a prince, but a tyrant, and the subjects are to consider him in no other view.[18]

In order to gain international legitimacy and military support to stand against Spain, William of Orange offered the sovereignty of the United Provinces to the Duke of Anjou, brother of the French King. William was assassinated in Delft in 1584, and a year later, the Dutch offered sovereignty to King Henri III and when he refused, they offered it to Elizabeth I of England. She declined, but elected to sent 6,350 foot troops and 1,000 horsemen under Robert Dudley, Earl of Leicester. The "Treaty of Nonsuch" (August 20, 1585) marked the first treaty between European states and was signed by the Dutch and the English. The Spanish planned to send their famous Armada against the English, but in 1588, it was defeated, and thereafter a permanent split became more firmly established between north and south. Peace between the Dutch rebels and Spain did not come until the Twelve Year Truce (1609–1621). The Dutch Republic was established, and it endured until 1795.[19] The tenacity of a small group of people in defending their local rights and culture is amazing.[20] The motto of the new Dutch Republic became "strength through unity" (*Eendracht maakt macht*, literally "unity makes power"). The Peace of Westphalia in 1648 granted the Dutch Republic permanent international recognition and peace with Spain.

### The Golden Age

The new Republic possessed some remarkable resources, despite its lack of what might constitute the elements of contemporary early modern governments: it had no strong monarchy, nor large tracks of arable land. The government was decentralized, and without a monarch, prime minister, or president, the stadholder had a limited role as a leader; his power was dependent on establishing strong ties with each province and the military. But it was this very decentralization that opened up markets and encouraged entrepreneurship. In this way, it possessed newer and more modern elements that would make it the first modern economy in Europe.[21] The Dutch Republic became the leader in trade and economic development and dominated Europe in the early modern period, the way that Florence or Venice had done in the 15th century, or the way that Britain would do in the late 18th and 19th centuries. There were several stages of economic development before the decline:

1. 1585–1622 was characterized by a consolidation of the unity of provinces, the accumulation of capital, and the successful establishment of colonies in the Americas, South Africa, and South East Asia;
2. 1622–1663 was characterized by a struggle to maintain the profitability of trade due in part to several significant wars with their growing economic competitors; and
3. 1670–1815 was characterized by stagnation and decline.

When the English and the Dutch defeated the Spanish Armada in 1588, an alliance was formed that lasted until the Peace of Westphalia in 1648; however, it was certainly strained after the English made peace with Spain in 1604. In addition to an alliance with England, new circumstances forged an alliance with France, as well. In 1589, Henri III, the last Valois King of France died and Henry Bourbon inherited the throne. As king of Navarre, a small kingdom on the border between Spain and France, there was no love lost. But Henry was also a Protestant, and these factors made him a natural ally of the new Dutch Republic. In order to combat this new enemy, Philip II recalled most of his troops from the Netherlands and turned them against the new Bourbon king, inevitably granting much relief to the struggling United Provinces.[22] This early period was very significant for the new Dutch Republic because it gave the Republic limited recognition as an established government and allowed it to consolidate its economy.

After unsuccessful attempts to grant sovereignty to either the French or the English, Maurice of Nassau, son of the murdered William the Silent, became the new military leader and stadholder. Maurice was supported by the most powerful politician of the time, Johan van Oldenbarnevelt. As "Land's Advocate" of Holland or, later, "Pensionary," he also served as chairman of the regional States' assemblies, which meant that he was responsible for all official correspondence for the Republic. Maurice was able to reclaim the eastern provinces, and he became the best military general of the age. Serious differences arose, however. Oldenbarnevelt was firmly committed to an alliance with Catholic Spain, whereas popular opinion favored reliance on Protestant England. When a split in the Reformed Church placed Oldenbarnevelt on the weaker side—he supported the "Remonstrants," a breakaway group following Jacob Arminius—Maurice acted quickly to bring unity to the Republic and arrested, tried, and executed him in 1618. Although historical hindsight might partially validate his policies, Oldenbarnevelt's main problem was that he had subjugated the needs of the United Providences to the prosperity and rule of Holland. Holland was only one province, but by far the central leader of the Dutch Republic.[23]

The Dutch Republic was not only divided politically, but economically; it possessed two separate systems. The Maritime Provinces of Zeeland, Holland, Friesland, and Groningen comprised a modern, trade-based economy, while the inland provinces were traditional agricultural economies. The largest cities were located in the Maritime Provinces, as well, and this was the real source of power.[24] Its involvement in international trade and colonization was what gave it power. The Dutch possessed the largest merchant marine in the early modern period, and not only did they transport goods through Europe and the colonies, but they also created a large depot of supplies in the harbor cities of

Amsterdam and Enkhuizen that were formerly held by Brugge and Antwerp. This new marketplace became known as the *stapelmarkt*, and functioned as a clearinghouse and entrepôt for European goods. With a near monopoly on Baltic grain, great stores of textiles, and other goods, such as salt, metals, and lumber, the merchant could regulate prices despite the fluctuation in supplies. It has been universally recognized that modern capitalism had its beginning in this market.

In 1602, the Dutch East India Company (*Vereenigde Oostindische Compagnie* or VOC) was established by the government as a monopoly for Asian trade, and was organized after numerous previous companies had already paved the way in Asia. What set the VOC apart from any earlier colonization was its modern means of financial operation. In 1609, it established the Amsterdam Exchange Bank as a means to raise capital, and it became the first joint-stock company in the world with the founding of the Amsterdam Stock Exchange. It raised more than six million guilders, an astonishing amount for the time, and issued bonds with a term of between three and twelve months. The VOC established central offices in Batavia, the main city on the island of Java, where they traded and set up colonies to collect spices. They also traded with Japan and had offices in South Africa. At the height of its power, the VOC possessed 150 merchant ships and 40 war ships with 20,000 seamen and 10,000 soldiers, as well as some 50,000 civilians working for the company.

A replica of a VOC ship is anchored next to the new NEMO science museum in Amsterdam, which is designed to appear as a ship. Courtesy of the author.

The fishing town of Enkhuizen was once part of the powerful Hanseatic League and then an important VOC harbor. Due to harbor silting and changes in transportation, Amsterdam eventually became more important. A typical Dutch draw-bridge is in the foreground. Courtesy of the author.

In 1621, the West India Company (*Westindische Compagnie* or WIC) was granted a charter with a monopoly to trade in the West Indies (the Caribbean), Brazil, West Africa, and North America. The WIC had far less success than the VOC since Spain, France, and England had far greater competitive advantages, although due to its extensive fleet, the Dutch became the most successful slave traders until the British gained a larger share after 1700. Not all success came from far away trade: Dutch ships in the North Sea continued to move valuable commercial goods, and fishing proved very successful. The invention of new ships appropriate for a particular trade created great success in the herring and whaling industries.

Likewise, new techniques for agriculture allowed production to actually increase at the same time that a smaller percentage of the population was needed to work on farms. Only about 40 percent of the population was directly involved in agriculture, compared to many other European countries, where most of the population was needed for subsistence. Several factors made agriculture far more efficient than in many other areas of Europe: a greater use of fertilizers (from a large animal husbandry production, indus-trial organic wastes, and large urban "night soil"); new technology, such as windmills and irrigation; good transportation via rivers and canals; and ready markets for products due to rising populations. From the 1590s until nearly 1650, the Dutch exported many food products, including fish, meat, cheese, butter, fruit, beer, wine, tobacco, and Baltic grain through its urban depots.

Rapid growth and wealth began to come to an end when England imposed the Navigation Act in 1651, and this led to the First Anglo-Dutch War a year later. In defeat, the Dutch lost their freedom to manipulate foreign trade. Oliver Cromwell, Lord Protector of England, had a grudge against the Dutch because the stadholders were related to English royalty. When William II of Orange died, Johan de Witt became the Grand Pensionary of Holland in the absence of a stadholder, establishing the first stadholderless period, which lasted until 1675. De Witt pledged support for Cromwell by agreeing to stop the succession from the house of Orange. In this way, Cromwell hoped that he could further control the royalty in Britain, as well. A second Anglo-Dutch War (1665–1667) did not solve the problem of international trade, and in fact, the Dutch lost New Amsterdam and their colonies in North America. By 1672, a third Anglo-Dutch War included even more losses of the wealth in trade that the Netherlands had accumulated. The year 1672 was called the disaster year when France, Münster, and Cologne attacked the United Provinces. De Witt was lynched and, together with his brother Cornelius, assassinated.

England once again turned to the Netherlands for an alliance; this time, rather than attempting to suppress the house of Orange, they called upon William III to take over the English crown. William's mother was Mary, Princess Royal of England, and in 1677, for diplomatic purposes, he married Mary Stuart, his first cousin. When James II fled in 1688, William became King of England, Ireland, and Scotland, and stadholder until his death in 1702, after which the Dutch Republic entered its second stadholderless pe-riod until 1722. While the republic had entered the 18th century as a Eu-ropean power, it soon discovered that it could no longer compete with the growing states, which had far larger territories and populations. Even when William IV of Orange became stadholder, the Netherlands lacked its former purpose and unity. Dutch trade had been seriously curtailed, and the costs from successive wars with England and France meant that greater amounts of money had to be spent just to service the debts.[25] But a policy of neutrality bought the Dutch some relative security until the end of the 18th century.

A new political group called Patriots begun to formulate new ideas of society based on Enlightenment principles. They were heavily influenced by Jean-Jacques Rousseau's new *Contrat social ou Principes du droit,* claiming their natural freedoms from dynastic families with their restrictions and international connections, which stifled a free market and greater democratic rule. After Britain began to control North America, many Dutch ships entered the lucrative contraband of the black markets. While William IV attempted to support British interests, he was powerless to plug the leaks. In the States General, Joan Derk van der Capellen tot den Pol, a Patriot, went about establishing diplomatic relations with the American patriots—the first to do so—in their struggle against the British. In 1779, the young John Adams, future president of the United States, arrived in the Netherlands to negotiate a loan for the war effort. Retaliation came quickly when the British declared war on the Dutch in 1780. In October 1784, William IV left the Netherlands in order to disassociate himself from the Patriot cause. Despite losing the war, the Patriots rallied in support of locally organized militias called Free Corps, and finally the States of Holland suspended the stadholderate. But while matters worsened for William IV, his connection with the Prussians through his wife Wilhelmine, sister of Frederick William II, caused the Prussians to invade the Netherlands to restore order, and by 1787, William IV triumphantly re-entered The Hague. But the economic situation was still dire, and in 1791, the WIC and VOC were liquidated and their stocks and debts passed on to the government, although the government appointed a Council of Asian Possessions to continue to organize trade.

Events in France in 1789 would forever change Europe, and the weakness and proximity of the Netherlands to France spelled disaster for Dutch sovereignty as the French Revolutionaries began to take hold of a new government, with an interest in spreading their revolution to other countries. France had always considered its natural territory to reach to the Rhine on the east and the Low Countries to the north. In 1793, the National Convention in France declared war on the First Coalition (Britain, Austria, Prussia), which included the Netherlands. By 1795, the French controlled the Netherlands and soon the Netherlands became known as the Batavian Republic. Although it was a sovereign state, it also retained a position as a secondary state of the French Republic. The revolutionary committee formed a National Assembly with Pieter Paulus as its first President. At this, the British declared war, which was fought sporadically until 1802.

The new Batavian Republic instituted policies that were very similar to those of its counterpart France. Universal male suffrage for men over 20 was instituted, 126 new electoral districts rationally divided the population, and any privileged position the Reformed Church might have had in the old system was denied. The new constitution also banned all hereditary titles and privileges. While these new-found freedoms might have been welcome at first, by the time of Napoleon, France's policies toward its secondary states had become oppressive. In order to fight along so many fronts throughout Europe and the Mediterranean, by 1800, they required enormous sums of money in the form of some three million guilders a year from the Netherlands.

Since the Batavian Republic was still duty bound to support the French, the British declared war on the Netherlands again in 1803, and the war continued until the defeat of Napoleon in 1814. Most of this final war was due to the Continental Blockade, but the Netherlands lost many of its remaining colonial enterprises in South Africa, as well as its involvement in Caribbean goods. Napoleon wanted to further control his empires and from 1806–1810, he installed his brother Louis Bonaparte as King of the Kingdom of Holland, ending the short-lived Batavian Republic. Even though the Dutch took to Louis' leadership and care for Dutch institutions—he allowed a relaxation of some trade with Britain, and genuinely attempted to build up the Netherlands again—Napoleon annexed the Low Countries to France in 1810. This incorporation bled the Netherlands of all of its remaining wealth by instituting a tax of 100 million guilders a year, and this enormous debt would plague the Netherlands until well into the mid-19th century.

Napoleon's control of his lands outside France was weakened as he lost more and more wars and exhausted his resources. William VI of Orange had trained as a military leader, and fought against Napoleon in several battles. When Czar Alexander I saw that Napoleon was clearly in grave trouble, he organized a conference under William's chairmanship to determine the fate of the Netherlands. To his surprise, the influential Gijsbert Karel van Hogendorp asked for William's return to his native lands and declared that the Dutch would consider him more than a stadholder, raising him to royal status. In a peculiar way, the Dutch had learned that in the new balance of European politics, King Louis' royal reign had brought far more benefits to the land than other previous arrangements. William VI was proclaimed sovereign of the Netherlands in December 1813 and was crowned King of the Northern Provinces on May 30, 1814, although his internationally recognized appointment did not come until the Congress of Vienna had decided the fate of the Dutch in a final declaration in June 1815. He declared himself King William I of the Netherlands, and the new kingdom took its motto from the Princes of Orange: *Je Maintiendrai,* French for "I will endure."

### The 19th Century

The Allied powers at the Congress of Vienna were interested in creating a new balance of power in Europe that would permanently check French aggression. Austria, which had ruled the Southern Netherlands as a Habsburg power in the 18th century, relinquished any claims and accepted new territories in the Tyrol and access to the Mediterranean near Venice in its place. William I of the United Kingdom of the Netherlands was given sovereignty over both north and south Netherlands in order to create a larger buffer state. And therefore, at a time when many former monarchies strongly influenced by the French were doing away with monarchy in favor of more republican rule, the Netherlands had decided to reverse its former system. In addition to restoring a united Netherlands of north and south, which now included the Bishopric of Liège for the first time, the question of Luxembourg arose, as well. The city of Luxembourg possessed a very strategic fortress that had to remain neutral, and the deal was struck that William I would trade his lands of Nassau, which Prussia had eyed for years, for Luxembourg, creating a contiguous state.

Although Great Britain gave funds to the Netherlands to build up fortresses against the French, William deferred this money toward his plan for economic revitalization. He became known as the merchant king for his ambitious plans to rebuild the infrastructure with new, more efficient canals, restructured education, and provided generous support for manufacturing. In 1824, William formed the Netherlands Trading Company (NHM), and although it was not directly part of the government, it worked closely to try to recover international markets. Yet William inherited an enormous national debt that was elevated by having assumed the debt of the VOC and WIC, as well as the tax burdens imposed under Napoleon. Despite his desire to develop all of his new lands, he favored the north and never really allowed the south equal representation: the south had a population seven times larger than the north, but William allowed only an equal number of delegates in the new government, which was bicameral but hardly parliamentary. He also established the Netherlands Bank and the Netherlands General Society for the Promotion of National Industry in 1821 to finance industrialization, and his own guarantee of dividends and personal investment led to some economic success. William's autocratic rule angered the south by attempting to promote the Dutch language over French, and his own connections with the privileged Reformed Church could not find favor in predominantly Roman Catholic regions. He also attempted to demand that the south pay an unequal share of the national debt.

By 1830, growing opposition and resentment in the south came to a head in Brussels. Influenced by the liberal revolution in Paris of that year, the Belgians declared independence on October 4. Although troops were sent to quell the protest, it became apparent that a serious breach had occurred, and they could no longer control the southern regions. Leopold of Sachsen-Coburg-Gotha was chosen as King Leopold I of Belgium. While the powers of Europe recognized Belgium, William I attempted further campaigns to retake the south, without success, and finally accepted their independence in 1838; shortly thereafter, he abdicated the throne to his son William II. On April 19, 1839, the Treaty of London recognized the independence and neutrality of Belgium, and established the independence of the Grand Duchy of Luxembourg and Duchy of Limburg, which were both greatly reduced in size due to the territories that Belgium, France, or Prussia acquired. They remained a de jure separate polity in personal union with the King of the Netherlands, who became the Duke, and the duchies remained part of the German Confederation until it was dissolved in 1866.

William II inherited a dire economic situation from continued debt repayment, and an agrarian crisis in the 1840s brought additional hardships, but the newer infrastructures helped restore wealth. Finance and trade, some of the oldest institutions, would again allow success. Britain had returned the East Indies colonies in 1815, and the Dutch soon established a new "cultivation system." Rather than merely collecting spices, a new system of cultivation selected a limited number of important cash crops for the European markets, such as coffee, sugar, and indigo, and this system raised nearly 30 percent of total national revenues. This fostered a high degree of capital and shipbuilding speculation, which eventually helped to reduce the national debt.

In 1848, liberal and democratic ideas once again spread throughout Europe, and William II realized that he needed to revise the constitution. Johan Rudolf Thorbecke became one of the most important liberals of the 19th century for his role in creating new structures; he was largely responsible for writing the new constitution. Starting in 1848, the Netherlands introduced a truly parliamentary government with a First Chamber (*Eerste Kamer*) composed of representatives chosen by the provincial states, and a Second Chamber (*Tweede Kamer*) with representatives chosen directly from the electorate. This government re-organization became a key element in recovering a more dynamic economy. In place of the older aristocratic regents and patricians who had been in power since the beginning of the Republic, the new players were the "notables" who had arisen because of wealth and to some degree, because of education.

This evolution from a more authoritarian monarchy to a parliamentary monarchy characterized the second half of the 19th century, and a greater voice for the workers through trade unions and male suffrage, economic reforms, and educational reform dominated social life. William II's new policies were not democratic, but were based on the census records of the most wealthy. Therefore, by mid-century, only 3.5 percent of the male population could vote, and it was not until 1896 that an amendment to the Constitution increased male suffrage to 49 percent and to 70 percent by 1916. Liberal policies allowed for the growth of labor unions, and in

1871, the first national union was founded: the Dutch Working Men's Association. From this time forward, many different associations formed within trades or under religious or socialist ideologies.

In 1866, the Netherlands faced a dilemma about its connections to Luxembourg and Limburg. Prussia had been increasing its hegemony and a Prussian garrison of 4–7,000 had represented the German Confederation in Luxembourg to ensure neutrality, but William II considered selling Luxembourg to France to rebalance the power. The 1867 "Conference in London" removed Luxembourg and Limburg from the German Confederation, thereby settling the issue. William's brother Prince Hendrik became the stadholder, but in 1890, when William III died, and had no male heirs, the hereditary title of Grand Duke, and his personal union, was passed on to the Nassau-Weilbourg line to fulfill the rules under Salic Law.

William II revised the antiquarian monetary system with the introduction of a standardized guilder, and he took other measures to create a more transparent governmental economic policy. "Since the late 16th century, this has been one of the most successful economies in the world. It has been amongst the top in terms of per-capita product or income, but never underwent an industrial revolution of the kind which typified the experience of its neighbors Britain, Belgium, parts of France, and Germany."[26] A closer look at the Netherlands in the late 18th and 19th centuries, however, reveals some striking fluctuations in the success of the many sectors that make up the economy. While the Netherlands had clearly been a leader in the pre-industrial world, it was one of the last Western European countries to eventually create modern industry. The reason for this industrial retardation lies in the fact that the Netherlands has always served in a supportive role for larger economies. In the pre-industrial world, they became the principal transportation system for central European agricultural products, and distributed the many products coming from the Baltic throughout Europe, and later, spices from Southeast Asia. The decline in Golden Age wealth had come after England and France had grown and developed overseas colonies. Caught in a complex series of wars, the Netherlands could not maintain its worldwide system of trade. When England and Germany began to industrialize, however, it was again the Netherlands that could concentrate on transportation and the supply of specialty goods to support growing populations and economies. Until World War I, the Netherlands experienced a period of peace under a neutral policy.

Second only to England, the Belgian Industrial Revolution at mid-century kept pace with the growing European economy, as opposed to that of the Netherlands. Belgium found success in new industrial products, in contrast to the Netherlands, where the once prosperous agricultural products were no longer competitive.[27] While international trade opened new markets for agricultural products, it was vulnerable, and the Netherlands suffered under the potato famine just like Ireland: food prices rose to record levels. When a ready supply of wheat and potatoes was not available, farmers placed a greater concentration on livestock, and dairy production increased, especially of butter and cheese, as well as of pork, sheep, and some beef. The agricultural sector experienced highs and lows based on the international market and competition, due partially to a lack of planning and in the form of flexible responses to market forces and demands.

One of the key reasons that the Netherlands lagged behind other industrialized states was its lack of natural resources. In addition to wood, iron, or other elements, they lacked any sources of energy, such as coal. Wind and water power could not keep up with industrialized demands, nor could the older burning of peat for fuel offer modern production what it needed, even though the price of peat was kept artificially high in the early 19th century due to the massive building of new canals. The earlier autocratic government of William I had also heavily taxed any importation of coal in order to protect the peat industry, but by mid-century, there was still no legislation with the foresight to consider a newer means of supplying greater energy. Industry also needed rail lines, and the Netherlands allowed private enterprise to develop with no state system until after the 1860s. Only after World War I would a national system develop, yet World War II completely devastated the rails, and only after the war could the Dutch rebuild a very modern, successful, and nationally owned railway institution.

In 1890, William III died, and since his three sons had experienced premature deaths, his wife Emma became Queen Regent until their daughter Wilhelmina reached the age of 18 in 1898, becoming the first queen of the Netherlands. Queen Wilhelmina would reign for 50 years, and became loved by her subjects, and showed great courage in World War I and II. The 1870s had marked a watershed in the Dutch economy. Despite the earlier success of agriculture, an agrarian depression occurred, lasting until the early 20th century, and in its place, industry finally grew. Colonial policy also changed and opened up more private enterprise, which led to a new and greater variety of crops, as well as the discovery of oil. The Dutch economy also developed via the emerging special interests groups centered along either Protestant or Catholic religious lines, or via socialist ideological lines connected with the poorer urban and rural groups. Cooperatives developed throughout the country from grass-roots organizations, and from a low of only 4 percent in 1893, by 1910, 44 percent of the workers were involved in cooperatives.[28] Cooperatives allowed farmers to optimize markets and raise capital, as well as to obtain insurance and gain knowledge through joint discussion. One example of these successful banks is the Rabobank, one of the top 25 banks in the world today, with 9 million customers in 35 countries.[29]

A good example of the new cooperation of government with manufacturing is the success of the margarine business. The government repealed the patent on margarine, after which the competitors Jurgen and van den Bergh joined forces in the Margarine Union to produce butter for insatiable English and German markets. Dutch companies also learned to cooperate with many English companies. In 1929, the Margarine Union merged with the British Lever Brothers to form Unilever, now one of the largest companies in the world, with over 87 subsidiary companies under several divisions. Likewise, oil production for the Royal Dutch Petroleum Company in Southeast Asia had lagged far below the oil companies of America, but after it was disestablished under antitrust legislation, Royal Dutch joined the British Shell Transport and Trading Company in 1907 to form Royal Dutch Shell, with the Dutch retaining 60 percent of the shares. Another example of government working to help new companies develop is the founding of Royal Philips Electronics N. V. In 1927, Philips acquired the British valve company, and in 1932, a German tube manufacturer, to create a large company with multiple electronic products. In 1927, Philips also produced the first radio broadcast to the Dutch East Indies.

## The 20th Century to the Present

The Netherlands remained neutral during World War I, but because of its proximity to the aggressor Germany, it felt great shock waves from the war; refugees cost the country 37 million guilders. Prior to the war, the country had deep divisions between the older nobility and merchant elites who still ran the country, and comprised a new middle class that had emerged in the nineteenth century, and a working class that had very few opportunities and little representation. In addition, deep rifts existed between a variety of Protestant groups, Roman Catholics, and a growing number who had identified more strongly with Socialist and even Communist workers parties. Abraham Kuyper, Prime Minister from 1901–1905, and quite active in society before and after his tenure, helped design a social system in which all of these separate bodies could be officially recognized by the government through separate political parties, schools, labor unions, clubs, and even hospitals. This new system of "pillarization" characterized the Netherlands until the 1960s.

Twentieth-century Netherlands grew from an agrarian and trade-based economy to a more industrial and service sector economy. Prior to the wars, labor unions and increased male suffrage grew slowly, and the new constitution of 1917 marked a watershed for granting real rights to the working classes. Universal male suffrage was finally assured, and an amendment in 1922 included all women, as well. In addition to voting rights, parliament also passed laws limiting the work week to 48 hours. But nothing could prepare the Netherlands for the international depression that was thrust upon them in the 1930s, as a result of which strikes and riots occurred, and the socialist party gained more adherents.

Long before the 1929 stock market crash in America, banking had suffered in the Netherlands as a result of World War I. The public had come to distrust the system after thousands of refugees flooded their shores and all silver coinage went out of circulation. To bolster the economy, the Netherlands Bank produced small denominations of one and two and a half guiders to stem the tide. There were some successes: Royal Dutch Airlines (KLM) was established in 1920; Philips Electronics acquired a larger share of the market; chemicals, porcelain, and other products began to take off; and agriculture had been transformed from wheat to vegetables, feeding the needs of Britain and Germany. Though the Netherlands was not immediately affected by the 1929 crash in the United States, large-scale unemployment eventually caused riots. Hendrikus Colijn, Prime Minister, sponsored the Labor Fund with a loan of 60 million guilders to support the economy. The real problem was that the Dutch tried to stay on the gold standard much later than other states, and in 1936, when France finally devalued its currency, the Dutch had to devalue the guilder, as well.

If World War I was a great hardship, World War II was worse when German forces began a blitzkrieg in Luxembourg, Belgium, and the Netherlands on May 10, 1940. On May 13, the Dutch Queen Wilhelmina departed for London and remained in exile until the end of the war. But the Queen heartedly supported the resistance from London and made regular radio addresses to the Netherlands on *Radio Oranje*. The Germans bombed Rotterdam on May 14, killing 900 Dutch, even though an act of capitulation had been signed. Martial law was quickly proclaimed throughout the country as an enforced conformity, and Arthur Seyss-Inquart, an Austrian Nazi, was appointed head of the government. Every man between the ages of 18 and 45 was forced to volunteer for work in German factories if the demand arose, and strict food rationing was enforced. Quite a few Dutch, however, believed that the Germans would be successful in defeating the Allies this time. The Dutch Prime Minister, Dirk Jan de Geer, tried to negotiate a separate peace treaty with the Germans, but eventually, Queen Wilhelmina had him removed from office, installing Pieter Gerbrandy in his place and thereby supporting an open resistance. The National Socialist Movement sympathized with the Nazis and grew to a high of 100,000 members; it was the only party allowed by the Germans. Among its members, 20,000 enlisted in the German army. The Germans built a line of defense along the North Sea called the Atlantic, and more than 20,000 houses were demolished, with 65,000 people relocated.

The destruction of Rotterdam in 1940. Courtesy of the National Archives.

Many Dutch resisted the Nazis. In addition to work slow-downs and strikes, the organized resistance performed much needed intelligence, subversion and guerilla attacks, as well as hiding as many Jews as possible. Jews were especially hard hit under German occupation. Many Jews lived in big cities, but the small size of the country and the absence of forests and mountainous areas made it more difficult for them to hide. Many Dutch nationals known as *onderduikers* (literally to dive under) attempted to hide the Jews. There were four independent resistance groups, and the LO (*Landelijke Organisatie*) had roughly 15,000 members looking after some 300,000 people in hiding.[30] Betsie and Corrie ten Boom, living in Haarlem, serve as an example of how many risked their lives to help people based on their Christian ethics. They hid Jews behind a false wall in the attic of their father's watch shop until they were arrested. Betsie, who remained very courageous, died in the concentration camp, while Corrie lived to tell her amazing story in the book and film *The Hiding Place*.

Still, an estimated 75 percent of the almost 140,000 Jews living in the Netherlands were killed by the Nazis, the highest percentage in Europe. At first, transit camps were created on Dutch soil, namely Westerbork, Amersfoort, Schoorl, Ommen, and Vught, but then the Nazis opened concentration camps, as well. By June 1942, however, most Jews were deported to Germany and Poland, and very few ever returned. Anne Frank's well-known story parallels the experience of thousands of Dutch Jews, and in 1942, when she was just 13, she began to write her diary in a small room hidden from the public. Just before the end of the war, conditions declined even further, and the winter of 1944–45 led to as many as 30,000 deaths due to starvation, cold, and disease. In 1945, the Allies began their final push, called Operation Market Garden, and they entered the Netherlands from the south and from Zeeland. On May 6, 1945, the Germans signed an act of surrender.

The infrastructure of the Netherlands after World War II was in utter chaos. Farms, houses, industry, ships, trains, and food supplies were destroyed. While the Dutch government worked vigorously to recover, one of its solutions was to encourage emigration, and in the 1950s, 560,000 migrated to the United States, Canada, South Africa, Australia, and New Zealand. Although Queen Wilhelmina was very popular during the war, her inability to come up with a policy to retain the East Indies colonies led to her abdication to her daughter Princess Juliana in 1948. The Japanese had already destroyed Dutch governance during their occupation in World War II, and after the war, nationalist leaders, such as Sukarno and Muhammad Hatta, convinced many Indonesians to seek independence. After much fighting, the Dutch government recognized Indonesia in December 1949, followed by the smaller colony of New Guinea in 1961, and the former South American colony of Suriname in 1975.

The Marshall Plan for Europe brought relief to the Netherlands, and the Low Countries of Belgium, the Netherlands, and Luxembourg formed the Benelux Customs Union in 1948, a market for approximately 28 million people, and in 1951, they added three more states to form the European Coal and Steel Community. The European Economic Community was formed in 1957, and by 1962, all agricultural goods had established price levels, followed in 1968 by the removal of many tariffs on trade. This European-wide cooperation led to the 1992 Maastricht Treaty establishing the European Union. In addition to Philips, Shell, and Unilever, new companies with an international competitive edge have been founded, including Ahol Foods (Albert Heijn Holdings), acquiring stores throughout Europe, Asia, and North and South America.

The Dutch have always been known for their banking, and the merger of the ABN (Algemene Bank Nederland, with roots in the NHM of 1824) with the AMRO (Amsterdam and Rotterdam banks of 1964) created the 15th largest bank in the world by 2007. In addition to the Rabobank, the ING bank was established in 1991 out of a merger between the Nationale Nederalanden and the NMB Postbank Group, with direct roots in banks from 1845, but also in the 1743 Kooger Doodenbos Company. With its major international banks and companies, the Netherlands is ranked 16th in the world for GDP, and 10th in GDP purchasing power parity.

The modern Netherlands has been an active partner in all major international multilateral organizations. Although neutrality had limited success in World War I, the experience of German occupation and the atrocities committed on Dutch soil convinced the Dutch to set another course for foreign policy. In 1920, the League of Nations established the International Court of Justice in The Hague, and the Dutch became founding members of the United Nations in 1945 and of NATO in 1949. The Hague continues to sponsor key international organizations, such as the Organization for the Prohibition of Chemical Weapons (OPCW). It is the leader in unearmarked assistance to UN humanitarian initiatives, and approximately half of the country's development funds go to Africa.

The necessity of cooperation, established as far back as the Late Middle Ages, has continued to comprise an element of contemporary Dutch politics. The Dutch political scientist Arend Lijphart has analyzed this system through the concept of "consociational" democracy based on the political system in the Netherlands for over 100 years, with roots throughout its history.[31] This political cooperation and consensus building has developed into a situation where many distinctive groups compete for recognition and representation in government, but each realizes that no one group could ever dominate. From the 1960s onward, there was a process of de-pillarization in which the original groups, Protestant, Catholic, Socialist, and Liberal, began to dissolve into multiple political parties. Today, there are 13 political parties with some representation in the Dutch and European Parliaments, with four parties sharing substantial ministries and administrative posts.

The Dutch government is a parliamentary monarchy, and the current Queen Beatrix took office in 1980; the heir apparent is her son Prince Willem-Alexander. The monarch is the head of state, and in addition to forming a cabinet, must co-sign all laws, although the policy has been for the Queen to refrain from an active role in legislative matters and, rather, seek to offer a non-partisan and moral role to promote unity.

## NOTES

1. Another theory suggests that the word "Holland" comes from the Celtic language used by the many monks who made their way from the islands of the contemporary United Kingdom and Ireland to the continent. Therefore, "ol" is derived from the Celtic "olatu," meaning waves, "la" is taken from "alaitu," meaning to fill with joy, and "and" is derived from "andar," meaning speeding; thus, "Holland" translates to "speeding the waves fills us with joy." See E. F. Legner, "Dutch Language Development," University of California, Riverside, http://www.faculty.ucr.edu/~legneref/bronze/dutch.htm.

2. Extensive digging for peat in the 12th century created a lake, and from 1609 to 1612 windmills pumped the water out, creating a grid of canals and dikes, as well as very good farm land. UNESCO has praised this engineering feat for its creative and innovative planning and the positive relationship that it engenders between humankind and water.

3. See Simon Schama, *The Embarrassment of Riches: An Interpretation of Dutch Culture in the Golden Age* (Berkeley: University of California Press, 1988), 44.

4. See UNESCO World Heritage Sites, Retrieved August 18, 2008, "The Defense Line of Amsterdam," http://whc.unesco.org/en/statesparties/nl.

5. See P.H. Nienhuis, *Environmental History of the Rhine-Meuse Delta: An Ecological Story on Evolving human-environmental Relations Coping with Climate Change and Sea-level Rise* (New York: Springer, 2008).

6. See DeltaWorks, Retrieved May 27, 2008, http://www.deltawerken.com/English/10.html?setlanguage=en.

7. See U.S. Census Bureau, Retrieved May 29, 2008, http://www.census.gov/population/www/ancestry.html.

8. See Centraal Bureau voor de Statistiek, Retrieved February 15, 2008, http://www.cbs.nl/nl-NL/menu/methoden/toelichtingen/alfabet/a/allochtoon.htm; *Facts and Figures of the Netherlands: Social and Cultural Trends 1995–2006*, ed. Theo Roes (The Hague: The Netherlands Institute for Social Research, 2008), Retrieved February 18, 2008, www.scp.nl/english/publications/books/9789037702118/Facts-and-Figures-of-the-Netherlands.pdf.

9. Theo Roes, ed., *Facts and Figures of the Netherlands: Social and Cultural Trends 1995–2006* (The Hague: SCP, the Netherlands Institute for Social Research, 2008), 13.

10. See Centrum voor Onderzoek and Statistiek, Rotterdam, May 27, 2008, http://www.cos.rotterdam.nl/.

11. See Dutch Ministry of Foreign Affairs/Nederlandse Ministerie van Buitenlandse Zaken, Retrieved May 27, 2008, www.minbuza.nl/en/welcome/DutchCitizens, dutch_nationality/how_can_i_acquire_dutch_nationalityx.html.

12. See Council of Europe, "European Charter for Regional or Minority Languages," http://conventions.coe.int/Treaty/EN/Treaties/Html/148.htm.

13. See J. C. H. Blom and E. Lamberts, eds., *History of the Low Countries,* trans. James C. Kennedy (New York: Berghahn Books, 1999), 109.

14. The southern provinces below the Rhine-Meuse delta were Brabant, Flanders (Flemish- and French-speaking Walloon), Artois, Cambrai, Namur, Mechelen, Hainault, Limburg, and Luxembourg. The Bishopric of Liège formed a territory surrounded by other southern provinces, but was not incorporated into the official collection until it was captured by France in 1795. The northern provinces included Holland, Zeeland, Utrecht, Gelderland (Duchy of Guelders), Overijssel, Groningen, Drenthe, and Friesland.

15. See Guido Marnef, *Antwerp in the Age of Reformation: Underground Protestantism in a Commercial Metropolis, 1550–1577,* trans. J. C. Grayson (Baltimore, MD: The Johns Hopkins UP, 1996).

16. See Jonathan Israel, *The Dutch Republic: Its Rise, Greatness, and Fall 1477–1806.* (Oxford: Clarendon Press, 1995), 139.

17. A "One Hundreth Penny," a new 5 percent sales tax, and a "Tenth Penny." See Jonathan I Israel, *The Dutch Republic: Its Rise, Greatness, and Fall, 1477–1806* (Oxford: Clarendon Press, 1995), 166; Willem Pieter Blockmans, Walter Prevenier, Elizabeth Fackelman. Edward Peters, ed., *The Promised Lands: the Low Countries Under Burgundian Rule, 1369–1530*, trans. Wim Blockmans, (Philadelphia: University of Pennsylvania Press, 1999).

18. "Act of Abjuration" (*Plakkaat van Verlatinghe*, July 26, 1581), University of Leiden, February 16, 2008, http://www.let.rug.nl/~usa/D/1501–1600/plakkaat/plakkaaten.htm.

19. The official title was the Republic of Seven United Netherlands Provinces, or *Republiek der Zeven Verenigde Nederlanden/Provinciën.*

20. See Schama, *The Embarrassment of Riches,* 35 (". . . they held a sacred title to their land.").

21. See Jan de Vries and Ad van der Woude, *The First Modern Economy: Success, Failure, and Perseverance of the Dutch Economy, 1500–1815* (Cambridge: Cambridge University Press, 1997).

22. See A. T. van Deursen, "The Dutch Republic, 1588–1780," in *History of the Low Countries*, eds. Blom and Lamberts, 145 (". . . through this order Philip unwittingly saved the Republic.")

23. See Israel, *The Dutch Republic*, 246; and Deursen, "The Dutch Republic," 164.

24. deVries and van der Woude, *The First Modern Economy*, 593.

25. Ibid., 682. ("after 1713, interest payments absorbed over 70 percent of Holland's tax revenue, . . . ")

26. Michael Wintle, *An Economic and Social History of the Netherlands 1800–1920* (Cambridge: Cambridge University Press, 2000), 69.

27. See Jan Luiten Van Zanden and Arthur van Riel, *The Strictures of Inheritance: The Dutch Economy in the Nineteenth Century* (Princeton, NJ: Princeton University Press, 2004), 194.

28. Ibid., 285.

29. Based on the principles of the German financier Raiffeisen, who established the first cooperative bank, the Dutch established the Cooperative Central Raiffeisen Bank, which later merged with the Cooperative Central Farmer's Credit Bank (*Boerenleenbank*). Eventually, these two merged into the Rabobank (Ra-bo-bank), specifically in 1972.

30. See Arblaster, *A History of the Low Countries*, 228.

31. See Arend Lijphart, *The Politics of Accommodation: Pluralism and Democracy in the Netherlands* (Berkeley: University of California Press, 1968).

# 2

# Religion and Thought

### Indigenous Celtic and German to Christian Religions

The indigenous people of the Netherlands practiced various forms of tribal and pagan religions. Many of these beliefs were tied to nature and the powers that they assumed controlled their lives and destinies. Some Germanic and Celtic practices were later taken up by Christians and sacralized as new rituals; thus, a distinctive northwestern Christianity began to grow. Christianity had been introduced into the Netherlands under the earlier Franks by Saint Amand in the Scheldt River region. He founded the monasteries of St. Peter (630) and St. Bavo (642) in Ghent, and his tomb in Saint-Amand-les-Eaux (near Tournai) became a place of pilgrimage. Saint Willibrord went further north to the Frisians, establishing a bishopric in Utrecht in 695, and later establishing a significant monastery in the south at Echternach in Luxembourg.

The spread of Christianity was undoubtedly connected with the Franks' interest in expanding their hegemony further north. Christianity would only slowly take root among the common people, and many reversals and renewals occurred. This was certainly the case with Saint Boniface, the patron saint of Germany and the Netherlands. Born Winfrid in the Kingdom of Wessex (England), he led a missionary to the continent. His first attempt to convert the Frisians in 716 ended in defeat, partially because the Frankish king

Charles Martel was battling the Frisians under King Radbod. Winfrid turned his attention to the Saxons, and in 1723, he chopped down the great oak tree dedicated to the god Thor; widespread conversion occurred as a result. To demonstrate God's power, like the Old Testament prophet Elijah, Winfrid retained the sacral image of the tree, but showed its Christian significance in the cross of Jesus Christ, whereby the *Tannenbaum* reclaimed its ritual significance for Christmas. Winfrid was given the name "Boniface" by Pope Gregory II and the title of archbishop of Germany, as well. After great success in Germany and with the Franks in 754, he again set out to missionize the Frisians, and to take over the vacated bishopric of Willibrord, who had died in 744. This time, he successfully converted many Frisians, but not all followed his message, and he was murdered in 755. By the eighth century, the bishopric of Utrecht was firmly established, with dioceses in Deventer and Haarlem.

Once Christianity took root among the nobility of the Netherlands, it was used for this group's own local interests, and its members had little contact with the universal church. Dirk II, Count of West Frisia (later renamed Holland), built the Abbey of Egmond in 922 near the modern city of Alkmaar in North Holland. Like Charlemagne's renaissance in Aachen, the monastery was responsible for developing the Dutch language in its growing scriptorium, and had links with other northern monasteries. Indeed, the name "Egmond" is comprised of the prefix "eg," which means to create, "mo," which means skillfully, and the suffix "ond," which refers to common inheritance.[1] In 1024, the Holy Roman Empire granted the title of Prince to the bishops of Utrecht, and the northeast section of the Netherlands, including the provinces of Utrecht, Groningen, Drenthe, and Overijssel, was part of this new theocracy. Other areas of the Low Countries also developed powerful local monasteries and bishoprics. The largest was the Bishopric of Liège. Lambert of Maastricht (Tongeren) had been appointed bishop by the Franks, and upon his death, the new bishop, Hubert, moved the See to Liège, and eventually the territory grew into a great Prince-Bishopric as a result of significant donations or land purchases. The Bishopric of Liège was squeezed between the Duchy of Brabant and Luxembourg, and although it was not officially part of the 17 provinces of the Low Countries, it was involved in local politics, and defended its territory. Although it retained its autonomy, and in time was recognized as a great place of learning, the Bishopric of Liège was officially part of the Holy Roman Empire. Working within the bishopric was Rupert of Deutz (c. 1075–1130), a scholar of liturgy, poetry, and scripture, as well as a mystic; his commentaries were used extensively to guide religious art and interest in the Bible. Liège was also recognized for its tradition of the feast of Corpus Christi, which was instituted for all of

Christendom by a former archdeacon who became Pope Urban IV in 1261. The power of Liège extended even further when another archdeacon became Pope Gregory X in 1271.

By the time the Renaissance began, the 17 provinces had only four dioceses: Utrecht, subject to Cologne, and Tournai, Arras, and Cambrai, who were all subject to Reims. Some of the low-lying areas of Flanders were settled by numerous monasteries, each order had a different focus. The new Cisterian monastic order preferred to venture into the wastelands of Europe and establish missionary outposts. The order was strict in terms of its disciplines and emphasis on sanctification. It developed the lands for agricultural use, and many of the lay brothers built dikes to maintain the reclaimed land. The goal of new mendicant monasteries was to minister to the growing urban centers in Flanders and Holland. The Dominicans performed very successful mission work in the Low Countries, and they established great houses in

The Amsterdam Historical Museum entrance off the Kalverstraat in Amsterdam is located at the old Orphanage established in 1520, and this doorway was built in 1581. Courtesy of the author.

Lille in 1224, Ghent and Leuven in 1228, and Utrecht 1232. As an order of preachers, the Dominicans were quite effective in bringing a more personal faith and piety to ordinary people.

### Devotio Moderna

In the early 14th century, a religious renewal known as the Modern Devotion (*Devotio Moderna*) incorporated lay piety with the local revivals of Augustinian monasticism (another new mendicant order) and northern Renaissance humanism. The history of the Brethren of the Common Life illustrates the local piety that was developing in the Low Countries, yet this phenomenon affected all of northern Europe. Geert Groote was a popular preacher who ministered throughout the eastern and central cities of Deventer, Zwolle, Kampen, and Zutphen, but also had some influence further west in Utrecht, Amsterdam, Leiden, and Delft. After spending his earlier years studying and enjoying the wealth of the times, he converted sometime around 1374 under the instruction of a Carthusian monastery. Although he never joined the Carthusians, Groote adopted their philosophy of living a more simple life with a special personal devotion to Jesus Christ, and he preached against the contemporary corruptions of the period, such as simony, concubinage, and empty ritual. His preaching angered some churchmen and nobility, and the Bishop of Utrecht was forced to prohibit his ministry. Groote founded a new-style community of lay believers (often made up of the poor) who, like the tertiary orders of the Franciscans, were allowed to devote themselves to a life of piety and good works without taking full vows. The name, the Brethren of the Common Life, denoted their focus: they were a community devoted to piety in common life. But Groote knew that he needed to connect the Brethren to an established religious order for Church approval, and he determined that the newer Augustinian order would be the best connection.

In the year 1256, a new mendicant order had been established using the rule of St. Augustine. The rule had been used by a few monks already, such as Norbert of Xanten, who established a monastery in Prémontré in northern France in 1120. Subsequent conferences sponsored by the Pope as a result of the Gregorian reforms developed the rule into a regular order that counter-balanced the Dominican and Franciscan orders. Groote visited the well-known mystic Jan van Ruysbroec, who was the prior of the Groenendaal Augustinian canons near Brussels, and who was inspired by what he saw there. Groote was determined to found an Augustinian canon in the north, but he died prematurely from the plague that struck in Deventer in 1384. His followers, under the leadership of Florens Radewyns, continued his plan and opened an Augustinian canon house in Windesheim, between Deventer and Zwolle, in 1387. Windesheim became the chief house of more than 86 various houses by the end of the 15th century; "canons" denoted priests following the Augustinian rule, while "convents" were religious women who took vows.

The Brethren of the Common Life became the central force in religious and social renewal throughout the Low Countries and northern Germany. Many of the established orders did not like their methods, yet they had papal protection from several popes. The Brethren established centers with scriptoriums and some of the first printing presses, which distributed Christian literature, and they were determined to support the laity through early education. They blurred the line between monks and laity by encouraging the reading of scripture and personal piety, and encouraged the dignity of regular work, rather than the contemplative medieval life. Among the well-known figures representing this movement was Thomas à Kempis, who wrote one of the most universally read books of Christian devotional literature, *The Imitation of Christ*. Many later reformers, such as Erasmus, Martin Luther, Cardinal Nicholas of Cusa, and Rudolf Agricola, credited their early education and piety to their attendance at the Brethren's primary schools.

The newer Augustinian thought was integrated with Renaissance humanism, and it stood against late medieval scholasticism, which relied on ancient Stoicism and reason. For Augustinian humanists, the body was not the inferior part; it contained a will and a heart that could be renewed. A special emphasis was placed on reading and studying the Bible—by scholars and ordinary laity alike. "Augustinian humanism attacked the spiritual elitism of the Stoic tradition, both in its loftier forms and in its application to government; and it was thus more sympathetic to those populist movements that found religious expression in the dignity of lay piety, political expression in the challenge of republicanism to despotism."[2] While the Augustinians and Brethren did not have political motives, the established Church in the Empire often saw them as subverting its tradition and power.

Another religious movement that contributed to a distinctive Low Countries spirituality was the founding of the beguines. These philanthropic communities cared for women, especially the many widows and orphans resulting from the Crusades. There were not many options for women at the time; noble women had the option of marriage or a convent, but many poor women were without means and could barely survive. The beguines allowed them to live together in a monastic-like setting without taking full vows, and they were more democratic and freer than regular nuns. Some of the first communities appeared in the Prince Bishopric of Liège under the direction of the reforming priest Lambert Le Bègue in the middle of the 12th century. Like Groot, he preached against simony and many other abuses in the Church, as well for reading the Bible in the vernacular and pledging devotion to the Eucharist. He encouraged the founding of the beguines around 1170, and by 1250, they had spread throughout the Low Countries, Germany, and Italy. In contrast to convents, beguines did not have any universal rules or leadership, and each community was autonomous. There was a new quest to return to the *vita apostolica,* or the original and early Church, in light of the increasing wealth and power of the institutionalized Church. The fully established beguines had a church, cemetery, hospital, and residences located within an enclosed courtyard (*hof,* and *begijnhofs* in Dutch). The largest and most well-known *Beguinages* were located in Ghent, Mechelin, Brussels, Leuven, Bruges, and Amsterdam. Like the Brethren of the Common Life, the beguines were often brought up on charges of heresy due to their ambiguous status under the Church until they found a defender in Cardinal Jacques de Vitry (c. 1230s). One of the greatest writers of the time was Hadewijch of Brabant, who lived in several beguinages throughout Brabant, and her extensive poems about her visions and mystical experiences became well known.

## RENAISSANCE, REFORMATION, AND THE DUTCH REPUBLIC

### Erasmus and Humanism

Renaissance humanism had developed into two branches by the early 16th century. The earlier Italian humanism focused on new methods to uncover ancient wisdom, and scholars rediscovered Greco-Roman philosophy, literature, and politics. Later, northern European, Christian humanism used the same methods to uncover biblical texts and the early church fathers. New vernacular translations of the Bible were written in French and Dutch, with reference to the original Hebrew and Greek versions, often bypassing the official Latin version of the Roman Church. By far the most important Christian Humanist in the Low Countries was Desiderius Erasmus of Rotterdam, known throughout Christendom. Educated in Paris, where humanism had become the dominant study applied to theology by 1450, Erasmus advanced study of the Bible with his translation of the New Testament in 1516. Reflecting Augustinian thought, Ronald Witt has aptly summarized Erasmus' primary focus on the "philosophy of Christ," reflecting Netherlandic piety: ". . . the grounding of the true word of Christ in the 'viscera of the mind.' This intimate contact transformed the human will into a creative source for acts of love within this world."[3] This new focus implicity highlighted the abuses, misuse of hierarchical powers, and empty rituals in the contemporary Church. Erasmus never renounced the Church in Rome, but his humanism and calls for reform certainly reflect a growing uneasiness with the practice of religion in the Low Countries on the eve of the Reformation.

## Protestantism: Lutheran, Calvinist, and Anabaptist

In the early 16th century, Low Countries' traditional authority and jurisdiction was called into question by many. Religion and politics were intertwined, as the established Church retained many of the functions that the modern state has since taken over, and this concentrated social power in the hands of an elite group. While Pope Leo X, in his *Debitum Pastoralis* of 1520, had attempted to grant the Bishop of Utrecht local autonomy so no one would challenge his authority, anticlerical challenges called for more freedom for the laity and also for local autonomy. Yet, the Netherlands was not without its own influences on the rest of the Church: Adriaan Florenszoon Boeyens of the Netherlands was Pope Adrian VI for one year prior to his death in 1523. He had been educated by the Brethren of the Common Life and followed its goal to reform the church. He became the tutor of the future Charles V and was later sent to Spain as a bishop, where he was commissioned as Grand Inquisitor of Aragon by 1516. In 1527, the Prince-Bishop of Utrecht, Hendrik II of Bavaria, sold his property to Charles V, and these lands were passed on to the Habsburgs; therefore, with papal approval, Charles could appoint a bishop. Although he had some knowledge of the culture, he reneged on the long-standing agreement for local autonomy and increasingly centralized the state in Brussels, appointing his sister Mary of Hungary to rule.

While the new ideas of Martin Luther flourished just over the border in Saxony and throughout the German lands, acceptance of his teachings came quite late to the Low Countries; one might have expected a quicker response, given the fact that he was an Augustinian monk and a humanist scholar who called for reform. Because Luther's protest against the abuse of indulgences could cost the empire valuable revenue, Charles V used all of his energies to try to quell Luther. That may have eventually made Luther's ideas more attractive to the people of the Low Countries since literacy rates were so high in the merchant cities where printing abounded, as well. But then again, by the early 16th century, reform had been present for a long time, and the rise of wealth, yet the relative lack of great religious demonstrations, slowed the progress of the Reformation.

More appealing to some Netherlanders was a concern for the poor and peasant population. Menno Simonzoon was a Frisian priest who had grown up in an area where the Saxon dukes had fought bitterly with the dukes of Guelders over control of the free areas of the northern Netherlands. In 1536, he broke with the Catholic Church over the question of baptism, preferring the doctrine of adult baptism practiced by the growing Anabaptist movement that had begun earlier in Switzerland. In their reading of the Bible, the Anabaptists did not understand it to teach infant baptism, but rather, based on literal examples, only recognized adult baptism in the first-century church. Menno began to travel extensively throughout Europe, partially as a result of his "illegal" activities, which most overlords rejected, yet his influence over the poor was great. His Anabaptist followers were called *Mennisten* and later Mennonites. In contrast to both Catholic and Protestant reformers, Menno disconnected his church from any magisterial control and concentrated rather on discipleship within the community of believers, shunning political office, the bearing of arms, and oath taking. They agreed with the Protestant reformers, however, in stressing personal conversion, Bible reading, and a direct relationship with Jesus Christ. Menno appealed to the northern Netherlanders in particular because his writings captured their language and social situation at the time. Although many Mennonites contributed large sums of money to fight the Spanish, because of persecution by Catholics and Reformed in the Low Countries, vast numbers migrated to Eastern Europe to create isolated communities where they were left alone.

The Reformed movement came slowly to the Netherlands. Long before the Protestant churches were established, preachers came to the large merchant towns to speak of a reform in the historic Christian Church, based on the newest humanist methods of recovering the original Gospel. Antwerp was one of the largest merchant cities of the time, with its population growing from 89,000 in 1556 to 100,000 in 1568.[4] Since the Inquisition was strong in the south, those who followed the Reformed at first had to meet clandestinely and their gatherings were referred to as "churches under the cross." From 1562 onward, Antwerp attracted thousands who thronged to hear Reformed Calvinist preaching, and while some left the Catholic fold for the Reformed community, many remained in a "broad middling group" (crypto-Protestants) that was very attracted to the message, but felt no need to seek permanent membership outside the Catholic Church.[5] In the French-speaking cities of Tournai, Mons, Valenciennes, and Lille, which were closer to the persecuted Huguenot churches of France, more permanent Reformed congregations established thriving organizations. Guido de Brès, a minister who was active in all of these locations, published a new doctrinal statement in the Belgic Confession in 1561 to articulate the most important biblical truths of the Christian faith.

In 1555, Charles V abdicated to his son, Philip II, as King of Spain and ruler of the Habsburg Netherlands. Unlike his father, Philip was not raised in the Low Countries and consequently, he knew very little of its culture and history. While Charles had attempted to root out heretics, the actual numbers of persecutions were very small—from 1521–1550, there was an average of only 13 convictions a year—compared to his son Philip's fury from 1561–1564, when that number rose to 264 a year.

Until then, Reformed preaching had appealed to the urban merchants and artisans, but the persistence of Spanish rulers in dominating religious and political institutions brought the nobility into the fight. In 1565, the League of Compromise, under the leadership of Hendrik Brederode and with the support of the Sea Beggers (*Gueux*), presented a petition to Margaret stating that if she would dismantle the Inquisition, end religious persecution, and open the States General, they would agree to support the crown and Church. But the Inquisition continued, and many Reformed in the French-speaking south were forcibly reconverted by the sword, or lost their lives. In August of 1566, a fiery sermon of protest called for an end to the papal idolatry, and wholesale destruction of Church property ensued with an iconoclastic fury. By the autumn of 1566, so many members of the nobility had taken up the cause of rejecting the Roman Catholic Church, and accepting the new Reformed faith, that it was called the "Wonderyear." William of Orange-Nassau, the most important noble, courted the Reformed, even though he would have liked a permanent plural state. By 1567, the struggle was beyond repair: two of the most loyal nobles of the crown, Egmond and Horn, were beheaded by the Duke of Alva, followed by another 18 nobles. More than 1,000 people were executed, and another 11,000 were banished from the region. Within a year, more than 60,000 Netherlanders had made a mass exodus to either Emden in East Friesland, Cleves in the Rhineland, or England.

Emden, part of greater Saxony, was home to many Reformed by 1571, and the first synod was held in order to officially organize a renewed church, which marked the beginning of the Reformed Church in the Netherlands. Not only Spain, but France increased its persecution, and in 1572, the St. Bartholomew's Day Massacre occurred in Paris, leaving more than 2,000 dead there and an estimated 5–10,000 throughout France. As a result of this polarization, the States of Holland forbade Catholic worship in 1573, despite the fact that many Catholics had been equally opposed to the harsh measures taken against ancient liberties in the Low Countries. Following the synod in Emden, the city of Dordrecht in Holland sponsored a synod to organize an ecclesiastical institution situated more directly in the heart of the struggle for freedom. In Flanders, Ghent declared itself a Calvinist Republic in 1577, and Brussels and Antwerp formed revolutionary committees and governments. By 1579, the seven northern provinces declared independence from Habsburg, Spain. The mottos of the new republic reflect this dual call for freedom and religion: *Haec Libertatis Ergo* ("This is for the sake of freedom") and *Haec Religionis Ergo* ("This is for the sake of religion").[6] Catholicism was forbidden to be openly practiced in the north, and after the archbishop of Utrecht

The New Church (Nieuw Kerk) in Delft took the entire 15th century to build. In 1584, William the Silent was entombed here in a mausoleum designed by Hendrick and Pieter de Keyser, and since then, all members of the royal family are buried in the crypt. Courtesy of the author.

died in 1559, he was not replaced until 1602. Despite William of Orange's attempt to mediate a truce, he was murdered in 1584, silencing any moderate voice. All of the southern provinces fell to the Spanish, and more than 200,000 Reformed moved north.

Another synod in The Hague composed a final agreement with the new Republic to make the Reformed Church a "public church," where marriage, care for the poor, and baptism would be officially recognized by the state, without making it a state church; it became a "monitorial rather than magisterial" church.[7] Even as the war with Spain raged on, the Renaissance was encouraging great strides among Dutch scholars. Often called the father of the Dutch Renaissance, Dirck Volckertszoon Coornhert was a philosopher, theologian, and politician, as well as a copper engraver; he constituted an example of how many scholars followed a craft and devoted themselves to learning. Like Erasmus, Coornhert never left the Catholic Church, although he despised Spanish rule, but labored endlessly to reform it through personal piety and humanist scholarship. Together with the Spiritualists, Sebastian Franck and Caspar Schwenckfeld, he insisted on tolerance because he believed in human perfectibility (the ability to completely obey God). Coornhert labored endlessly to spread his ideas through numerous publications and high-profile debates. He translated Homer, Cicero, Seneca, and Boethius into Dutch. He was also given the position of secretary of the city of Haarlem, and produced the manifesto that William the Silent used against the Spanish. He was known for promoting tolerance at a time of heightened polemics.[8]

In 1618, one of the most important national synods met in Dordrecht to address doctrinal issues, and establish catechisms and confessions, together with the Heidelberg Catechism (1563) and the Belgic Confession (1561). The synod approved the "States Bible" that recognized a national language comprised of a combination of the dialects of Holland and Brabant, translated directly from Hebrew, Greek, and Aramaic. The synod also settled a great internal struggle within the larger Reformed Church over the nature of salvation and predestination. Jacob Arminius, a theologian teaching in Leiden, questioned Calvin's interpretation of divine predestination because

The Zuiderkerk in Amsterdam was the first church built specifically for Protestant use in 1611. Courtesy of the author.

he felt it could not account for human responsibility; God's choices appeared too arbitrary. In his mind, a just God elected those people who he knew would believe, thus underlining a person's choices. By contrast, the Calvinists, led by Franciscus Gomarus, designed a five-point doctrinal statement, "The Canons of Dordt," that has become famous for the acronym TULIP: Total depravity, Unconditional election, Limited atonement, Irresistible grace, and Perseverance of the saints. Because the Calvinists included representatives of Reformed churches from Switzerland, Germany, France, and Britain, the Canons of Dordt became internationally recognized as central teachings.[9] This theological impasse threatened to divide the new state, so the government wanted a common agreement, and their eventual support for the Calvinists was based partially on the political exigencies of the time. The synod concluded that the Calvinists had won most of their concessions, but a spirit of tolerance eventually led to the recognition of a variety of Protestant churches. The Remonstrant Church, known for its document of protest, followed Arminius' teachings, and small Lutheran and Mennonite churches were also able to practice their faiths.

Although the initial Union of Utrecht that formed the first Republic attempted to safeguard the Catholic Church in the north, the polemical battles caused by the revolt against Spain weakened the resolve for religious peace. There was a pragmatic mood in the republic: "Article 13 of the Union of Utrecht decreed a 'don't ask, don't tell' form of freedom of conscience, which provided space for alternative religious groups to maintain a low-key presence in the Republic. This was true even for Catholicism. Although Mass had been declared illegal, priests continued to serve their congregation in secret, supported by an underground network of pious women, *klopjes*, who were successors to the Beguines."[10] Recognizing that the Catholic Church had lost its territory in the new Republic, Pope Clement VIII declared it a "mission church" under the control of an apostolic vicar; a titular bishop with no jurisdiction over provinces looked to Mechelen until the restoration of 1853. Because the central site of the Reformed Church was located in the Netherlands, no other Christian religions were allowed to build churches in large cities, but instead had to meet in smaller quarters that did not resemble churches. The two most famous "churches" were the Catholic "Our Lord of the Attic" in the Amsterdam Beguinage, and the Remonstrant Church in a one-time hat store called "The Red Hat" (*De Rode Hoed*) and located on the *Keizersgracht* (street) in Amsterdam.

In time, there was also division within the Dutch Catholic Church. In the 1630s, Catholic theologian Cornelius Jansen underlined the Augustinian doctrines of election and complete reliance on God's grace for salvation, something that the papacy found to be too similar to the Calvinist and Lutheran doctrines. It also drew from the older spirituality of the Low Countries, which was conscious of personal piety and accountability to a community of believers. In many ways, they were the Jesuits' number one enemies. As Jansenism grew in the Low Countries and France, neither the papacy nor vigorous Jesuit activity could completely control the movement that eventually formed the Old Catholic Church, with Utrecht rather than Rome as its center. The Old Catholic Church was established when Petrus Codde, the apostolic vicar of Utrecht, supported Jansenist ideas. In 1701, the Pope suspended him, eventually excommunicating his followers as well. Many Dutch Catholics underlined the 1520 agreement to allow no outside ecclesiastical interference and declared an independent Old Catholic Church in the Netherlands. They continued to inform the Pope of the election of an archbishop of Utrecht, but refused to acknowledge any Vatican decisions. In 1725, the Dutch banned apostolic vicars in support of the Old Catholic Church in Utrecht, despite the fact that many Dutch Catholics remained loyal to Rome. For the most part, the majority of Catholics resided in two southern provinces of Brabant and Limburg and thus, they enjoyed some local privileges. The Jesuits were able to gain widespread support among the nobility for their excellent education, both at the primary and secondary levels, including religious education.

The character of Dutch religion can be identified in this early period: Dutch spirituality remained localized, more personal, and communal, and was open to new ideas. The majority found themselves situated in a broad middle ground, with a more pragmatic attitude toward ecclesiastical organizations and traditions. Whether Protestant or Catholic, a tradition of simple piety, lay involvement, and an Augustinianism continued to give Dutch Christianity a distinctive character and, compared to other states, relative tolerance. If the state restricted religious practices in public, it did not trample on freedom of conscience. If the language that developed surrounding religion is an indicator of its character, it is interesting that the word *godsdienst* (religion), literally meaning "to serve God," denoted the practical piety whereby religion meant service to God in works that supported the community.

Justus Lipsius (Joost Lips) represents an interesting case for the Netherlands in his attempt to reconcile Stoic ideas, especially the Roman philosopher and statesman Seneca, with Christianity in contrast to the prevailing Augustinian thought. Born in Brabant, he taught in Leiden from 1579–1590, and his book *On Constancy* showed how the ideal republic must be administered through reason by magistrates who are in control of their emotions, and able to create strong discipline among its citizens and to protect itself with a strong military. In this age of revolution, his ideas resonated with many people, but his application of Stoicism eventually underlined the importance of a complete religious unity that denied the pragmatic tolerance of the Dutch Republic. Although he was supported by the University of Leiden, he returned to teach in Leuven, where he more publicly assented to the importance of the Roman Catholic Church.

The pragmatic and limited tolerance, based on "a mixture of sentiment, tradition, and expediency," allowed Jews greater freedom than any other state at that time.[11] By 1600, the Sephardic Spanish and Portuguese Jews began to arrive in Amsterdam, where they could openly practice their faith again. They brought with them great skills as merchants, and because of their ability to speak Hebrew in addition to their Iberian languages, they had important connections to the Mediterranean world, the Middle East, and throughout Europe.[12] While largely restricted to Amsterdam at first, they contributed to the wealth of the entire Republic, and for their support of the house of Orange-Nassau, they were protected by the stadholders. Due to the violent religious wars that had erupted in central Europe by the mid-17th century, the Republic experienced its second great influx of Jews from the German lands, the Ashkenazim. In contrast to the highly skilled and wealthy Sephardic Jews, the Ashkenazim were poor and unskilled; they settled in very small communities throughout the Republic, where they were hawkers and peddlers. Only later did some of them acquire skills and prosperity, especially within the diamond industry, as the wealth of the Republic increased by the late 17th century.

### Science and Philosophy

The Renaissance in the Low Countries spawned great scientific and intellectual study. Because of their struggle with the sea and their necessary cooperation in land reclamation and management, plus their active trade, which was supported by an enormous fleet of ships, the Dutch understood the importance of technology in continually fulfilling their needs. The extensive merchant activity and industry produced a pragmatism that encouraged new discoveries. The Reformed encouraged scientific discovery, and many theologians practiced science in order to gain an understanding of their creator.

Hugo Grotius is famous for his *Mare Liberum* (*The Free Seas,* 1609), for he used knowledge of international law to claim that beyond the immediate state borders, the seas must be free for transportation and trade. This certainly benefited the Dutch view of world trade and served the interests of the VOC, and it also stood to restrict the monopolies that the monarchies of Europe wanted to maintain. The Englishman John Seldon countered this claim, but as many more states with interests in world-wide exploration entered the fray, another Dutchman, Cornelius Bynkershoek, offered the workable solution of a three-mile limit surrounding the coastline. Grotius was actively involved with the Netherlands' government, but he found himself embroiled in the events of 1618, which were triggered by the doctrines of the Reformed Church. He was asked to draft a paper working out the ways in which the government would benefit from demanding only the minimum doctrinal tenets, leaving individuals free to pursue their conscience on many religious matters. But the heightened political tensions of the times, characterized by the threat of war and the intrigue of government power plays, wed him solidly to both Johan van Oldenbarnevelt and the Arminian Remonstrants. The stadholder, Maurice of Nassau, had been undermined by Oldenbarnevelt's decisions, which excluded him, and he chose to accept the orthodox Calvinist Canons of Dordt. Oldenbarnevelt was arrested and executed, and Grotius was placed in prison, though he later escaped and fled to France. Grotius remained determined to support the validity of Christianity, and while in France, he published *On the Truth of the Christian Religion,* dedicated to his patron, the King of France.

Philip Landsbergen, a Reformed minister, is a good example of how the Reformed Protestants generally embraced the scientific method. Landsbergen was one of the best scientists to describe the heliocentric view of the universe. He was convinced that astronomy required far more direct observation than previously prescribed, and he used the new instruments being invented in the Low Countries to more carefully examine the movement of the planets. In 1619, he published *Progymnasatium* (*Preparatory Exercise of the Restored Astronomy*), and over the course of the next 10 years, he published several books defending Copernican science as a theory, although he felt Copernicus had lacked enough observations to properly defend himself. In another popular book, *Bedenckingen* (*Considerations*), published in 1629, Landsbergen developed a Christian cosmology in which he proclaimed a "three heavens" theory based partially on Aristotle and partially on Corinthians 12:2, in which St. Paul discusses a third heaven where God dwells (the first being the planets, and the second being the fixed stars), yet it is beyond human capacity to observe it.

In a thriving urban landscape where education, literacy, and trade in fine goods were at their height by European standards, the Dutch thrived in inventing instruments for scientific inquiry. Christiaan Huygens (1629–1695) was a mathematician, astronomer, and physicist whose father had been a friend of René Descartes. Educated in Leiden and Breda, Huygens discovered the moon of Saturn and described its rings in 1655. He also applied his knowledge of instruments to make far more accurate clocks than were previously available. He patented the pendulum clock in 1657, and due to his fame as a scientist, he acquired a position in the French Academy of Sciences in 1666. Anton van Leeuwenhoek (1632–1723) is known as the Father of

Microbiology, and through careful observation, he studied bacteria, spermatozoa, and blood flow, and was the first to study muscle fibers. In order to see these microorganisms and cells, Huygens reportedly invented over 400 types of microscopes, although few examples remain today.

In addition to early scientific discoveries, the Dutch were also interested in studying the wealth of nations and how republics differed from the predominant monarchies, with their strictly controlled economies. Pieter de la Court wrote one the best known books on economics prior to Adam Smith; his *Interest van Holland*, published in 1662, was a critical assessment of economic success in the Netherlands based on free competition and a republican form of government. Like other Dutch scholars, he had studied the earlier success of the Republic of Venice and concluded that its strength lay in its political organization, which allowed an open market and curbed the dominance of any ruling family. He also admired the German free cities for their ability to defend themselves against larger powers—all of which appealed greatly to this small republic.

An earlier scholar had also argued in favor of the Dutch Republic, using historical support. Petrus Cunaeus, the pen name for Peter van der Kun, was a professor of Latin and jurisprudence at the University of Leiden, but his interests turned to Hebrew texts. In his well-known book *The Hebrew Republic,* he identified important elements of a modern republic in the ancient Jewish kingdom, and through the work of Josephus, Maimonides, and the Talmud, he claimed that its political ideas were superior to those of Greece and Rome. Rooted in Reformed theology, Cunaeus and others developed a "Dutch Hebraism" that could justify the Dutch Republic as God's chosen people, a modern Israel which had been justified in taking the "promised land." In a very practical way, the Dutch had also chosen Hebrew names, such as Abraham, Isaac, and Jakob, to identify with Israel. This typology would greatly influence the American colonies, especially through the Puritans, who would also go on to claim God's providential design for a new nation: a chosen people.

## THE ENLIGHTENMENT

### Nadere Reformatie

There has been a cycle within Christianity whereby new movements of piety and practice have been followed by institutional development; very often, what follows is a loss of the original religious fervor to the play of political, economic, and social interests that have become central to society. Once the synod of Dordrecht established a privileged church, some Dutch pastors and theologians wanted to return to a concentration on spiritual growth through community and practice. Contact with English Puritans brought a new movement to the Netherlands that is known as the *Nadere Reformatie* or the Further Reformation. In following the goal of pietists and Puritans for a *praxis pietatis*, Willem Teellinck (1579–1629) is often called the father of Dutch pietism. He lived for a time with a Puritan family in England and came into contact with their family worship, personal prayer, fasting, and philanthropy. After studying with both Gomarus and Arminius in Leiden, he had a very successful pastorate in Middelburg, Zeeland, where many were awakened through his fervent preaching. He became an important voice in support of the Canons of Dordt. Gisbertus Voetius (1589–1676) was a student of Gomarus' as well, and he also came under the influence of Teellinck's piety. He became a professor of theology and oriental languages at the University of Utrecht in 1636, and was the most important voice for Calvinism in his day. Greatly concerned with the new philosophy of anti-Aristotelianism introduced in the Netherlands by Descartes, he set out to underline the importance of defending the historic Calvinist tradition, which adhered to the belief that all substance is endowed with a meaningful design. He also fought Arminianism, which he believed undermined the notion of predestination for a return to salvation through good works. Aligned with the house of Orange, the Voetians often tried to institute public morality in a more liberal society that did not favor strict controls, such as enforcement of the Sabbath. Wilhelmus à Brakel (1635–1711) is another example of a Dutch theologian with strong ties to the English Puritans. His book *The Christian's Reasonable Service* (*De Redelijke Godsdienst*) was a very practical guide to lay spirituality that was widely recognized in the Netherlands and Britain. Dutch Pietism continued as a movement until the mid-18th century.

## The Philosophers

It is difficult to judge early modern tolerance by today's standards, but it is certain that its practice in the Dutch Republic was the most advanced in Europe: philosophers and radical thinkers flocked to the Netherlands in the 17th and 18th centuries. The Dutch Enlightenment radically altered the religious tradition by calling into question the authority and authorship of the Bible and all religious phenomena, such as miracles, prayer, sacraments, divine providence, and eventually the Trinity. At best, many enlightened philosophers created a radical break between faith and reason. In 1618, René Descartes, born in France, became a mercenary soldier in the service of Maurice of Nassau, Prince of Orange, who had organized the successful revolt against Spain. While stationed in Breda, he met the mathematician Isaac Beeckman, who encouraged him to pursue his scientific studies. After some time in France, he returned to the Republic in 1628 and remained there for 21 years, teaching at the universities of Franeker, Leiden, and Utrecht, where he had the freedom to publish all his books. As a mathematician, scientist, and polemical writer, he has become known as the father of modern philosophy for his bold attempt to break with the philosophical tradition and advance his own propositions, the most famous being: "I think, therefore I am." In his principal work, *Discourse on the Method* (1637), his radical rejection of the principles of a meaningful direction and the end of being, which were fundamental to the Aristotelian system, got him in trouble with many authorities of his day. He also undermined the authorities with his assertion that knowledge could only be understood from an individual experience, rather than from natural philosophy. The University of Utrecht, under its rector Gisbertus Voetius, condemned his writings, and the Pope placed his works on the *Index Librorum Prohibitorum* (list of prohibited books).

But not all Reformed theologians rejected Cartesian thought. Johannes Cocceius (1603–1669), who developed the system of Covenant theology, taught Hebrew philology and exegesis at the universities of Franecker and Leiden. In the 17th century, it was not uncommon to hear the title "Cartesio-Cocceianism" partially because there were some affinities, but also due to the ire of Calvinist orthodoxy, which found the acceptance of doubt as applied to theology very unsettling. Cocceius had a so-called rational and liberal approach to the history of God's covenantal relationship with humanity, which was continually unfolding. He believed that the Bible was complex and could not always be taken literally, and he used his great philological skills to discover which prescriptive rules still applied to his era and which were no longer applicable. What most troubled the orthodox was his insistence that miracles could no longer exist. Some theologians tried to mediate a middle path between the Coccians and the Voetians, such as Herman Witsius, who taught theology at the Universities of Franecker, Utrecht, and Leiden. His attempt at reconciliation in *The Economy of the Covenants between God and Man* (1677) was never fully realized, however.

Baruch Spinoza was by far one of the most important Dutch philosophers, and his ideas have international significance, though for most of his life he worked as a lens grinder, and most likely died from life-long inhalation of fine fragments. His philosophy combined Cartesian metaphysics with elements from Stoicism and medieval Jewish rationalism. It is this combination that caused the Jewish community to excommunicate him in 1656. Rather than rely on God's divine providence and activity in the world, Spinoza taught that virtue and happiness, the real salvation, could be achieved through a control of the passions (*apatheia*)—a solid Stoic argument. God could not be distinguished from nature, and Spinoza's biblical criticism questioned divine authorship. In the end, his separation of theological speculation and philosophy demanded that society make purely rational choices to curb human self-interest, ideas he certainly acquired from Thomas Hobbes.

Balthasar Bekker (1634–1698) became known throughout Europe for his book *The World Bewitched* (*De Betoverde Weerld,* 1691) because he not only denied the existence of the devil, demons, and angels, but presented a detailed, systematic study of the Bible in doing so. His book came at a time when Europe had come through the height of the witch craze, and most people not only believed in supernatural beings, but also believed that their activity among humans had been increasing for the last few centuries. Bekker's book was instrumental in quelling the witch hunt, but it had dire consequences for the tradition of Christian mystery and the belief in God's direct activity in the world. Even more devastating was his assertion that the Bible contained only figurative speech and poetic license in reference to supernatural beings. In the end, both Voetians and Cocceians accused him of spreading the atheism of Hobbes and Spinoza.

Like Descartes, Pierre Bayle was born in France in 1647, but spent a good part of his life in the Netherlands, where he had more freedom to publish his radical ideas. Unlike Descartes, however, he was raised as a Calvinist, but vacillated between a conversion to Roman Catholicism and a reconversion to the Reformed faith. Following Spinoza, Bayle created a dualism between faith and reason, whereby any belief in God could not be claimed through rational thought. He began to teach in a school in Rotterdam in 1681, and remained in Rotterdam until his death in 1706.

## THE 19TH CENTURY

### New State Church and the Réveil

When the French successfully invaded the Dutch Republic in 1795, the relationship between church and state was one of the first societal constructs to be changed. Although the Reformed Church in the Netherlands was never a state church, the government funded all maintenance of church property and paid the salaries of ministers. In turn, the government had the right to be involved in the appointment of ministers and used the church to promote civic peace and national morality; public days of prayer were regularly called for, and a blessing on agriculture occurred in spring and autumn. The Reformed had become the church of the Fatherland, a public church, and the government obligated a certain level of morality. The first acts of the new assembly disestablished the Reformed Church as a privileged church and guaranteed full religious freedom. When Napoleon came to power, he wanted to maintain good relations with a moderate religious body which could help promote civic morality and peace. In 1809, the first real census of religious affiliation was taken in the Netherlands, and it found that 55 percent of the population of 2.2 million belonged to the Reformed Church.[13]

The return of the Netherlands to an independent sovereign state in 1815, after Napoleon's defeat at Waterloo, restored the Reformed Church and increased its connections to the state. One of the first things that King William I did was to make Sunday observance a law, and in the *Algemeen Reglement* (General Regulations) of 1816, he gave official status to the *Nederlands Hervormde Kerk* (Netherlands Reformed Church) under the direction, care, and oversight of the King. Rather than being merely a church in the Netherlands, the Reformed Church was now "the" Church. Article 9 of the *Algemeen Reglement* states: "Concern for the interests of Christianity in general, and the Reformed Church in particular, maintaining its teachings, the propagation of religious knowledge, the promotion of Christian morality, the preservation of order and unity, and the cultivation of love for the King and Fatherland, must always be the primary objective of all who are in charge of administering various ecclesiastical bodies."[14]

A new wave of art and scholarship also emerged after 1815 in the form of the Romantic movement. Romanticism reacted to the rationalism of the Enlightenment and to the doctrinal disputes within the confessional churches. The Groningen School represented an attempt to see God's revelation as an organic development in scripture and in nature. Petrus Hofstede de Groot, who taught theology at the University of Groningen, penned *Truth in Love: A Theological Journal for Cultured Christians* in 1837 to show that Jesus was the perfect example of God's progressive revelation. Yet, he departed from Christian Trinitarian orthodoxy in his claim that Jesus only appeared as a human in order to show the way to God. In this manner, the Groningen school was latitudinarian and continued the tradition of the Enlightenment. Philip Willem van Heusde, an influential Dutch philosopher and professor of literature and history at the University of Utrecht, also promoted this theology. He attempted to explore the mysteries of the Christian faith through philosophy, and in employing Platonic ideas, he envisioned Christianity as a quest for human perfection, or a deeper self-understanding of the divine spark in everyone. The Groningen school developed theological liberalism throughout the 19th century.

But Romanticism also took Christianity in a different direction. With roots in Scotland and Switzerland, the *Réveil*, a European-wide religious revival, came to the Netherlands through the ministry of the newly appointed chaplain to King William I in Brussels, the Swiss pastor Jean Henri Merle d'Aubigné. He had studied in Berlin with the church historian August Neander and with the theologian Friedrich Schleiermacher, arguably the most important theologian of his time. The Groningen school and the *Réveil* were united in (1) desiring a heart-felt religion, and (2) the belief that revelation came through scripture and history. They differed on the normative value of the Bible as literal history; also, the majority of the *Réveil* leadership was from the aristocracy. William I warmly embraced Merle's fervent preaching, though by 1830, it appeared that the novelty had somewhat worn off, although his Prussian wife, Wilhelmina Frederika, continued her support. Many Dutch theologians and intellectuals embraced this new piety that combined Reformed orthodoxy with connections to the *Nadere Reformatie,* but with newer Romantic elements. Willem Bilderdijk is a good example of the older generation of Dutch that was loyal to the house of Orange yet searching for order in the rapidly changing world of the French Revolution. When William of Nassau-Orange was re-established, Bilderdijk became a staunch advocate for a return to the strong, restored Reformed Church. He was attracted to the *Réveil* for its orthodox doctrinal base, but as a poet, his Romantic feelings found expression in heart-felt appeals.[15] Bilderdijk's poetry and inspiring speeches greatly influenced the young students Abraham Capadose and Isaac da Costa, who as, Sephardic Jews, converted to Christianity as a result. Bilderdijk had taught philosophy and law to da Costa in Leiden. In turn, da Costa's friendship with Willem de Clercq led to his conversion. As secretary, and later director of NHM national trading company, de Clercq held an important position in the recovery of the Netherlands economy. Da Costa and de Clercq would later adopt the poetry tradition of Bilderdijk. They became universally recognized as important Dutch poets, despite the fact that their conservative religious views as leaders of the *Réveil* were not shared by everyone. Not only were they masters of the Dutch language, but they also drew upon a long history of Dutch Christianity in the tradition of the Brethren of the Common Life and Erasmus, whereby a deep respect for personal piety and conscience was able to thrive in a pluralist religious marketplace.

Romanticism and the *Réveil* inspired the famous Dutch historian Guillaume Groen van Prinsterer to reconstruct the history of the "Fatherland," the language used in Dutch historiography until recently. Much had changed as a result of the French Revolution, and national identity was again in question. Groen and others developed a plan to restore the Netherlands to its former greatness through a rejection of French revolutionary calls for freedom and liberty, and instead pleaded for a return to the older order, which was supported by divine providence. Underlying the theme of Dutch Israel, Calvinist historians living in a plural state could still claim the uniqueness of their nation and *volk*: "it was taken very literally as a fleshly nation consisting of both saints and sinners. This view enabled preachers to regard the Dutch as a unified community of baptized believers, paradoxically disobeying the Law under the covenant of grace."[16] Employing the Romantic concepts of an underlying organic spirit that made itself manifest in history, Groen envisioned the Dutch national spirit as led by the work of God's Spirit. Groen worked out his idea of the Dutch nation in his *Handbook of Dutch History* (1846), and his conclusions on events in post-French Revolutionary Europe were further developed in *Unbelief and Revolution* (1847). He was a secretary to William I from 1829–1833, and he remained in politics throughout his life, eventually helping to found the "Confessional Union" in 1864, which led to the influential Anti-Revolutionary Party.[17]

Despite the fact that leaders of the *Réveil* combated the Groningen school and liberalism within the Reformed Church, they remained members. Some conservatives could no longer remain, however, and in 1834, a Secession (*Afscheiding*) occurred under the leadership of Hendrik de Cock (1801–1842), who fronted a small group protesting what they saw as liberalism in the established church. Because of his preaching (of what he saw as doctrinal orthodoxy), and with a large local following, the Reformed Church suspended his license to preach, which raised a bitter struggle within the Church. When Heinrich Scholte, another pastor embracing Cock's orthodoxy, attempted to preach in his church, things came to a head. The Reformed Church did not comment on their theology, but silenced them for their perceived disruption in the state church. Both pastors refused to recant and subsist from preaching, and they signed an Act of Secession in 1834, soon forming their own churches, which were eventually recognized as the Christian Reformed Church in the Netherlands in 1869. This group represented many of the poor, and the Dutch government persecuted them for their intransigence by reinstating an older law limiting groups to under 20 persons and forcing them to quarter troops in the area, paying large fines for any infractions. Only when William II signed the 1848 constitution would they have limited freedom to worship. Scholte and about 800 faithful emigrated to Iowa in the United States, establishing a large farming community there.

### Freedom of Religion and Catholicism

The new constitution of 1848 not only gave limited freedom for dissent within Dutch Protestantism, but led to emancipation for Roman Catholics, as well. The revision of the constitution was headed by four liberals and one Catholic, and chaired by Jan Rudolf Thorbeke. With this, the *Algemeen Reglement* that regulated the state church was revised by 1852, and the election and calling of elders, deacons, and preachers were given to local congregation. In 1853, Pope Pius IX recovered the Catholic hierarchy with Archbishopric in Utrecht and subordinate bishops in Haarlem, 's-Hertogenbosch, Breda, and Roermond. Given the more liberal policies established in 1848, as well as the complete freedom provided to the Catholic Church in the Netherlands, a wave of fear ran through the Protestant community. Pope Pius IX's letter *Ex qua die arcano* of 1853 warning of the "weeds of Calvinism" did not help with this transition.[18] Together with several massive protests, known collectively as the April Movement, a conservative Reformed petition bearing over 250,000 signatures was circulated, calling for maintenance of the Calvinist character of the Netherlands. Protestant martyrs from the 16th century were recalled in support of the protests, including Johannes Pistorius, who died at the stake under Margaret of Austria in 1525.

A struggle continued within the Reformed Church. In 1864, Groen van Prinsterer formed a "Confessional Union" of *Réveil*-minded theologians and scholars who wanted to maintain orthodoxy in opposition to the modern liberals, who saw some doctrines as no longer relevant. In their minds, the Bible was no longer a normative standard, even though it contained some important historical accounts. In the spirit of the times, the "moderns" believed that the Word of God was revealed within each individual conscience, and should not take the form of a public debate. Abraham Kuyper, a journalist, theologian, pastor, and politician, brought this debate to a head in the 1870s when he was able to launch a vigorous defense of orthodoxy in the public sphere, not just the pulpit. In 1879, he formed the Anti-Revolutionary Party (ARP), the first modern political party in the Netherlands, and in 1880, he was instrumental in establishing the private Free University of Amsterdam, becoming a professor of theology and its first President. Kuyper's movement came out of the *Réveil*, and had initially been established as a pact between the people, the monarchy (Orange), and God. But its constituency was no longer the elite; Kuyper's appeal was to the rising lower-middle class and to those who felt they could no longer work with the liberal. Modern powers in the Reformed Church began to disassociate themselves from the monarchy. In 1886, the *Doleantie* (those with grievances) separated from the established church, and in 1892, founded a new denomination called The Reformed (*Gereformeerde*) Churches (GKN) in the Netherlands after merging with many *Afscheiding* churches from 1834 forward. When Kuyper began to attack capitalism in 1891, leaning instead toward Christian socialism, the right wing of his party broke away in 1893 to form the Christian Historical Party. Kuyper went on to become prime minister from 1901–1905, and throughout the 20th century, the ARP became one of the most influential political parties until merging with the CDA in 1980.

In an interesting twist, the long struggle between Protestants and Catholics over the liberal program of establishing more public schools in place of parochial schools finally brought them together. In the 1860s, a great controversy in education called the School Conflict (*Schoolstrijd*) arose. An 1878 Elementary Education Act raised the standards for education, but did not provide any subsidies for denominational schools; this brought together Protestants and Catholics, and within a year, small subsidies were found. Unhappy with either Christian or liberal solutions, the Social Democratic Union was formed in 1881 to represent socialist workers who wanted a radical redistribution of wealth. This set the stage for a division in the Dutch nation for over 50 years into Protestant, Catholic, Liberal, and Socialist ideological camps called pillars (*verzuiling*). In 1889, a new school law granted subsidies to all private schools, and the new constitution of 1917 gave full funding to both public and private schools.

## 20TH CENTURY TO THE PRESENT

### World Wars and Religion

After the Reformed Church split, not all orthodox chose to go with Kuyper, and the main spokesman for the orthodox who remained was Philippus Jacobus Hoedemaker, a minister in Amsterdam. He believed that it was necessary to remain in the historic Church in order to demonstrate unity and persuade others of the covenantal relationship that was at the heart of God's calling. In agreement with Cyprian, the early Church father, the Church was conceived as a school for sinners that must remain a *volkskerk* (people's church) in the Netherlands. Some within the Reformed Church believed in highlighting ethical practices and community, perceiving doctrinal statements as less relevant to the concerns of the modern world; in 1921, the Ethical Union was formed. Liberal theology had grown throughout the 19th century, and it became strong in the Reformed Church of the Netherlands. The Church stressed freedom of conviction and personal faith experiences, rather than discussions of sin and grace. Under the leadership of Henrik Roessingh, Gerrit Jan Heering, and Henrik Tjakko de Graaf, the Union of Liberal Reformed was established in 1913.

Dutch Judaism began to thrive in the 19th century, given this group's increasing freedom to practice their religion. Jews gave their support to the monarchy in exchange for more liberal policies and protection, but by the end of the 19th century, the growing socialist movement was the most beneficial factor in their livelihood. In 1830, there were approximately 46,000 Jews of both Sephardic and Ashkenazi decent; by 1899, that number topped 104,000. With greater anti-Semitism on the rise throughout Germany and other eastern European states, Jews flocked to a more tolerant Netherlands, and by 1941, the nation housed a high of nearly 150,000 Jewish residents. The majority lived in North and South Holland, with nearly 80,000 residing in Amsterdam alone. The Nazi Holocaust eliminated 75 percent of the Dutch Jewish population, one of the highest in Nazi-occupied Europe. In

1947, only 13,000 Jews remained, but by 1966, the number rose to 30,000. As a result, one-third of Dutch Jews has a non-Dutch background. It appears that an equal number of Israeli Jews have immigrated to the Netherlands as Dutch Jews have emigrated to Israel. Many Jews have intermarried and do not choose to affiliate with any congregation. The Dutch Israelite Church is the largest group of practicing Jews, with over 5,000 members representing Orthodox Judaism. The Union of Liberal Synagogues is a smaller group, and the Portuguese Israelite Religious Community is the smallest. Recent figures suggest that about two percent of the Dutch population was Jewish, with a total of approximately 73,000.

### Liberalism and Secularization

The critical study of religion and philosophy in the Netherlands followed general European scholarship throughout the late 19th and 20th century. G.J.P.J. Bolland was a self-taught scholar who revived Hegelianism in the Netherlands; he produced *Hegel* (1898) and began to publish Hegel's works. He was part of a group of "radical critics" that included A.D. Loman, W.C. van Manen, and G.A. van den Bergh van Eysinga, who used criticism to claim that the Pauline letters were not authentic and that Jesus was a historical construction. They fought against what they felt was a dominant *domineesfilosfie* (pastors' philosophy). In the early 20th century, Gerardus van der Leeuw became an internationally recognized scholar for his contribution *Religion in Essence and Manifestation: A Study in Phenomenology* (1933), which developed the work of Edmund Husserl in contrast to popular neo-Kantianism. Dirk Henrik Theodoor Vollenhoven and Herman Dooyeweerd represented a movement within neo-Calvinism to develop a unique Reformational philosophy, whereby fundamental Christian thinking starts with a philosophical grounding in God's creational purposes. The most significant Dutch Protestant theologians of the 20th century were Herman Bavinck, Klaas Schilder, Willem Visser 't Hooft, Herman Ridderbos, and Harry Kuitert, and the most significant Roman Catholic theologians were Sebastian Tromp, SJ (Society of Jesus), and Franz Jozef van Beeck.[19]

On October 31, 1945, the established Reformed Church (NHK) held a truly national synod, the first since 1619, to restructure the Church in the modern state. The new Church order that became official in 1951 was free from governmental influence, a reversal of the nature of the established Church tradition dating back to 1816. At the same time, it purported to be a *volkskerk*, a church of the people, rooted in the history of the Dutch nation and its religious character. While some differences existed between the Reformed Church and the Reformed churches of the *Doleantie* (GKN), there was general consensus on the importance of the doctrines of the Canons of

Dordt. The new NHK wanted to position itself at the center of society, due not to an official status, but as a moral and ethical guide (to members and non-members) of the Dutch nation. While many independent Reformed denominations (GKN) continued to follow Kuyper's model of antithesis, the NHK broke out of the pillarized model and became actively involved in lobbying for freedom for colonial possessions and the rejection of nuclear weapons in order to bring about more peace and justice. Other differences existed; for example, by 1966, the NHK had paved the way for women to become pastors, or undergo university training to become pastors. While GKN churches continued to stress the traditional subjects of biblical languages, exegesis, history, and theology, the NHK increased sociological and psychological studies as a means to serve the church and world. But all churches found their place in the world increasingly problematic after the 1960s as secularization, individualization, and relativism dramatically increased.

Church membership and church attendance in the Netherlands for both Protestants and Catholics were extremely high until 1960. In 1960, the NHK comprised 28 percent of the population, with the GKN churches at 9 percent, and the Catholic Church at a high of 40 percent; only 18 percent of the population was officially unchurched. The very rapid membership decline that occurred in the Netherlands, which experienced one of the greatest declines in Europe, though more so in terms of church attendance, took place between the mid-1960s and the end of the 1990s. By way of comparison, in 1970, 80 percent of the GKN regularly attended worship services, 33 percent of the NHK attended, and 63 percent of Roman Catholics attended mass. By 1999, a more rapid decrease than any other country occurred: while the GKN churches managed to maintain attendance at 45 percent and the NHK had 25 percent, the Roman Catholic Church had only 8.8 percent attendance, even though almost 32 percent of the Dutch population claimed they were Roman Catholic. By 2006, although the Catholic Church could claim 26.6 percent of the population, the official research agency of the Church could only account for 1.2 percent of mass attendance.[20] Catholics had always been isolated from the realms of political power, and until recently, had been largely restricted to two of the southern provinces (Brabant and Limburg). They found themselves liberated by the rapid dissolution of the pillars in the 1960s, and with equal opportunities in Dutch society, they are now rarely distinguishable, to the consternation of their bishops and priests, from modern secular Netherlanders. Andrew Greeley suggests that Vatican II released Catholics from the pillarization (*verzuiling*) model, but left them with few new models since they had previously relied far too much on the political structure.[21] But monitoring church attendance is not the only way to determine interest in religion; like many other Western countries, spirituality (a deep sense of self with others and sensitivity to some mysteries in life) is still high in the Netherlands, yet traditional doctrinal beliefs and rituals are seen as more irrelevant.[22]

In the early 1960s, some leaders of the NHK and the GKN began to discuss merging. By 1986, definitive steps had been taken to include the Evangelical Lutheran Church and other Protestant groups, such as the Mennonites and Remonstrants, in a movement call *Samen Op Weg* (literally together on the way). In 1990, a basic church order was agreed upon, but it took several years to agree on the particular elements of a church union. On May 1, 2004, the Protestant Church of the Netherlands (*Protestant Kerk Nederland*, or PKN) was established, and it represented 12 percent of the Dutch population. Many GKN churches did not join, and they represented six percent of the population. Certainly ecumenical activity has permeated Christian churches, and some theologians and artists have widespread appeal among all Christians, such as the Catholic theologian Henri Nouwen, and the music and lyrics of Huub Oosterhuis.[23]

### New Immigrants, New Religions: A Question of Tolerance

During the period of declining churches, Dutch society viewed itself as increasingly tolerant of variant ideas in a pluralist society. Although church attendance dropped, the legacy of a Christian nation provided the nation with basic values and a distinctive culture. Dutch society was based on tolerance, but a quiet yet strong set of customs ensured a smooth transition. By the 1980s, however, tensions increased between native-born Dutch and thousands of non-European immigrants, most of whom were Muslim. While Christianity in the Netherlands was characterized by a 400-year-old record of separation of church and state, Islam had little experience in a secular society. The government, which invited Muslims as guest workers, went out of its way to respect and communicate with foreigners in their own language. But many workers did not return home, nor did they learn the Dutch language and become inculcated into Dutch society. Remaining marginalized and separated in urban ghettos, many second-generation youths became frustrated with their perceived lack of opportunity, and some turned to radical Islam as a means of identity. Guest worker programs ceased in 1973, but immigration continued, mainly from Morocco and Turkey. In 1971, there were 54,000 (0.4%) Muslims in the Netherlands, but by 1980, that figure reached 236,000 (1.7%), and in 2004, a high point of 944,000 (5.8%) was attained.[24] Many, if not most, Muslims have now found a thriving home in the Netherlands, with some serving in local government and many beginning to attain education and well-paying jobs. But a small, vocal, and violent few have created widespread tensions and caused many Dutch citizens to reconsider the limits of tolerance. Certainly the tragedy that happened in New York City on September 9, 2001, set off alarms of coming disasters throughout Europe, and the Netherlands became concerned about its growing immigrant population. The Eurobarometer Poll of 2005 illustrated the underlying sense of religion in the Netherlands: 34 percent of Dutch citizens responded that they "believe there is a God"; 37 percent answered that they "believe there is some sort of spirit or life force"; and 27 percent answered that they "do not believe there is any sort of spirit, God, or life force."[25] While each century has its own unique context and issues, religion in the Netherlands has always been a matter of individual conscience over institutional homogeneity. A pragmatic attitude, born in a tragic mix of politics and religion in the 16th century and nurtured in the success of free market commerce and trade, still prevails. At the same time, the Dutch have felt especially motivated to demonstrate that their communal society, ordered by a sense of collective agreement and equality, should to some degree be shared by other nations. It is not hard to discover much of the Dutch Republic's aspirations in the new American republic of 1800, and Dutch Calvinist thought has influenced Protestantism more than any other philosophy. And in an interesting twist, the secularized, "religious fervor" of the Purple Coalition was quite evangelistic about its multicultural welfare state, and a tolerant and permissive culture.[26]

## COMMUNITY: PILLARIZATION AND THE POLDER MODEL

In the period leading up to World War I, the Netherlands emerged as a nation that had made significant changes to its socio-economic structure. By the end of the 19th century, national identity meant different things to different groups, and within this pluralism, distinctive groups created their own subcultures and demanded formal participation in governing and responsibility.[27] The liberal political and economic policies of the late 19th century began to offer a greater share to the population, and the older regents and notables took a backseat in terms of policy making. The 19th century had been an era of nation building throughout Europe, and various groups vied for legitimacy and recognition. The major issue of school funding for both public and Christian schools had led to an alliance between Protestants and Catholics, yet in the end, they each created a separate sphere where they built an entire sub-culture within the larger society. At the same time, the working classes began to formally participation in economic and political organization, especially with the rise of several socialist labor unions. Many workers with strong Protestant and Catholic beliefs joined their own labor unions, which were supported by the churches and remained reformist by nature. A growing number of workers, however, had no firm connections to any church; rising socialist ideas attracted them instead. Abraham Kuyper appealed to the lower-middle class

Reformed, whereas the Catholics formed their own labor unions, inspired by Leo XIII's papal encyclical *Rerum Novarum* of 1891. In 1900, the Reformed, under the direction of A. S. Talma, established the Christian Labor Secretariat as a national organization for labor, and in 1909, it became the Christian Trades Union. In 1909, Catholics established the Bureau for Roman Catholic Trades Organization as another alternative national organization.

Domela Nieuwenhuis was the first socialist leader to organize workers and the first socialist in parliament. He began as a Lutheran preacher, but lost his desire to remain in the ministry in 1879, and by 1881, he was actively involved with Henri Polak as co-founder of the Social Democratic Bond (SDB), the earliest organization of workers fighting for universal suffrage and using strikes to pressure the government. He spread his ideas in his newspaper, *Right for All,* and his radical notions led to a great riot in Amsterdam in 1886 called the "Eel Riots," in which 20 people died. He gained widespread support in Friesland, where many workers were strongly affected by the Agrarian depression. From 1888 until 1891, Nieuwenhuis tried to promote change as an elected official in the Lower House of Parliament, but his disillusionment led him to adopt more anarchist beliefs. He had many supporters within the SDB, but a faction, under the leadership of Pieter Jelles Troelstra and Frank van der Goes, eventually established a more moderate movement called the Social Democratic Labor Party (SDAP). Although Nieuwenhuis continued to fight in a radical manner, his organization was declared illegal, and tensions rose between his anarchist methods and the reformist trends of Trolstra and Goes, who believed that workers could become partial owners of industry.[28] Workers began flocking to the SDAP in great numbers, and the SDB was forced to join the SDAP in 1900. A major rail strike in 1903 caused a bitter division in terms of any common goals that Christian and socialist workers and trade unions might have had. Abraham Kuyper was prime minister at the time, and he took a very hard line against the strikers, employing harsh treatment for their actions.

Any significant changes were postponed by the disruption engendered by World War I. The liberal Prime Minister Cort van der Linden spearheaded the Pacification of 1917, whereby the socialists and radicals received universal male suffrage and the Christians received full funding for schools. In the Lower House election, the two Protestant parties (ARP & CHU) won 11 and 10 seats, respectively, the Roman Catholic party (ABRK) won 25 seats, the Liberals (LU) gained 22 seats, and the Social Democrats (SDAP) acquired 15 seats, giving socialists a definitive voice for the first time. For the next 50 years, these four basic groups created sub-cultures within society called pillars, known in Dutch as *verzuiling*, meaning pillarization. In this way, each distinctive group had a voice in society and a stake in government.

The theory and motivation behind *verzuiling* came from confessional thought; that is, both Protestant and Catholic thinkers continued to affirm that distinctive communities centered around fundamental religious truths needed to be maintained in the face of growing relativism and loss of faith. The reaffirmation of religious communities had developed in a 19th-century struggle to fight secularization and the excesses of the new state absolutism, born in the French Revolution. The state, in their minds, wanted to increasingly gather all social institutions under its power and guidance. Abraham Kuyper developed a notion of sphere sovereignty, whereby God had ordained specific human institutions to carry out His will, including church, family, and other community organizations, such as schools, unions and cooperatives in areas like science, art, and business. The state and government are also said to be ordained by God under this philosophy (Romans 13), yet within their jurisdiction, these entities have the limited task of bringing justice to all disputes, defending the weak against the strong, and encouraging all people to participate as citizens. Therefore, each God-ordained sphere has a unique place in this organic view of society; they act as mediating structures, and cannot be eliminated through state absolutism. Likewise, Catholics developed the concept of subsidiarity based on the Thomistic natural law that inspired Pope Leo XIII's 1891 encyclical *Rerum Novarum* and Pope Pius XI's encyclical *Quadragesimo Anno* (meaning 40 years after *Rerum Novarum*) in 1931. Pius XI wrote: "Inasmuch as every social activity should, by its very nature, prove a help (*subsidium*) to members of the body social, it should never destroy or absorb them. The State should leave to other bodies the care and expediting of matters of lesser moment. . . ."[29] Thus, Protestants and Catholics were unified in maintaining separate structures and minimizing the role of government at the local level.

No particular party could ever capture a majority of votes in the Netherlands, and therefore, all elected governments required coalitions of several parties. Before the 1950s, the largest Protestant, Catholic, and Liberal parties dominated government to the exclusion of the Social Democrats. Rudy Andeweg and Galen Irwin have summarized this succinctly: "The Netherlands is a country of minorities, which is without doubt the single most important characteristic of Dutch politics . . . The largest percentage ever received by a single party is 35.3 per cent of the vote . . . and this left the party still 22 (out of 150) seats short of an overall majority in the Second Chamber of Parliament."[30] Since the 1930s, the normal connection between the pillars has demonstrated an elective affinity toward certain services (political parties, broadcasting, newspapers, healthcare, trade unions), as illustrated in Table 2.1.[31]

Pillarization continued until well into the 1960s, and the Netherlands developed a consociational democracy whereby a consensus model existed between the four basic players: Protestants (NHK & GKN), Catholics,

**Table 2.1**

| Pillar Group | Political Party | Broadcast | Newspaper | Health Care | Trade Union |
|---|---|---|---|---|---|
| Roman Catholic | KVP: *Katholieke Volkspartij* | KRO: *Katholieke Radio Omroep* | *Volkskrant* | White/ yellow Cross | NKV: *Rooms-Katholieke Werklieden Verbond* |
| Dutch Reformed [NHK] | CHU: *Christelijk-Historische Unie* | NCRV: *Nederlandse Christelijke Radio Vereniging* | *Trouw* | Green/ Orange Cross | CNV: *Christelijk Nationaal Vakverbond* |
| Gereformeerd [GKN] | ARP: *Anti-Revolutionaire Partij* | NCRV, EO: *Evangelische Omroep* | *Trouw* | Green/ Orange Cross | CNV |
| Socialist (working class) | PvdA: *Partij van de Arbeid* | VARA: *Vereeniging van Arbeiders Radio Amateurs* | *Het Parool/ Vrijevolk* | Green Cross | FNV: *Federatie Nederlandse Vakbeweging* |
| Liberal (middle class) | VVD: *Volkspartij voor Vrijheid en Democratie* | AVRO: *Algemene Vereniging Radio Omroep* | *NRC, Handelsblad* | Green Cross | MHP: *Vakcentrale Voor Middengroepen en Hoger Personeel* |

Liberals, and Socialists. Each group had its own schools (Liberals and Socialists attended public schools), newspaper, labor union, sports team, clubs, insurance companies, and social welfare. It was very possible that someone could experience almost every aspect of life, from birth through old age, within a distinct sub-culture with little contact with others. Arend Lijphart has called this a "politics of accommodation."[32]

The 1960s radically changed the structure of Dutch society. With the great success of the Dutch economy after World War II, the Dutch looked for more laborers. The guest worker program brought many Turkish and Moroccans workers, and in the process of decolonization, the Netherlands opened up citizenship for a time to Indonesians, Surinamese, and Dutch Antillians.[33]

A process of depillarization (*ontzuiling*) dissolved the older sub-cultures. Religious adherence and identification declined rapidly after the mid-1960s, and a vast number of new immigrants changed the composition of the population, thereby eliminating the distinctiveness of the former pillars. The many social revolutions of the 1960s, such as the youth movement, women's liberation, gender and sexual movements, and the environmental pushes, led to further erosion when the traditional pillars had no sufficient responses. The voting age was lowered from a high of 23 to 18, and new political parties appealed to the growing population, which wanted more social welfare and freedom. The traditionally strongest political parties, representing Protestants, Catholics, and traditional Liberals, became involved in new coalitions with more progressive liberal and socialist groups. The KVP, CHU, and ARP Christian parties realized that they needed to work in closer cooperation and amalgamated into the Christian Democratic Appeal (CDA) in 1980; they found limited success, as they still led successive coalition governments. With the loss of support for the Protestant and Catholic parties, and increasing economic success, the Catholic and Protestant parties were excluded from the coalition government in 1994, and swift changed occurred within a few years. The Purple Coalition included the social democrats (PvdA), the progressive liberals (D66), and the conservative liberals (VVD), with Wim Kok forming three governments in the years 1994–2002. The color was a mixture of the symbol of red socialists with liberal blue and brought many changes to traditional values in terms of the issues of abortion, euthanasia, drug control, environmental problems, and gender.

Despite depillarization, the purple coalition operated according to the consensus model and surprised Europe and the world by creating a working alliance between employers, labor unions, and the government called the "Polder Model." The government established a Social Economic Council (SER) to discuss labor relations, which had roots in an earlier agreement dating back to 1982, the Wassenaar Accords. The polder model was hailed throughout the West as a successful way to bring various sectors of the economy together to work for greater profit and accord. While employment in the European Union grew by 0.6 percent, and the United States could boast of a 1.7 percent climb, the Netherlands' employment increased by 2.6 percent.

By 2002, the social welfare system throughout Europe could no longer afford to support its former policies due to financial crises, but a return to older policies in the Netherlands also highlighted a reaction to the increased immigration of non-Europeans from different cultures. The significant influx of Muslims and Africans became the target of some new political parties, such as the Populist Party founded by Pim Fortuyn. Although he was murdered by a radical Muslim, his party has held several seats. Many more discussions have arisen over immigration and the national identity with the murder of Theo van Gogh, the radical film maker, and the status of the African immigrant Ayaan Hirsi Ali who wrote the script for "Submission" and was a member of the Second Chamber until she decided to leave the country in protest over the heated debates about her social views and even her legality as a citizen.

Whether due to the new model or the growth of global markets, the Netherlands' economic success continued, with a high of seven percent growth in 2000. In an effort to encourage the integration of immigrants, the Dutch embraced the notion of a multicultural society. The government translated many documents into the native languages of immigrants, granted liberal welfare funding, and set up organizations to support local leadership. However, after 2000, the economy fell, and by 2003, its growth had slowed to only two percent. The Netherlands was greatly affected by the drop in U.S. markets, and by the September 11, 2001, terrorist attacks. Given the shrinking economy, the great influx of guest workers and immigrants produced new fears. In 2002, Prime Minister Kok stepped down amid concerns that the Netherlands had been compliant in the massacre in Srebrenica. The polder model and the Purple Coalition came to an end.

## Change and Continuity: The Limits of Tolerance

In the wake of heightened fears about the economy, the environment, security, and the place of increasing numbers of immigrants, Pim Fortuyn burst on the scene with an appeal for a defense of the traditional Dutch institutions that protected ethnic Dutch from multiculturalism, globalization, and the influx of Muslims in Europe. In early 2002, he formed his own party, the *Lijst Pim Fortuyn* (LPF), with the goals of adopting a stricter policy on immigrants, fighting crime, dismantling big government, increasing educational spending, and improving healthcare. However, his racist rhetoric against Islam, his flamboyant displays of homosexuality, and far-right political plans enraged as many people as they attracted. But far more shocking than Fortuyn's rhetoric was his assassination on May 6, 2002, by a radical animal rights activist who claimed to be defending Muslims, though he was not one. The Dutch public could not believe that a political murder could happen in the modern Netherlands; it was clear that the social structure had changed. In the wake of the new experiment that had begun in 1994, a new coalition government was formed between the CDA, the VVD, and the LPF, which had captured 26 of the 150 seats. The CDA leader, Jan Peter Balkenende, became Prime Minister and formed a cabinet, but after only 86 days, it disbanded, and support for the LPF vanished. In the new elections of 2003, the CDA again took the lead and Balkenende instituted a harder line with forced assimilation policies, yet since 2006, he has formed a new government with the PvdA and become far more progressive.

Shock and controversy surrounding immigration and the integration of Muslims into Dutch society continued. Ayaan Hirsi Ali entered the political scene as fast as Fortuyn had. Fleeing political oppression in Africa, she arrived in the Netherlands in 1992. She used the name "Hirsi Ali" instead of her real name, Hirsi Magan, in order to receive political asylum since she was allegedly fleeing an arranged marriage, which did not constitute grounds for asylum. She quickly assimilated into Dutch society after learning Dutch in a remarkably short time, and received a Master of Arts (MA) degree in Political Science from the University of Leiden in 2000. Having become involved in politics through a PvdA think-tank, Hirsi Ali was responsible for studying Muslim immigrant issues, and she was shocked to learn that many traditional customs, such as female circumcision, had continued to be followed even in Europe. By 2003, she had switched to the VVD party and successfully ran for Parliament. After 9/11, she began to doubt whether Islam could ever integrate in secularized Europe, as she was horrified by the rash statements of Osama bin Laden and the reaction of the Muslim world to terrorism. Influenced by *The Atheist Manifesto* by Leiden philosopher Herman Philipse, Ali denounced Islam and the concept of God. Like Fortuyn, she began a campaign to demonstrate what she felt was the backwardness of Islam by exposing its worst practices. She wrote a script for a film produced by the avant-garde filmmaker Theo van Gogh called "Submission," translated from the Arabic word "Muslim," and it turned the suggestion of religious piety into an issue of social and political coercion. Broadcast in August 2004, the film greatly offended Muslims, not merely because of its ideological claims, but for its blatant overlay of the Qur'an with nude women's bodies, which was reminiscent of van Gogh. He was murdered in broad daylight on November 2 by a young Moroccan Muslim, with a note threatening Hirsi Ali, as well, pinned to his chest. As a reaction to this problem, the Minister of Immigration and Integration, Rita Verdonk, began to take a tough stance on immigration. Hirsi Ali was one of her critics, and in 2006, Verdonk began to question her status in the Netherlands since Ali had already declared that she had lied about her name and circumstances. This led to an attempt to deny her citizenship, but it very quickly became a divisive political struggle, and Verdonk reconsidered. In the end, she lost her own position in the VVD party, as well as her Parliamentary seat. Since then, Hirsi Ali has been under protective custody and has been hailed by some for her indictment of Muslim terrorists.

Opposition to Islam continued with the film "Fitna" produced by Geert Wilders, who is a Member of Parliament for the Party for Freedom, having been first elected under the VVD in 1998. His platform is reminiscent of Fortuyn's policies; he wants to severely restrict all non-Western immigration, and like Fortuyn, he has the ability to garner media attention and dominate Parliamentary debates. "Fitna," the Arabic word denoting a trial of faith, raises the question of free speech, as the film explores the incompatibility of

Islam and the West. In a conciliatory manner, Prime Minister Balkenende condemned the film with the statement: "The Dutch government stands for a society in which freedom and respect go hand in hand. Such a society demands dedication and commitment. We oppose extremism. Anyone who breaks the law is dealt with firmly. Let us solve problems by working together. Let us reach out to others and build confidence and trust. Let us conquer prejudice. We shall surely succeed."[34]

These recent efforts to find a new balance between the integration of well-meaning immigrants and security and vigilance against terrorism has raised serious questions about the limits of Dutch tolerance, a characteristic element of its national identity for three centuries. Ian Buruma's reflections offer one possible way to understand the tensions: from a neo-conservative viewpoint. He grew up with Theo van Gogh and had access to the elite of the Netherlands, but left the country in 1976 and is a professor at Bard College in New York. Reminiscent of Alexis de Tocqueville as a social critic, he has outlined the underlying problem of European and Dutch society compared to American society.

Europeans are proud of their welfare states, but they were not designed to absorb large numbers of immigrants. Immigrants appear to fare better in the harsher system of the United States, where there is less temptation to milk the state. The necessity to fend for oneself encourages a kind of tough integration. It is for this reason, perhaps, that immigrants from Africa or the Caribbean often express contempt for African-Americans, who feel, for understandable historic reasons, that the state owes them something. Immigrants cannot feel that kind of entitlement in the United States. But in Europe, at least, some do.[35]

At the same time, there has been some progress in integrating Muslims into Dutch society, as demonstrated by the work of Ahmed Aboutaleb, who was born in Morocco. He worked for Dutch radio, served as an information officer for the Ministry of Welfare, Health, and Cultural Affairs, SER, and CBS, and was then appointed to the Amsterdam municipal executive as an alderman for Work and Income, Education, Youth, Diversity, and Urban Policy, under the direction of the Jewish mayor Job Cohen in 2004. In 2007, Mr. Aboutaleb became State Secretary for the Work and Income, Education, Youth, Diversity, and Urban Policy under the Balkenende IV government. In 2006, the Dutch government introduced a new test for perspective immigrants that must be completed in their own country. At a cost of Euro 360 (U.S.$508), there is an extensive language examination, and a film representing the liberal society of the Netherlands with scenes that would potentially offend Muslims, such as two gay men kissing and nude beaches. All EU countries, Switzerland, the United States, Canada, Australia, New Zealand,

and Japan are exempt from the test. Critics claim that this test is designed to offend Muslims and keep them away from the Netherland, effectively constituting outright discrimination against Islam.

Opinions about the extent and effect of changes due to secularization, liberalization, immigration, and globalization vary widely within the Netherlands. Some writers lament the loss of solidarity and balance created by a long history of religion and politics under the house of Orange, and mediated in the 20th century through pillarization. Leon de Winter, a novelist and social critic, is more pessimistic about the loss of "a disciplined, civic society, confident enough to provide space for those with different ideas," and he concludes that "Netherlands no longer exists."[36] By contrast, Geert Mak, a popular writer, has offered some interesting and optimistic assessments of the current struggles in the Netherlands. In his estimation, there are three major transition periods that loom large at the moment: (1) "The fundamental political and religious transition," or the transition from an intensely religious and pillarized society to a secularized and liberal society, where religious and the old political parties no longer play a role; (2) The manner in which urbanization has changed the way people live, and the growing *Randstad* of urban conglomerates, wherein large waves of immigrants and technology thrive, changing the landscape; and (3) The transition away from the welfare state, as the liberal social systems that created a firm safety net have fallen to record lows, validating the growing fears of the aging population about security. Yet, Mak claims "no multicultural disaster [is] going on" as a result of immigration, and "no serious problems" are occurring as a result of the transition to urbanization.[37]

## NOTES

1. See Dutch Language Development, Retrieved May 8, 2008, http://www.fac ulty.ucr.edu/~legneref/bronze/dutch.htm.

2. William J. Bouwsma, *A Usable Past: Essays in European Cultural History* (Berkeley: University of California Press, 1990), 54.

3. Ronald G. Witt, in *Handbook of European History, 1400–1600, Late Middle Ages, Renaissance, and Reformation*, Vol. 2: *Visions, Programs, and Outcomes* (Grand Rapids, MI: Eerdmans, 1994), 117.

4. Compare the populations in 1600: Paris, 400,000; London, 200,000; Flanders and Brabant 3 million; and Holland 2 million.

5. See Guido Marnef, Antwerp in the Age of Reformation: Underground Protestantism in a Commercial Metropolis, 1550–1577. trans. J. C. Grayson (Baltimore, MD: The Johns Hopkins University Press, 1996).

6. See Arthur Eyffinger, "'How Wondrously Moses Goes Along With the House of Orange!': Hugo Grotius 'De Republica Emendanda' in the Context of the Dutch Revolt," *Hebraic Political Studies* 1.1 (Fall 2005): 71–109.

7. Simon Schama, *The Embarrassment of Riches: An Interpretation of Dutch Culture in the Golden Age* (Berkeley: University of California Press, 1988), 62.

8. See Gerrit Voogt, *Constraint on Trial: Dirck Volckertz Coornhert and Religious Freedom* (Kirksville, MS: Truman State University Press, 2000).

9. See Herman Hanke, Homer Hoeksema, and Gise J. Van Buren, *The Five Points of Calvinism* (Reformed Free Publishing, 1976), http://www.prca.org/five points/index.html.

10. Paul Arblaster, *A History of the Low Countries* (New York: Palgrave Macmillan, 2006), 138.

11. Peter van Rooden, "Jews and Religious Toleration in the Dutch Republic," in *Calvinism and Religious Toleration in the Dutch Golden Age*, eds. R. Po-Chia Hsia, and H.F.K. Van Nierop (Cambridge: Cambridge University Press, 2002 ), 132. "Augustine had justified the presence of Jews in the Christian Europe by enlarging upon Paul's speculations about their special status in God's dispensation." (p.136)

12. See Hans Bots and Jan Roegiers, eds. *The Contribution of the Jews to the Culture in the Netherlands* (Amsterdam: Holland University Press, 1989); Jonathan Israel and Reiner Salverda, eds. *Dutch Jewry: Its History and Secular Culture (1500–2000)* (Leiden: E.J.Brill, 2002).

13. See Karel Blei, *The Netherlands Reformed Church, 1571–2005*, trans. Allan J. Janssen (Grand Rapids, MI: Eerdmans, 2006), 54.

14. See *Algemeen Reglement* (General Regulations) of 1816, Retrieved May 20, 2008, http://www.kerkrecht.nl/main.asp?pagetype=onderdeel&item=90.

15. See Gerrit TenZythoff, *Sources of Seccession: The Netherlands Hervormde Kerk on the Dutch Immigration to the Midwest* (Grand Rapids, MI: Eerdmans, 1987), "God had assigned the Netherlands a unique place as the Israel of the North. The House of Orange was the messianic center of this Israel. The Groningen School, on the other hand, considered the Netherlands to one of the places in which God was educating part of mankind." (p. 107)

16. Joris van Eijnatten, *God, Nederland en Oranje: Dutch Calvinism and the Search for the Social Centre* (Den Haag, CIP, 1993), 50.

17. He also wrote the massive volumes: *Archives et correspondence de la maison d'Orange* (12 vols., 1835–1845).

18. See *Aprilbeweging*, The Hague: National Archives of the Netherlands, http://www.nationaalarchief.nl/content/jaartal/1800–1900/1853Aprilbeweging.asp (March 11, 2008).

19. See Arie L. Molendijk. *Emergence of the Science of Religion in the Netherlands* (Leiden: Brill, 2005); Gerardus van der Leeuw, *Phänomenologie der Religion* (1933); *Religion in Essence and Manifestation: A Study in Phenomenology*, trans. J. E. Turner. 2 vols. (New York: Harper & Row, 1963); Peter J. Steen, *The Structure of Herman Dooyeweerd's Thought* (Toronto: Wedge, 1984); John H.Kok, *Vollenhoven: His Early Development* (Sioux Center, IA: Dordt College Press, 1992). Louis Berkhof and Corneilius van Til were Protestant theologians born in the Netherlands, but they immigrated to the United States and spent their careers there, although their influence on the Netherlands was significant.

20. Statistics vary depending on how the data is gathered, but general consensus can be found in several publications. See Erik Sengers, ed., *The Dutch and Their Gods: Secularization and Transformation of Religion in the Netherlands since 1950* (Hilversum: Uitgeverij Verloren, 2005); *The Roman Catholic Church in the Netherlands at the beginning of a new millennium*, Report of 2004, www.bisdomhaarlem.nl/docs/2004/adliminarapport.htm (May 10, 2008); KASKI (research institute at the University of Nijmegen), www.ru.nl/kaski/kerkelijke/statistiek/ (May 10, 2008); and Michael Gilchrist, "Growth of a 'New Church': the Dutch Experiment," *AD2000*, www.ad2000.com.au/articles/1988/jul1988p14_564.html (May 20, 2008). In 1960, 316 priests were ordained, and only 11 left the priesthood; in 1970, only 48 were ordained and 243 left the priesthood. See Rudy B. Andeweg and Galen A. Irwin, *Governance and Politics in the Netherlands* (New York: Palgrave Macmillan, 2002), 37.

21. See Andrew M. Greeley, *Religion in Europe at the End of the Second Millennium* (New Brunswick, NJ: Transaction Publishers, 2003), 198.

22. See Anton van Harskamp, in *The Dutch and Their God's: Secularization and Transformation of Religion in the Netherlands since 1950,* ed. Erik Sengers (Hilversum: Uitgeverij Verloren, 2005), 50.

23. Henri J. M. Nouwen (1932–1996), a Dutch Catholic priest and well-known writer who wrote 40 books on spirituality and life that are very popular among both Protestants and Catholics throughout the West. He is best known for *The Wounded Healer, The Return of the Prodigal Son, and The Inner Voice of Love*. He taught for 20 years at the Menninger Foundation Clinic in Topeka, Kansas, the University of Notre Dame, Yale University, and Harvard University. He spent the last years of his life in Toronto in the L'Arche community for handicapped people.

24. See the Centraal Bureau voor de Statistiek, Retrieved May 20, 2008, www.cbs.nl/nl-NL/menus/themes/vrije-tijd-cultuur/cijfers/religie/default.htm.

25. See the Eurobarometer 2005, Retrieved May 22, 2008, http://ec.europa.eu/public_opinion/archives/ebs/ebs_225_report_en.pdf.

26. See Ian Buruma, *Murder in Amsterdam: The Death of Theo van Gogh and the Limits of Tolerance* (New York: Penguin Press, 2006), 217, discusses "the idea that Holland is the world's moral beacon."

27. See Michael Wintle, *An Economic and Social History of the Netherlands 1800–1920: Demographic, Economic, and Social Transition* (Cambridge: Cambridge University Press, 2000), 288–289.

28. See Domela Nieuwenhuis Letters, The International Institute for Social History, Retrieved June 2, 2008, http://www.iisg.nl/collections/domela.php.

29. *Quadragesimo Anno*, as cited by Paul E. Sigmund, "Subsidiarity, Solidarity, and Liberation: Alternative Approaches in Catholic Social Thought," in *Religion, Pluralism, and Public Life: Abraham Kuyper's Legacy for the Twenty-First Century* (Grand Rapids, MI: Eerdmans, 2000), 210.

30. Andeweg and Irwin, *Governance and Politics,* 17.

31. Andeweg and Irwin, *Governance and Politics,* 20, 24. In 1977, most members of the KVP, CHU, and ARP formed a Protestant/Catholic party, the CDA (*Christen Democratisch Appèl*).

32. See Arend Lijphart, *Politics of Accommodation*, 2nd edition (Berkeley: University of California Press, 1975). See also M.P.C.M. van Schendelen, ed. *Consociationalism, Pillarization, and Conflict Management in the Low Countries* (Meppel, 1984); J. E. Ellemers, "Pillarization as a process of modernization," *Acta Politica* 1 (1984): 97–116; Hans Daalder, "On the Origins of Consociational Democracy Model," *Acta Politica* 1 (1984): 129–144.

33. Today there are approximately 300,000 Turks, 250,000 Moroccans, 300,000 Surinamese, 100,000 Dutch Antillians, and 25,000 asylum seekers a year. See Irwin Anderweg, *Governance and Politics*, 38–39.

34. PM Jan Peter Balkenende, news release, March 27, 2008, Retrieved www.gov ernment.nl/News/Press_releases_and_news_items/2008/March/Government_s_ reaction_to_Wilders_film (April 4, 2008).

35. Ian Buruma, *Murder in Amsterdam: The Death of Theo van Gogh and the Limits of Tolerance* (New York: Penguin, 2006), 203.

36. Leon de Winter, "Tolerating a Time Bomb," The New York Times, July 16, 2005, http://www.nytimes.com/2005/07/16/opinion/16winter.html.

37. Geert Mak, lecture, "What About the Netherlands," www.geertmak.nl/ english/123.html (July 7, 2008).

# Society: Social Issues and Lifestyle

## HEALTH AND SOCIAL WELFARE

In the monastic tradition of the Cisterians, Dominicans, Augustinians, Brethren of the Common Life, and the Beguines, by the late 16th century, Protestants and Catholics in the Netherlands had established organizations to provide social services for the poor and elderly. It was the responsibility of the churches to raise money and provide the necessary care. It was also common to have almshouses, called *Hofjes*, where poor, elderly women could live. Often, wealthy patrons donated property or funding, and these houses were situated in small courtyards with gates protecting them from the street. Many had chapels for worship and reflection. By the 18th century, they became secularized, and residents would pay a certain rent to live there. In addition, many cities established a guest house (*gasthuis*) where poor and disabled people, as well as traveling pilgrims, could sleep. Orphanages also provided a much needed place for children in need of institutional care and the fulfillment of their basic needs, although life at orphanages was hard and food was very scarce. Some orphanages attempted to teach simple skills, such as weaving and spinning or other crafts for boys. In cities, the mentally ill were confined to a "mad" house, or *dolhuis*. The Dutch developed a well-defined sense of social welfare based on their belief in the importance of community, forged from mutual dependence over centuries of cooperation to control their precarious physical environment and ensure political independence. The government played only an indirect role by creating a means through which churches and private donors funded many different institutions that served local needs. Compared to many other countries at that time, charitable work in the Netherlands was advanced and reflected the need to help the large numbers of refugees that had landed on the country's shores. Because they were so highly urbanized, had acquired sufficient wealth, and understood the necessity of communal activity—both to ward off the sea and enemies who wanted their land—they became well-known as one of the exceptional models for civic behavior.[1] In many ways, the early modern Netherlands was a nation of immigrants and refugees, and its success was derived from the integration of all people in the form of nation building.

In the modern Netherlands, charity and welfare have continued under various auspices. Nineteenth-century society did not have the same care for the poor, and due to the agricultural crisis, many poor rural residents suffered greatly. Until modern industry developed better pumping stations, the Netherlands lacked good sources of drinking water, and water-related illnesses, such as malaria and cholera, were far too common, especially in the polder areas. By 1860, the availability of quinine helped reduce malaria, and widespread vaccinations stopped the spread of smallpox. As was the case in many countries, the sheer numbers of physicians was significant for healthcare, and due to economic and educational opportunities, the ratio of doctors to the general population was the same in the 1850s as it is now.[2] In 1865, the government became more directly involved in healthcare by launching state inspections (through the Law of State Inspectorate) and by monitoring and researching contagious diseases (1872 Contagious Diseases Act), which came as direct responses to several epidemics: cholera (1866–1867), typhoid (1869–1871), and smallpox (1870–1872). By 1901, the government had established a Central Health Council to provide oversight for all private, government-funded health initiatives and research.

Unlike in many other countries, however, the government remained disconnected from any national health plans. By the early 20th century, pillarization had taken root, and each confessional and ideological group provided their own healthcare systems. During the 19th century, the Green and White Cross organization had been neutral, serving small sectors of society. In the province of Limburg, however, the Green Cross became a Catholic-managed institution in 1913 due to the overwhelmingly high percentage of Catholics residing there. The province of Brabant, the other Catholic region, established its own healthcare system in 1916 under the White-Yellow Cross, representing the papal colors. By 1923, the two provinces had merged their healthcare systems into the National White-Yellow Cross. While the Green Cross remained neutral, and served all others, the Protestants established the

Green-Orange Cross in 1946, and the Green Cross served mainly the Socialist and Liberal pillars. These healthcare systems grew slowly throughout the 20th century: in 1910, only three percent of the Dutch population belonged to any society, but by 1940, that number had increased to 36 percent and in 1957, it reached a high of 57 percent.[3] However, with the collapse of the pillars, new forms of healthcare came into being.

In the early 20th century, the Netherlands became a welfare state (*Welvaartsstaat*). Willem Drees, a Social Democrat, became the Franklin D. Roosevelt of the Netherlands when he rescued the economy during his tenure as Prime Minister from 1948–1958. He became known as "Father Drees" for his popularity and his design of the welfare state. Shortly after the economic boom that occurred in the wake of World War II, the Old Age Pension Law of 1957 guaranteed retirement income for citizens over the age of 65, who had 50 years of residence in the Netherlands, with contributions from earned income. In 1982, the Wassenaar Accord began to curb the costs of welfare, as unemployment has risen to a high of 11 percent. In the next decade, taxes were lowered and business was deregulated, but social benefits were also reduced. An expanded law allowed for disability payments of up to 70 percent of the citizen's former income through 1998, and also enabled survivors to collection their spouses' pensions. By the 1970s, however, the cost of maintaining a welfare state was increasing beyond affordable levels, becoming one of the most expensive systems in the world.

Today, the Ministry of Health, Welfare, and Sport administers a new universal healthcare system (*uitkering*). By 1998, the Netherlands had the highest per-capita GNP funding for social services in Europe. Care for all citizens falls under three integrated areas: healthcare, benefits for all employees and their families, and pensions and family allowances. In 2006, the government mandated an obligatory health insurance plan with a clear set of rules for administering care; all healthcare is administered through insurance companies that cannot refuse care to any high-risk patients. All employers supply 50 percent of the costs, with the other 45 percent coming from the individual and five percent derived from the government; all premiums have a flat rate of about 100 Euros (U.S.$142) per month. All children under 18 are covered for free, and those earning below the minimum wage are subsidized with a "care allowance." Basic coverage includes treatment by a general practitioner, specialists, ambulance and hospital care, prenatal and midwife services, dental care for children and specialist dental care for all, prescription medicines, short-term psychiatric care, and paramedic care. Most citizens take out additional medical insurance to cover normal dental care and any other elective treatments, including long-term care. The Dutch tradition of Christian charity and care has also translated into a substantial foreign aid cost. Consistent with the tradition of social care has been cooperation between nonprofit organizations and governmental entities providing regulations. Since the 1990s, the Dutch have increasingly experimented with market forces and competition to manage costs and seek more efficient and equitable means for universal coverage.[4] The Netherlands is one of the world's leaders in foreign aid, with approximately 0.8 percent of its GNP given to development assistance, making it the sixth-largest donor nation.

In 1933, the Dutch government established the Ministry of Social Affairs and Employment. World War II had nearly destroyed the infrastructure of the economy, with a third of all industry ruined, and 60 percent of the transportation system unusable. The Netherlands received one of the highest amounts of funding from the Marshall Plan, a total of $1,127,000,000, which helped jump start the economy again. Indeed, the Dutch economy became very successful, despite the loss of colonies that had served as reserves of natural resources and trade for over 300 years. By the 1960s, the Dutch economy was growing so rapidly that thousands of workers from Italy, Spain, and then Turkey and Morocco, as well as the former colonies of Indonesia, Surinam, and Netherlands Antilles, immigrated to the Netherlands. To improve the economy, the government also established the SER (Social-Economische Raad/Economic and Social Council of the Netherlands) in 1950, since the Catholic KVP and the social democratic PvdA could not agree on how deeply the government should regulate the economy. The SER allowed unions, employers, and the government to work together to ensure maximum involvement from all members. This corporatist model brought success, yet it could not withstand the damages caused by the oil crisis of the late 1970s, as well as changing demographics. Unemployment was at 10 percent in the 1970s, given rising inflation and wage cuts. Unions agreed to a shorter work week, which dropped from 40 to 38 hours. With these reforms, employment increased by 1.8 percent each year from 1984–2000. The economy slowed to a halt again in the years 2000–2003, and then steadily climbed thereafter. In 2007, a new Working Hours Act eliminated any set working hours as the government allowed market forces to play a more significant role. In the present Dutch government, the SER plays a diminished role that is mainly advisory.

Like other Western countries, the Netherlands has developed a comprehensive system of unemployment benefits, social security, and pensions. The government provides funds for the basic social security of all citizens under social welfare benefits (*sociale voorzieningen*), and the AOW law (*Algemene Ouderdomswet*) is designed to create a foundation for retirement benefits. The amount of funding is dependent on active employment in the

In the foreground is the Maurits house built in 1640 for Prince Johan Maurits, Governor General of Dutch Brazil, which is now a museum of Golden Age masterpieces. The highest building in The Hague, the Hoftoren, stands in the rear, and houses the Ministry of Education, Culture, and Science. The smaller building, rounded at the top, is the Ministry of Health, Welfare and Sports. Courtesy of the author.

Netherlands, with two percent accrued for every year of employment from age 15–65. In cases where AOW funds are not possible, or where they are not sufficient, National Assistance Act (ABW, *Algemene Bijstandswet*) funds are open to Dutch citizens and recognized foreign residents. Workers also build up additional funds through social insurance benefits (*sociale verzekeringen*). These funds are available through contributions by employees, which are compulsory. Under national insurance, the state provides survivor pensions, many child benefits, and disability payments, as well. For example, under the child care benefits system, parents receive a fixed amount per month for every child under the age of 19. In 2004, the government reformed the system by placing more emphasis on personal responsibility for finding work and saving for the future. The Reformed Social Assistance Act also places more responsibility on local authorities in the administration of social assistance.

## SOCIAL PROBLEMS AND TOLERANCE (CONTROVERSIAL ISSUES)

Community and social welfare have been key characteristics of Dutch society for centuries. With a history of ethnic, religious, and regional diversity, Dutch society was built on the concept of tolerance, a necessary ingredient within this loose confederation of provinces. Underlining tolerance was a more pragmatic attitude based on a merchant and trade economy that had to interact with a diversity of people: it was good business. The early modern Dutch Republic practiced tolerance within the limits of its larger context, meaning that certain Christian principles were fundamental to the morals of society, as recognized by Protestants, Catholics, or dissenters.[5] The reality of tolerance, however, resulted in freedom of conscience far more often than freedom of practice. In contemporary Dutch society, greater freedom of practice has now become the new norm. Whereas older Dutch terms might refer to tolerance as *verdraagzaamheid*—meaning a quarantining of the other, which could denote passive resistance—in the language of recent debates about tolerance, the word *gedogen* is now used, meaning an active tolerance wherein a secularized, pluralist culture recognizes a wide variety of lifestyles or practices as socially acceptable.[6] The Dutch are at the forefront of social engineering, especially regarding persistent social problems that are not ameliorated by strict legal actions. The underlying laws recognize or accommodate deviance, which means that some practices may remain illegal, but if the practice remains within reasonable limits set by the government, no direct prosecution will occur. For this reason, Dutch society on the whole has been internationally recognized as one of the most "liberal" societies today, along with Scandinavia. That does not mean that there are no conservative groups within the Netherlands, as the variety of Dutch political parties attests, and it can be argued that a vocal minority pushes tolerance to its limits. The Netherlands certainly has a reputation for openness: the sex trade is openly practiced in the Red Light District in Amsterdam, where coffeeshops serve marijuana without censure, and free needles are given out to drug addicts. In the 1960s, the establishment reacted quite differently to new ideas and practices than, for example, the United States. Rather than resist, the Dutch elites, who had always viewed themselves as tolerant and ready to accept change, formally incorporated radical groups into public discussions and governmental initiatives with characteristic consensus.

### Prostitution and the Sex Trade

One internationally known social problem in the Netherlands is prostitution, although the Red Light District in Amsterdam has also become a major tourist attraction. It is sometimes referred to as the "Wall" since the district is located in an old 15th-century neighborhood where the old city wall protected the inhabitants from outside invaders and, along the Wall, marginal people were quarantined. Today, the Red Light District is an experiment in social engineering, wherein the practice of prostitution is tolerated with the goal of controlling the spread of disease and crime. Prostitution is certainly nothing new, for it has been present throughout the history of civilization, not only in the Netherlands. In some ways, it was tolerated in order to curb men's desires and protect honorable women from rape or entanglement. When Napoleon reorganized the Netherlands, he required all prostitutes to declare themselves free of disease or else they could not practice. Previously, medical exams were harsh, and many poor women without power could be subjected to trials as suspected prostitutes by irate men or rejected lovers. Prostitutes were marginalized from society, and the Dutch government continued the Napoleonic plan of registration and medical exams. Nineteenth-century society attacked prostitution from two angles: on the one hand, the Protestant and Catholic moral teachings were heightened by religious revivals, thereby condemning it on religious grounds, and on the other hand, socialists and feminists condemned it based on human rights and equality issues. By the end of the century, the abolitionist movement against prostitution had grown, and the Dutch government was forced to abolish any kind of legal regulation in 1912. Therefore, for the first half of the 20th century, while it was illegal to own a brothel, prostitution was somewhat tolerated. Before the 1970s, most prostitutes were lower-class, white Dutch women, but with growing prosperity, Southeast Asian women were brought to the Netherlands, and then later Latin Americans and African. When the Soviet Union dissolved, Eastern European women joined the mix.

Decades of debate and the introduction of newer political parties into Parliament increased the pressure to formally address the issue. An organization called *De Rode Draad* (The Red Thread) became an advocacy group in 1985, and worked to have prostitution recognized as a profession; by 1988, it was recognized as such, giving prostitutes half-legal status. By 1999, more than 75 percent of Dutch citizens favored the legalization of brothels. Finally, on October 1, 2000, brothels and prostitutes gained full legal status. There are some major qualifications for that legality, however, and that is one of the reasons for their final acceptance. Since the 1980s, fears have grown that human trafficking is on the rise, and that underage girls and illegal immigrants were being coerced into this practice. In addition, organized crime, drugs, and other illegal activities often followed an unprotected industry that was ever-present. The Ministry of Justice declared that prostitution was ". . . legal, provided that they do their work on a voluntary basis and possess the legal residence permit required for employment." A further caveat was that ". . . although prostitution is legalized on certain conditions, at the same time the penalization of particular forms of prostitution has been made more severe."[7] Therefore, the government set up a quota system, strict locations for brothels, and camera surveillance, together with medical exams and spot checks. The issue of prostitution is not settled, and fears of violence in the Red Light District and underground criminal rings require constant surveillance and research to understand whether the related crime can be controlled.

### Euthanasia

In April 2002, Dutch law ruled that doctors who practice euthanasia would not immediately be prosecuted. This has come as a shock to the international community, many of whom perceive this ruling as a bold step toward devaluing human life, especially members of religious communities. The Dutch Ministry of Justice has underlined the uniqueness of the situation by pointing out that euthanasia is not legal, but that if doctors follow strict guidelines, they will not be held directly responsible, and although euthanasia is considered punishable, nothing will be done. This is another example of *gedogen* resulting from a consensus decision by a secular, pluralist society. The guidelines are clear and strict, and a key step in any case is to determine the patient's voluntary desires and condition. The patient must have a hopeless physical diagnosis whereby intractable pain over a sustained time period renders their quality of life almost nil. A second doctor must confirm the condition of the patient, as well, and a report is then sent to the regional review board. Once the report has been read by the review board, it is finally sent to the Public Prosecution Service, where officials determine whether or not to prosecute.

### Pro-Life Versus Pro-Choice

While the Protestant and Catholic political parties dominated the government until the 1990s, and Dutch Catholicism became a model of church attendance and vitality, secularization spread rapidly in the early 1960s. In 1952, the Dutch Reformed Church declared that the use of contraception was morally acceptable, and then against the Vatican's wishes, Roman Catholic Bishop Beckers declared himself in favor of birth control in 1963, when the first contraceptive pill was made available for sale. Elevated to Cardinal in 1960, Cardinal Alfrink also guided Dutch Catholics in opposition to Rome, yet wanted to keep the lines of communication open, especially after Pope Paul VI condemned artificial contraceptives. But despite this openness, the KVP Catholic political party lost half of its members in the years 1965–1968. In the 1980s, the Vatican attempted to restructure the Church by bringing in conservative bishops and weeding out radical ones. But, in many ways, the general feeling among many Catholics is that they are not so much angry at the conservatism of the Church as they simply feel that it is irrelevant. An overwhelming numbers of Dutch Catholics ignored Church teachings when they imposed a standard they had rendered unacceptable.

Far more controversial are the issues of defining the moment of life and determining whether a fetus has rights in relation to the desires of the mother. Any government decision is no longer a religiously motivated one, despite the Catholic or Protestant positions, but abortion has become a legal question, with many claiming secular moral and ethical values as the foundation of their arguments. The questions surrounding abortion as a social problem only emerged in the 19th century; in 1886, the Penal Code underlined its illegality, but did not have a well-defined procedure in place until the Morality Acts of 1911 barred any pregnancy termination, except in cases where it would safeguard the mortality of the mother. Despite the rapid secularization and liberalization of the 1970s, there was a split in public opinion until a 1981 abortion law was passed with a narrow victory of 38 "for" and 37 "against" in the Upper House, and 76 for and 74 against in the Lower House. Something of a compromise prevailed by restricting abortions to a limited number of approved hospitals and 16 clinics, limiting them to 24 weeks, and making counseling and a minimum waiting period mandatory. Despite being a liberal society, today, the Netherlands has the lowest abortion rate of all Western countries.[8]

A similar problem has arisen in the Netherlands and throughout the West regarding embryonic stem-cell research. Together with Brazil, Canada, France, Iran, South Africa, Spain, and Taiwan, the Netherlands allowed embryos from fertility clinics that are no longer needed for reproduction to be used for medical research.[9] The majority in these countries base their opinion of the use of embryonic stem-cells on the medical benefits, rather than on moral grounds or the embryos' rights. But concern is certainly widespread in these countries, as in more conservative countries, that using human embryos can lead to much more morally reprehensible uses, creating trafficking and human rights issues.

### Homosexuality

The current government has declared the Netherlands a gay-friendly country. The official SCP/Netherlands Institute for Social Research reported that "the Netherlands is the world leader when it comes to giving equal rights to heterosexuals and homosexuals."[10] This policy did not necessarily apply until after World War II. In the 19th century all homosexual activity was considered as "wrong loves" (*verkeerde liefhebber[ij]*) and was done in secret, and if discovered, punished. In 1911, the issue was addressed by increasing the legal age for homosexual contact from 16 to 21, yet few other protections existed outside a general rule against slander. In 1958, Catholic priests called for a general acceptance, and the Protestant HKN church followed suit in 1961 with a pamphlet titled "The Homosexual Neighbor." But no government recognition came before 1973, when the COC (*Cultuur en Ontspannings Centrum*/Center for Culture and Recreation), established in 1946 as a society for homosexuals, was officially recognized by the government, making them eligible for funding. In 1986, the government published their first "gay policy memorandum" suggesting full equality. It became very common to see and hear openly gay people in the media and on the radio and television, and within a decade, acceptance grew among the general population. Gay pride parades, especially those featuring floating barges on the country's many canals, have become a regular attraction in Amsterdam, and represent some of the largest in the world.

In 1997, the Dutch government created a category of "registered partnerships" in order to allow gays to gain the benefits of marriage partners, and in April 2001, same-sex marriages were legalized for the first time in any country. One could imagine a rush for a sizable portion of the marriage licenses to be from gay couples, and for the first month, six percent of all marriages were by gay couples, but then the numbers fell off sharply. Statistics Netherlands released estimates in 2006 on the number of same-sex marriages each year, with 2,500 occurring in 2001; 1,800 in 2002; 1,200 in 2004; and 1,100 in 2005. The Netherlands remained the world's leader in integrating homosexuals into society. Surveys that asked about the legitimacy of homosexuality in the Netherlands show that 78 percent were in favor of full rights for homosexuals, which was higher than Sweden's 74 percent, with the lowest percentage of any European state occurring in United Kingdom, where only 38 percent favored full rights. Outside Europe, 51 percent of citizens in the most developed country, Canada, supported full rights for homosexuals, compared to the United States' 40 percent. When asked about gay marriage, 82 percent of the Dutch were in favor, which was the highest in Europe; with Sweden's 71 percent as the next highest, while in Poland and Greece, the percentages were 18 and 15, respectively.[11]

### Drugs

As with prostitution policy, the Dutch government has tolerated certain soft narcotic drugs in order to curb organized crime, restricting the use of drugs to certain locations, monitoring use and abuse, and setting even tougher standards for hard drugs. Rather than viewing drug use as a criminal act per se, the government sees it as a health issue, and therefore, the policy of *gedogen* is practiced. Consistent with this policy, the Ministry of Health, Welfare, and Sports, and the Ministry of Justice, are involved in regulating illicit drugs. Although it is considered a misdemeanor, which can carry a fine, the use of small amounts of marijuana (cannabis) in what the Dutch call "coffeeshops" is not prosecuted on an individual basis, but the production, distribution, and sale of large quantities is strictly forbidden and enforced. Coffeeshops, as the signs read, may sell coffee or, more likely, tea, but the name is a facade for the sale of marijuana (cafés are where real coffee is served). The government appears to turn a blind eye to the origin of soft drugs in coffeeshops, but its real interest is cutting the connection between soft and hard drugs. In 2005, Parliamentary debate raised the issue of limiting marijuana production in order to control the quality, but it remains illegal. In tandem with the relaxed policy on soft drugs, the government takes a strict and enforceable position on hard drugs. The Netherlands is second only to Sweden in the EU for the amount of money spent per capita to combat illegal drug traffic. Roughly one-quarter is spent on the care and health of users, and three-quarters is devoted to law enforcement.

The Netherlands' policy on soft drugs is not appreciated by its nearby neighbors, who have tried to enforce their own stricter policies. Germany and France, like the United States, do not tolerate soft drugs, and are trying to adhere to the international treaties that regulate illicit drugs, such as the latest "United Nations Convention Against Illicit Traffic in Narcotic Drugs and Psychotropic Substances" of 1988. Dutch Parliamentary debates have entertained suggestions that the use of marijuana be restricted to citizens, but no practical solution has ever emerged to make this possible. Like prostitution, soft drugs draw many foreigners, who come to the Netherlands specifically to partake in this activity. Yet, it is significant that when one compares the use of soft drugs by young boys across countries, one finds that 9.7 percent of Dutch boys consume soft drugs once a month, whereas in Germany, this figure was 9.9 percent, 10.9 percent in Italy, 15.8 percent in the United Kingdom, and 16.4 percent in Spain. The Netherlands also has a lower number of reported deaths due to drugs than the EU average, most likely due to their extensive demand reduction programs. But despite government programs and a strict policy on hard drugs, the Netherlands remains a hub for international narcotics trafficking. Recent efforts have sought to restrict the increasing rise of THC (the intoxicating element) in marijuana, the cultivation and trade of "magic mushrooms," and the trade in cocaine arriving from the Dutch Caribbean islands.

## FAMILY AND GENDER

### Marriage and Family

Early modern Netherlands was divided regionally between many urban areas surrounded by countryside with very small villages. It was also divided between rich and poor, but unlike most other parts of Europe, there was a much wider range, from the very wealthy princes, dukes, and regent nobility to a growing middling group of urban merchants and skilled craftsmen, followed by poorer workers and rural peasants. The successful economy of the Dutch Republic in the 17th century created new opportunities for women and men, which made the place of women unique. Often, women had to be far more independent than in other countries since so many men went to sea for months on end.[12] While the majority of Europe was still based on an agrarian model, which limited travel and trade for most people, the Dutch had many more characteristics of a modern economy. Because of their extensive river systems and proximity to the North Sea and Atlantic Ocean, many men became sailors and fishermen, leaving women to run the households and supplemental businesses on land. An urbanized economy also created more skilled jobs for both genders, and in the Dutch Republic, some guilds were open to women born to the upper classes, which was often unheard of in many other areas of Europe. Depending on the craft or industry, there were even some guilds devoted exclusively to women, such as the peat tax collectors and the second-hand merchandisers.

The historic place of women in Western civilization in terms of their societal role was the domestic sphere: marriage and children. Common to other family patterns throughout Europe, in the Dutch family, men took the role of head of the household, and the nuclear units included husband, wife, children, and servants for the wealthier. Marriage also played an economic role in the intergenerational transfer of property. By the Renaissance, marriages came to be based more on affection, passion, and more equal unions, rather than on the medieval customs of arranged marriages based primarily on economic considerations.[13] Women also had to take a more active role in the economy and community because of the increased absence of men at sea for international trade or fishing, or the more complex urban textile industries, where many specialized jobs needed to be performed by women. The general religious attitudes also encouraged greater literacy and the development of individual conscience among women. Due to the religious awakening movement called the Modern Devotion, which supported the Brethren of the Common Life and the Beguine movements, girls and women had more outlets for education in practical skills and literacy within supportive communities. The Reformed Church, which became the dominant power in the Netherlands, underlined the importance of reading the Bible in the vernacular, listening to the word in sermon, and discussing the word in community, and women were included in these activities. The Dutch Republic had no established church per se, and while the Reformed Church had a privileged status, and the government greatly restricted other religious groups from practicing, it did protect freedom of conscience. Many travelers to the Netherlands commented on the relative freedom Dutch women had to go to work and purchase supplies without being accompanied by a man, which was still the standard practice in almost all other places.[14] There were also jokes about how many Dutch wives ordered their husbands around, and working-class women who needed to work long hours had a reputation for their combative characters.

While there were a variety of Christian churches in the Netherlands, the government instituted a civil ceremony for marriage. Whereas the Reformed Church attempted to restrict all marriage ceremonies to a religious service, all non-Reformed needed governmental approval. It was possible to have two ceremonies, and in the case of the Catholic Church's elevation of marriage to a sacrament, this allowed some possibilities for the peaceful co-existence of church and state. The Reformed Church had strict rules about declaring the "banns of marriage" whereby the engagement of a couple was publicly announced, making it almost impossible to break the arrangement once the bans had been read. The marriage ceremony was one of the biggest events in the life of a family. After the formal religious and civil ceremonies, a great feast featuring all kinds of food, music, and dance followed; some feasts endured for three days, and it was not uncommon for several couples to share the same feast in order to increase the volume of material, as well as the festival atmosphere.

Consistent with the Catholic Church's teaching and practice throughout Europe, divorce was impossible, except in extraordinary cases and where approval at the highest levels could be sought for an annulment. Marriages between different Christian groups were illegal, as were marriages to Jews or Muslims. Within the Reformed Church, following the teachings of John Calvin, divorce was possible in cases of adultery or clear abandonment. By the 17th century, it was also possible that women could bring up charges against men to dissolve a marriage or force the father of a child born out of wedlock to marry. Because of high mortality rates, it was common to see many remarriages. Life was especially hard for most Netherlanders due to the precarious nature of the land, increased travel at sea, the poor quality of drinking water, and a sometimes harsh climate. The average age of marriage was approximately 22 for women and 25 for men. If they were lucky, they remained married for 20–25 years before one or more of them died, thus very few extended families existed for very long. Infant mortality remained high until the end of the 19th century.

Marriage in contemporary Netherlands has been on the decline, as many couples do not see the need for formal ties. Before 1970, the Netherlands was a model for strong marriages: Reformed and Catholic teachings strongly supported the traditional understanding that couples came together to procreate. In 1970, only about three percent of births were out of wedlock, and by 1985, this number was still below 10 percent. Two factors radically changed the perception of marriage and the laws that restricted the union to heterosexual couples. The sexual revolution for women had already begun to put pressure on social norms in the late 1960s, and women made great strides in the 1970s, amalgamating with other liberal movements on housing, drugs, social welfare, and environmental issues. In its characteristic manner, Dutch pragmatism attempted to forge a moderate path between the traditional forms of marriage and an expanded category that allowed a variety of social unions. Same-sex marriage also became an increasingly important social issue among some radical groups. When the Christian political parties were no longer in the coalition government in 1994 (for the first time since 1913), the "Purple Coalition" of liberal (D66 and VVD parties) and social-democratic (PvdA party) parties opened a formal debate on the issue of marriage. In 1997, the Dutch government legalized registered partnerships, and on April 1, 2001, they approved same-sex marriages by a vote of 109–33 in the Lower House and 49–26 in the Upper House, thus eliminating the notion that marriage was for procreation. In 2003, out-of-wedlock births increased to 32 percent and have climbed every year since.[15] Most births outside marriage, however, are to couples who have chosen to live together rather than marry.

### Feminism

While it was common in the early modern Netherlands for young boys to become laborers or apprentices, young girls often became servants for wealthier households. The girls had to maintain the house, cook, buy materials, and interact with the family at meals. They were subordinate to the wishes of the family patriarch and matriarch, and had to remain within the boundaries of their lowly position; yet, in most cases, these servant girls were never physically punished where loyalty and discretion followed. But stories abounded about devious and unreliable girls, and it was not uncommon to blame servant girls for creating a stumbling block to a man's sexual desires. It is well known that Rembrandt abandoned his caretaker, Geertje Dircx, who had become his lover, but she was lucky to be able to legally charge alimony of 200 guilders. Unfortunately, however, Rembrandt had enough connections to have her committed to an asylum in Gouda for 12 years. In the early 1640s, he took his new caretaker, Hendrickje Stoffels, as his lover. Certainly, women were often victimized and did not have equal rights.

As with the revolutionary fervor nourished during the Enlightenment and the French Revolution, some Dutch women spoke out about their place in society. It was generally understood that women should not speak out in public, especially concerning science, religion, or politics. But Etta Aelders spoke to the French National Convention in 1790 regarding her *Discourse on the Injustice of the Laws in Favor of Men, at the Expense of Women*. She had been living in Paris for some time, and her salon became well known as a place where radicals met, and she herself had many different lovers. She had become a spy for both sides, periodically living in The Hague and spying on French emissaries or on the Dutch government in turn. Nurtured in the household of a democratic and anti-Orangist father who was a Mennonite preacher, Maria Aletta Hulshoff, known as "Mietje," had a far more direct impact on women's status in the Netherlands. Mietje became known for her high-profile trials during the French occupation of the Netherlands. Her pamphlets, such as *An Appeal to the Batavian People* in 1806, sought to continue the patriotic fervor that had originally swept the country, but waned with the rise of Napoleon. Although her family had tried to shield her from public trial by hiding her in Germany, she returned to face the opposition. William Bilderdijk and Valckenaer tried to defend her in the most acceptable manner of the times by claiming that that she had fallen into hysteria (a reference to the Greek word for uterus that consigned women to an unstable condition unfit for politics), she rejected this argument and decided to defend herself instead. Unfortunately, she actually had a nervous breakdown during the trial and this would consign her to prison; however, she once again escaped to Amsterdam and later exiled in New York. There, she wrote a pamphlet titled *Republicans' Peace Manual,* and upon returning to the Netherlands, she turned her attention to women's health issues, offering comments on hygiene and smallpox vaccinations. She often compared herself to Joan of Arc, and she died in 1846, just prior to the start of a more liberal democratic government.

Shortly after Maria Aletta Hulshoff's death, another Aletta was born: Aletta Jacobs. She became the first woman in the Netherlands to attain a university degree, and later became the first female physician, as well. Her father was a Jewish doctor from whom she learned classical Greek and Latin, and under the tutelage of her mother, she excelled at French and German. In 1871, she enrolled at the University of Groningen, and later pursued medical training at the University of Amsterdam, obtaining her doctor's degree in 1878. In addition to her practice, she worked with the government and the Dutch General Trade Union to teach women's hygiene and infant care. Jacobs was also instrumental in helping women seek voting rights through her leadership in the Dutch Association for Women's Suffrage. Her work on the international level later bore fruit in the 1915 Hague Congress, leading to the Women's International League for Peace and Freedom, and in her support for the International Women's Suffrage Alliance.[16] Another example of women's activism is found in the work of Christine de Bosch Kemper. To address the educational concerns of women, the Christine-Stichting Foundation was administered by a Mennonite board of directors in honor of Christine de Bosch Kemper, who had worked to educate young women since 1867. In 1880, she moved from Amsterdam to Amersfoort, where she established a free school that was open to all young women. These are only some examples of the many small opportunities women enacted in the 19th century to provide women with the education and training they needed.

In 1898, a National Exhibition of Women's Labor was held in The Hague. This represented the new power of bourgeois women, as 1,400 contributors demonstrated their rich contribution to the Dutch economy for more than 90,000 visitors. Women's groups were consciously trying to connect the importance of women in the economy with the necessity of granting them full citizenship and, therefore, full emancipation in the form of women's suffrage.[17] When King William III died in 1890, leaving no male heir, his daughter Wilhelmina was not yet ready to serve at such a young age, so her mother, Queen Emma, acted as regent until 1898. This decade of female monarchy greatly encouraged women's further participation in public life. Queen Wilhelmina reigned for 50 years, and was highly regarded as a strong leader. She stood firm against German occupation of the Netherlands and worked closely with Churchill to lead the resistance and reorganization of her government after World War II. By her own right, Queen Wilhelmina became an important voice for the substantive place that women now hold in the public sphere.

In recent decades, more economic and political opportunities have been open to women than ever before. In 2006, the Dutch Parliament had the third-highest percentage of women with 36.7 percent; only Sweden at 47.3 percent and Costa Rica at 38.6 percent were higher.[18] An example of a modern Dutch feminist who advanced the position of women is Hedy d'Ancona. In 1981, she was appointed *staatssecretaris* for issues centering on women's emancipation, and from 1989 forward, she held the Ministry of Welfare, Public Health, and Culture. She also served in the European Parliament and in the First Chamber of the Dutch Parliament (Senate) for the Labor Party. In public, she has been outspoken through her monthly magazine *Opzij,* and in the Man-Woman Society. Since 1995, she has been the chairperson of Oxfam Novib, the Dutch branch, and since 1999, she has served as vice-chairperson of Oxfam International, an organization that fights poverty and injustice around the world.

In 1982, the older Ministry of Economic Affairs transferred its oversight of social affairs and labor market policy to a new Ministry of Social Affairs and Employment that included all of the issues surrounding employment, social security, and the emancipation of women. Their task was to increase gender equality, giving women new opportunities to enhance their status and experience less victimization, and to increase the number of women that were gainfully employed. The goal was to make women economically independent, which means earning at least 70 percent of the minimum Dutch income. By 2003, approximately 41 percent of women in the 15–65 age range were deemed economically independent, and the new target is to reach 60 percent by 2010, although the Social and Cultural Planning Office of the Netherlands has expressed doubts about attaining this goal.[19]

## EDUCATION

### History of Education

Formal education has been a hallmark of the Netherlands, rooted in its religious and commercial interests in the Renaissance. The earliest Latin schools allowed the sons of the wealthy to learn the basics of a classical education, but university study was limited to the existing northern universities in Leuven, Paris, Oxford, or Cambridge. The Brethren of the Common Life movement had organized local schools where basic reading skills were taught in order to read and study scripture. Wealthy merchants, on the other hand, began to desire more training in arithmetic, bookkeeping, and foreign languages in order to increase their own commercial enterprises and pass them on to the next generation. After the city of Leiden withstood the Spanish siege and became a symbol of Dutch resistance, William of Orange granted a charter to the city to establish a university in 1575. Unhappy with their classical training in Latin, the wealthy merchants of Amsterdam attempted to open their own university in 1620, but they were only allowed to create an *Atheneum Illustre,* where they could devote study to more commercial interests. In 1632, they were able to establish the Amsterdam Municipal University, and despite the fact that they could easily raise far more funds than Leiden, Leiden retained its premier place as the most learned institution.

In addition to philosophy and theology, the study of science became an important aspect of university curriculum. The Reformation redirected primary and secondary education from the medieval interest in monastic and priestly education, designed for the religious and a select few, to an interest in the practical and personal piety of the masses. Throughout its educational history, the Reformed Church established "schools of the Bible" in order to highlight the central place of God's word and the wisdom that could be gained through scripture, thus building character. The emphasis was on religious education, and catechisms, creeds, and other religious sources were used along with the Bible. Girls and the poor were often given equal opportunities that previously, only wealthy sons enjoyed. This tradition is also reflected in universities to this day, where a distinction is made between the discipline of philosophy (*filosofie*) and wisdom studies (*wijsbegerte*, literally following wisdom). By the Golden Age of the 17th century, the Dutch Republic was one of the most literate states, and it is reported that in 1630, 57 percent of grooms and 32 percent of brides, and, in 1680, 70 percent of grooms and 44 percent of brides, were able to sign their names on marriage certificates.[20]

By the 19th century, girls and boys were equally encouraged to attend school, though at the higher levels, education was segregated, as was common in other countries. Higher education for girls included practical crafts, such as knitting, cooking, and other domestic skills, together with foreign languages, art, music, and other social skills. Very few girls had the opportunity to study mathematics, history, and ancient languages. Until the 1850s, all education was run by the various churches, and under the new monarchy, training in the morals and values of the kingdom was central. The liberal government that was established in 1848 under Thorbeke began to distance primary education from the churches and more schools became public and independent. In the liberal way of thinking, government funding should go primarily to public schools.

Although both Protestants and Catholics benefited from liberal policies in trade, union organization, and suffrage, the growth of secularized public schools, which reduced any religious education, created a profound struggle that stands as a case study in the realization of great differences within Dutch society. Protestants and Catholics set aside their differences when they joined forces to promote freedom for private religious education under the control of parents, a collaboration known as the *Schoolstrijd* (school struggle). The Primary Education Act of 1857 (the Van der Brugghen Law) proposed a stricter government system; it attempted to eliminate the possibility of competition from private education, yet by 1875, nearly 55 percent of all Dutch students were in Protestant schools, and 11 percent were enrolled in Catholic schools. In 1888, Protestants and Catholics formed an alliance, and helped create a new school law in 1889 that allowed the government to subsidize private schools. By 1917, the new Constitution created full funding for all schools, whether public or private; this was a compromise that the Liberals and Social Democrats were willing to make in exchange for universal suffrage and a share in the government. Today, Protestant and Catholics schools account for two-thirds of all schools, and public schools only one-third. In principle, any organization can apply for status as a school, and if approved, will receive full governmental funding. Recent new additions to the schools in terms of diversity are those organized around Islamic values and principles.

### Primary and Secondary Education

Today, education is compulsory for all children in the Netherlands. The country has developed a unique and multi-tiered system with the goal of offering a base line of education for all future citizens interested in equality, and a very specific education at the higher levels, depending on the field of study. Normally, many children start before the age of five by attending a nursery school (*Crèche*) until their fifth birthday. Formal schooling starts in the elementary school (*Basisschool*) and continues until age 12. This eight-year education is identical for all students, but a variety of more specialized training commences at the next levels. In 1993, a new *Basisvorming* law ("fundamental education") increased the amount of core courses for subsequent levels of education, as well. The new law stipulated that for the two years following *Basisschool*, all students should study the same 15 subjects and are required to demonstrate a passing grade. At this point, 14- or 15-year-old students must select from a variety of secondary school education, depending on their field of study or intended occupation.

Approximately one-third of the students select the LBO (*Lager Beroepsonderwijs*), or lower vocational education, which takes them through another three years of study in preparation for advanced vocational training in basic employment skills. Other students can select a number of other levels intended for more professional training. The MAVO (*Middelbaar Algemeen Voortgezet Onderwijs*), or middle-level general preparatory education, also requires three years of study, and a mandatory national examination in six subjects determines whether students can continue in higher education. If they pass the examinations, they can attend the MBO colleges (*Middelbaar Beroeps Onderwijs*), which require two to five years of study, depending on the vocation. Typical vocations are the administration of small businesses, secretarial training, technical areas, and agriculture and horticulture. The traditional designation of "college" in Europe is the equivalent of "high school" in the United States, and the Dutch name *hogescholen* (literally "higher" school) is the equivalent of specialized community college and university vocational education in the U.S. A second option for excellent MAVO students, and other students who have tracked through the *basisvorming* education with the intent of pursuing higher professional study, is the HAVO (*Hoger Algemeen Voortgezet Onderwijs*), or higher general preparatory education. Advanced students who enter the HAVO directly from *basisvorming* study for five years,

Bicycles (*fietsen*) are a primary means of transportation, and some have front compartments for supplies or children, with plastic covers used to keep out the rain. Courtesy of the author.

whereas students who had chosen MAVO first must complete another two years to increase their knowledge and training in order to arrive at the same level. Every student must pass a standard exam on six subjects, depending on the vocational field. Most students who have achieved good grades in HAVO training continue in the various *hogescholen*. Today, there are some 80 different *hogescholen* serving a variety of disciplines and sub-fields. In recent years, some of the *hogescholen* have increased their educational levels and offer the equivalent of university-type education.

A third option for students who have demonstrated the highest aptitudes and desire education leading to the most advanced fields is to select the highest level of secondary education after their *basisvorming* education, the VWO (*Voorbereidend Wetenschappelijk Onderwijs*), or literally Preparatory Scientific Education. All VWOs require six years of study in seven areas, with competency examinations given at the end. Two basic tracks exist, depending on the intended fields. The *Atheneum* track is typical for students going into the sciences, while the *Gymnasium* is for students in the arts and humanities. Often, a *Lyceum* combines the two VWO tracks for the first two years, and then more specialized training occurs. It is also common for one school administration and building complex to house the MAVO, HAVO, and VWO tracks together. The care and discipline of the Dutch educational system has paid off in recent international comparisons provided by the "Programme for International Student Assessment" (PISA). The Netherlands ranks ninth in the world in general science achievements, fifth in the world in mathematics, and third in "practical mathematics."

### University Education

University education has also been very important in the Netherlands. Given the diverse interest groups established in *verzuiling,* the small size of the population, and diverse educational needs, the Netherlands has organized its current system of 16 universities into three areas: state universities, private universities, and technological and professional universities. All universities receive full government funding. Among the state-run universities, the oldest are Leiden, the first university founded in 1575; Groningen, founded in 1614; and Utrecht, established in 1636. Erasmus University was founded in 1973, combining the older School of Economics with the School of Medicine in Rotterdam; Maastricht University in 1976; the Open University in Heerlen in 1984; and the newest state school, the University for Humanistics (*Universiteit voor Humanistiek*) in Utrecht, was founded in 1989, specifically for humanities degrees.

The private universities were formerly religious, with the Free University of Amsterdam (*Gereformeerde*) founded in 1880, and two Catholic universities, Radboud University Nijmegen (renamed in 2004 from the former "Catholic University Nijmegen"), founded in 1923, and Tilburg University, founded in 1927. The University of Amsterdam, founded in 1632, remains a municipal university, and the Nijenrode Business University was founded in 1946 by executives of leading companies, such as Akzo, KLM, Philips, Shell, and Unilever. In 1992, the Nijenrode Business University decided to reject governmental funding in order to control its selection process.

The remaining technological and professional universities include Delft University of Technology, founded in 1905 for a wide range of engineering and other technical applications; Wageningen University and Research Centre, the premier agricultural school founded in 1918; Eindhoven University of Technology, founded in 1957; and the University of Twente, founded in 1964 in Enschede. In addition to offering theology faculties, several independent theological schools have graduate programs, including Kampen

The University of Leiden's oldest building is simply called the Academic Building, located on the Rapenburg street; it is still used today. Courtesy of the author.

Theological University, founded in 1854. Kampen was formerly the *Theologische Hogeschool* from 1939 forward, but in 1944, a split in the Church produced a second theological school in Kampen, the Kampen Theological University of the Reformed Church (Liberated). In 1986, the older *Theologische Hogeschool* changed its status and title to that of a university.

Traditional degrees in Dutch higher education were changed to conform to international standards in 2004. The *hogescholen* award technical Bachelor's level degrees, such as B.Com. or B.Eng., after four years of study, but any further education at the Master's level requires one more year of "bridge studies" to acquire a Bachelor-level degree granted by a university. After three years of university study, students are granted either a B.A. or a B.Sc. degrees—formerly a *baccalureus* (*bc.*) degree—that qualifies them to apply directly to a graduate program. The traditional degrees are given as a prefix with a name. At the Master's level, there is the *doctorandus* (*drs.,* a degree similar to the PhD), the *ingenieur* (*ing.,* or engineer from a university of applied science, or *ir.* from a university), and the *meester in de rechten* (*mr.*, law, equivalent to LL.M.), and at the Doctorate level, there is the *doctor* (*dr.*, equivalent to a PhD). These degrees are still granted, along with their international equivalents.

Dutch universities are recognized in several well-known university-ranking systems, which vary depending on the nature of the education offered and other political issues. The two educational areas detailed below, among many, have received international rankings reserved for research universities and business and economic programs (science, medicine, law, and other fields could be added). In the "Academic Ranking of World Universities" (Shanghai Jiao Tong University) for the years 2003–2007, the University of Utrecht was ranked between 39–42, the University of Leiden between 63–78, and the University of Groningen was ranked at 84. The "Top 100 Global Universities" (*Newsweek* magazine) ranked only the University of Leiden at 83. The "Webometrics" ranking of the top European universities illustrates the level of many more Dutch universities: Utrecht is 8th in Europe and 63rd in the world; the University of Amsterdam is 17th in Europe and 93rd in the world; Groningen is 21st in Europe and 102nd in the world; the Eindhoven University of Technology is 45th in Europe and 161st in the world; Leiden is 56th in Europe and 180th in the world; The Free University of Amsterdam is 60th in Europe and 192nd in the world; Radboud University of Technology is 65th in Europe and 203rd in the world; and Delft University of Technology is 76th in Europe and 227th in the world. When ranking the study of economics and business, the University of Texas at Dallas' School of Management's "Top 100 Worldwide Business Schools Rankings Based on Research Contributions between 2003–2007" places Tilburg University at 52, Erasmus University's Rotterdam School of Management at 64, and Maastricht University at 99. Finally, the *Financial Times'* EMBA world rankings place the Tias Nimbas Business School, Tilburg, at 11, and the Rotterdam School of Management at 32.[21]

## NOTES

1. See Jonathan I. Israel, *The Dutch Republic: Its Rise, Greatness, and Fall, 1477–18* (Oxford: Clarendon Press, 1995), 353–354.

2. See Michael J. Wintle, *An Economic and Social History of the Netherlands, 1800–1920: Demographic, Economic and Social Transition* (Cambridge, MA: Cambridge University Press, 2007), 44.

3. Marco Strik, and Nel Knols, "Public Health, Private Concern: The Organizational Development of Public Health in the Netherlands at the Beginning of the Twentieth Century," *European Journal of Public Health* 6, no. 2 (1996): 84.

4. See Ary Burger, and Vic Veldheer, "The Growth of the Nonprofit Sector in the Netherlands," *Nonprofit and Voluntary Sector Quarterly* 30, no. 2 (June 2001): 221–246. Retrieved June 5, 2008, http://nvs.sagepub.com.

5. Willem Frijhoff, *Embodied Belief: Ten Essays on Religious Culture in Dutch History*. (Hilversum: Uitgeverij Verloren, 2002). Erasmus made the distinction between *fundamenta* (fundamentals that had to be unified) and *adiaphoria* (teachings that may allow some differences).

6. See a lively discussion of *gedogen* from Gijs van Oenen, the Department of Philosophy, Erasmus University, Rotterdam, Retrieved June 10, 2008, http://www2.eur.nl/fw/law/gedogen/ukindex.html.

7. Frans Leeuw, "Prostitution in the Netherlands Since the Lifting of the Brothel Ban," Ministry of Justice, the Netherlands, Retrieved June 13, 2008, www.wodc.nl.

8. See The Ministry of Health, Welfare, and Sport, Retrieved June 8, 2008, http://www.minvws.nl/dossiers/abortus/. See also E. Ketting, and A.P. Visser, "Contraception in The Netherlands: The Low Abortion Rate Explained," Retrieved July 7, 2008, http://www.ncbi.nlm.nih.gov/pubmed/797154.

9. See Walters, and LeRoy, National Academy of Sciences, 2004 and University of Minnesota, 2007, Retrieved June 4, 2008, http://mbbnet.umn.edu/scmap.html.

10. See Saskia Kueuzenkamp and David Bos, "Out in the Netherlands: Acceptance of homosexuality in the Netherlands" (SCP, 2007), 13, Retrieved June 14, 2008, http://www.scp.nl/english/publications/books/9789037703245/Out_in_the_Netherlands.pdf.

11. Kueuzenkamp and Bos, "Out in the Netherlands," 15–16.

12. See A. Th. Van Deursen, *Plain Lives in a Golden Age: Popular Culture, Religion, and Society in Seventeenth-Century Holland*, trans. Maarten Ultee (Cambridge: Cambridge University Press, 1991), 84.

13. See Howell, Martha, *The Marriage Exchange: Property, Social Place, and Gender in Cities of the Low Countries, 1300–1550* (Chicago: University of Chicago Press, 1998).

14. See Israel, The Dutch Republic, 677.

15. See Eurostat, Population Statistics (Luxembourg, 1996), Retrieved February 15, 2008, http://epp.eurostat.ec.europa.eu: In 1970, Spain had the lowest rate of out-of-wedlock births at 1.4, and Sweden had the highest at 18.6, with an EU-15 average of 5.6. In 1995, Italy was the lowest at 8.3 percent, and Sweden was still the highest at 52 percent, with the Euro-15 average at 23 percent. In France, the figure had reached 50.5 percent by 2007, while the U.S. had reached 37 percent in 2008.

16. See Aletta Jacobs, *Memoirs: My Life as an International Leader in Health, Suffrage, and Peace*, ed. Harriet Feinberg, trans. Annie Wright, Retrieved May 29, 2008, http://www.pinn.net/~sunshine/book-sum/jacobs2.html.

17. See Maria Grever, and Berteke Waalrijk, *Transforming the Public Sphere: The Dutch National Exhibition of Women's Labor in 1898*, trans. Mischa F.C Hoyinck, and Robert E. Chesal (Chapel Hill, NC: Duke University Press, 2004).

18. See Inter-Parliamentary Union, Geneva, Retrieved May 30, 2008, http://www.ipu.org/pdf/publications/wmn06-e.pdf.

19. See the Social and Cultural Planning Office of the Netherlands, Retrieved May 16, 2008, http://www.scp.nl/english/index.shtml.

20. See Cor Snabel, Retrieved June 23, 2008, http://www.olivetreegenealogy.com/nn/amst_edu.shtml.

21. See "Academic Ranking of World Universities" (Shanghai Jiao Tong University), http://ed.sjtu.edu.cn/rank/2007/ARWU2007_Top100.htm; Webmetrics Ranking of European Universities, http://www.webometrics.info/top500_europe.asp; and University of Texas at Dallas, School of Management, http://somweb.utdallas.edu/top100Ranking/searchRanking.php?t=w; *Financial Times'* EMBA Rankings, http://rankings.ft.com/emba-rankings. Retrieved June 23, 2008.

$$4$$

# Holidays, Leisure, and Housing

## OFFICIAL STATE AND RELIGIOUS HOLIDAYS

The Netherlands celebrates civil and religious holidays similar to those of many other European and North American states.

### New Year's Celebration

The Dutch celebrate the end of the year, calling December 31 "Old Year's Evening" (*oudejaarsavond*) or, often, "Old and New" (*Oud en Nieuw*), and January 1 "New Year's Day." Traditionally, many people watch special shows on television to commemorate the old and new years, including shows by well-known Dutch cabaret stars, who comment on Dutch social and political culture with much satire. Many eat copious numbers of *oliebollen,* which are small, round donuts with raisons, or *appelflappen* (apple fritters), and at midnight, they either drink champagne or *Glühwein* (the popular German expression for spiced wine, or, in Dutch *bisschopswijn*) in celebration. Although there are no official civil fireworks displays, it is common for many individuals to light their own smaller firework displays to bring in the New Year with a bang.

### Carnival and Lent

Forty days prior to Easter, the Dutch celebrate *Karnival,* sometimes referred to as *Vastenavond* (literally the fasting evening), the day before Ash Wednesday. It is most popular in the southern Netherlands, where the majority of Roman Catholics live, especially in the province of Limburg, where the *Rijnlandsche Carnival* (Rhineland Carnival) sponsors large parades featuring many different costumes that allow the "world to be turned upside down" as people humorously impersonate princes, participants in farmer's weddings (*boerenbruiloft*), or herring eaters (*haring happen*) to the delight of the crowd. The 's-Hertogenbosch Carnival is one of the oldest in the Netherlands, dating back to the Late Middle Ages. It has become popular to disconnect carnival from any original religious adherences and today, Rotterdam and Arnhem celebrate a "Mardi Gras" or Brazilian-type carnival in the summer months.

### Easter Season

Good Friday (*Goede Vrijdag*) is celebrated three days before Easter (*Pasen*). Although Good Friday is still recognized as a national holiday, it does not necessarily translate to a day off from work for many businesses. However, most companies and governmental institutions do suspend work for the long Easter weekend. The Dutch extend the Easter weekend with a celebration of Easter Sunday (*Eerste Paasdag*) and Easter Monday (*Tweede Paasdag*). Ascension Day (*Hemelvaartsdag*) is celebrated 40 days after Easter. In some areas, there is an older tradition called *Luilak*, literally "lazybones," practiced on the Saturday before Pentecost, when young people arise early and make loud noises to rouse people from their sleep, and then *Luilakbollen*, or Lazybones Cakes, are eaten. Pentecost (or Whit) Sunday (*Eerste Pinksterdag*) is celebrated on the seventh Sunday after Easter, followed by the second Pentecost Monday (*Tweede Pinkerdag*). All of these dates vary from year to year. For example, in 2008, Good Friday fell on March 21, Easter was on March 23, Ascension Day occurred on May 1, and Pentecost Sunday was on May 11.

### Queen's Birthday

The Queen's Birthday (*Koninginnedag*) is celebrated on April 30 each year. The date is based on the late Queen-mother Juliana's birthday (1909), and it also coincides with the accession to the throne of her oldest daughter Beatrix (1980), who is the current Queen. This day of national unity is celebrated in several ways. It is typical for people to sell goods at flea markets (*vrijmarkt*, or free market), but the most important events center around large parties and parades in which everyone dresses in orange, celebrating the royal House of Orange. This orange craze (*oranjegekte*) reaches its height in Amsterdam and The Hague, where live music fills the streets, overloaded barges carry revelers through the network of urban canals, and large amounts of Dutch beer and sausage are consumed. Queen Beatrix and her family regularly visit two or three different places in the Netherlands

Beatrix was born in 1938 and became Queen in 1980. Rijksvoorlichtingsdienst, afd/Royal Netherlands Embassy.

each year to sample the local flavor and culture offered in honor of the entire country.

## Liberation Day

On May 4 of each year, the Netherlands commemorates a day to remember the dead (*Dodenherdenking*) who gave their lives in wars, and at 10 p.m., everyone practices two minutes of silence. May 5 is a celebration called Liberation Day (*Bevrijdingsdag*), a reminder of the day in 1945 when the Nazi troops withdrew from the Netherlands and the country was liberated by the Allied forces. It is only customary to allow a day off from work once every five years for this national holiday.

## Beggar's Day

On November 11, Beggar's Day is celebrated, coinciding with the religious holiday of Saint Martin, or *Martinmas* in Dutch. It is common for children to visit their neighbors, carrying candles and lanterns (often made of hollowed-out sugar beets) asking for treats and candy as they sing. This is similar to the tradition of Halloween, but there is no direct connection to witches and goblins, nor is Beggar's Day connected to All Saints' Day on November 1, although since the 1990s, Halloween has grown in commercial value and been celebrated as well.

### Christmas

On the evening of December 5, the Dutch celebrate *Sinterklaas*, which translates as "Saint Nicolas," but is a separate day and celebration from Christmas. The traditional patron saint of children in the Netherlands is Saint Nicholas (*Sint Nicolaas*), and in celebration of his memory, on the evening of December 5, gifts—wrapped in surprises—are given to children, along with a poem that characterizes the person, often in the form of a humorous appreciation. It is also common for children to put out wooden shoes in which candy and treats appear by morning. There are also small parades and parties in which Saint Nicolaas is dressed in red robes and throws small gingerbread cookies (*peppernoten*) and candy to the crowd, accompanied by his companion *Zwarte Piet* (black Peter)—supposedly the "foreigner" who accompanied Sint Nicolaas when he came from Spain, although in recent years, many have eliminated this character due to the possible misunderstandings or charges of racism his presence might evoke. Some people have connected the American tradition of Santa Claus with the Dutch tradition brought to the new world of New York, formerly known as "New Amsterdam." The more religious tradition of Christmas (*Eerste Kerstdag*) is celebrated on December 25, and the following day, December 26, is Boxing Day (*Tweede Kerstdag*). Although Christmas was traditionally just a religious day, the Dutch have recently embraced the more secular and commercial tradition of Christmas that is more common in the United States.

## Sport

As in many Western countries, economic opportunities and leisure time allow Dutch citizens to get involved in an infinite variety of sports, and it is possible to categorize sports in three areas: (1) popular professional or national team sports; (2) popular recreational sports; and (3) sports that engender national identity. In recent years, overall participation in sports has been consistently ranked as follows (in relation to the country's approximately 16 million inhabitants): (1) *Voetbal* (football/soccer), with over a million; (2) Tennis (700,000); (3) Gymnastics (300,000); (4) Golf (300,000); (5) Field Hockey (185,000); (6) Equestrian (180,000); (7) Skating (160,000); (8) Swimming

(148,000); (9) Volleyball (128,000); and (10) Snow Skiing (126,000).[1] In addition to these top ten activities, many other sports are growing, such as rugby, basketball, baseball, judo, and other martial arts. Almost all water sports are very popular as leisure time activities, and clubs for sailing, boating, and rowing abound. There is even an "American football" team, the Amsterdam Admirals, who play in a professional European league. Almost all communities in the Netherlands have established public fields and club houses for various team uses, and the field houses include changing rooms, showers, and small cafés for snacks and drinks. About 30 percent of the Dutch are members of one of the more than 35,000 sports clubs. The following discussion highlights the most important sports that distinguish the Netherlands from other countries.[2]

### Cycling (Fietsen)

The Netherlands is one of the most cycle-friendly countries in the world, with thousands of miles of cycling paths over relatively flat land, and a social system that encourages the regular use of cycles for commuting to work or school; therefore, cycling is far more than merely a sport. For years, urban planners have made bicycling paths (*fiets paden*) an integral part of city designs, with separate or well-marked lanes for bicycles (in addition to road and pedestrian lanes) that are equipped with direction signs, stop lights, tunnels, and overpasses. Most children begin cycling to school, and many continue to do so throughout their lives in commuting to work and shopping, or for recreation (nearly 50 % of the Dutch plan cycle trips to the countryside). Nearly every train station in the Netherlands has bicycles for rent at a reasonable rate. Visitors to the Netherlands are amazed at the literally thousands of bicycles lined up at the large train stations, with hundreds found in front of schools and shopping districts, along with the sea of commuters who seem to head out in almost every kind of weather, armed with rain jackets, scarves, and hats. Cycling for recreation is also very common, and a well-marked network of paths allows travelers to traverse routes throughout the country. In the largest *Hoge Veluwe* Park in the eastern-central Netherlands, a system of "white bicycles" allows all visitors to grab any available, standing white bicycle for their use until they park it again at one of the stations.

Sports and competition has always been an extension of the love for cycling, and an extensive system of racing has been established for years, under the direction of the *Koninklijke Nederlandsche Wielren Unie* (Royal Dutch Cycling Union). Road bicycle racing, known as *Wielrennen,* (literally wheel racing), is very popular, and the largest race of the year is the Amstel Gold Race, which is part of the UCI Pro Tour competition. The most famous Dutch-sponsored professional cycling team is Rabobank, named after its main sponsor, the Dutch international bank, and has entered every Tour de France since its first

Bicycles (*fietsen*) at the Central Station in The Hague are typical of all train stations and public buildings in the Netherlands since they are the primary means of transportation within cities and towns. Courtesy of the author.

season in 1984. Several cyclists have gained an international reputation. In the 1960s and 1970s, Jan Jansen distinguished himself by winning the Vuelta a España (1967), and was the first Dutch rider to win the Tour de France (1968). Joop Zoetemelk won the Gold medal in the team time trial at the Olympics in Mexico City in 1968, and went on to win the Vuelta a España (1979) and the Tour de France (1980); he became the director of Rabobank for ten years. Erik Dekker raced for Rabobank in the 1990s, retiring in 2006, and won many significant stages in the pro tours. His teammate, Michael Boogerd, had a similar career, winning several important stages in the grand tours. Leontien van Moorsel is the most celebrated women's cycling champion, competing and winning many races early in the 1980s and continuing on until the 2004 Olympics. Recently, Marianne Vos won a Gold medal in the Olympic Track Cycling points race of 2008.

### Football (Voetbal)

The Dutch love sports, and they are willing to devote a lot of time and money to the planning and practice of individual and collective activities.

The most popular sport at the professional and recreational level in the Netherlands is *voetbal* (literally football, or soccer), with numerous levels for recreation and several levels for semi-professional and professional play. The *Koninklijk Nederlandse Voetbal Bond* (KNVB), the official Dutch Football Association, was founded in 1889, and since 1904, it has been affiliated with FIFA worldwide. The highest professional league, the *Eredivisie,* was established in 1954 and developed through 1956 to become a national competition. By 1990, the *Eredivisie* was sponsored by the PTT Telecom, which changed its name to the KPN in 1999, so that the official name, as of 2000, is currently the *KPN Eredivisie.* From 2002–2005, it was called the *Holland Casino Eredivisie* after a new sponsor, and since that time, it has been sponsored by the lottery (*Sponsorloterij*), but for legal reasons, it cannot use that name. Over the years, the *Eredivisie* has achieved international status at the bottom of the top ten leagues, but it has also produced some of the best players in the world. It has 18 clubs, with competitions taking place from August until May; the most successful have been AFC Ajax of Amsterdam, winning 29 titles; PSV Eindhoven, with 21 titles; and Feynoord of Rotterdam, with 14. The bottom club is relegated to the second division league, the *Eerste Divisie,* at the end of the season, and the top club of the *Eerste Divisie* is then promoted to the *Eredivisie.* The Dutch take enormous pride in their national team, as well, and they have earned a reputation as some of the most energetic fans in the world; when they support their teams, they wear outrageous orange costumes.

The most well-known Dutch player is Johan Cruijff, a striker, who was named "European Footballer of the Year" in 1971, 1973, and 1974, and demonstrated the method of "Total Football" (a fluid system with constant player replacement in every position) developed in the Netherlands by Rinus Michels (an Ajax coach). Several other players have contributed significantly to Dutch football, achieving international recognition: Marco van Basten, a defender, was also European Footballer of the Year three times (1988, 1989, 1992), FIFA World Player of the Year in 1992, and recently coached of the national team; Dennis Bergkamp, a midfielder, was selected for third place in the FIFA Player of the Year award twice, and in 2007, he became the first Dutch player to be inducted into the English Football Hall of Fame; Ruud Gulitt became the European Footballer of the Year in 1987; and Ruud van Nistelrooy, a striker, is currently the third-highest goal scorer in Champions League History, a league title he won three times. In addition, the three players with the most international caps for the national team are Edwin van der Saar, a goal keeper, with 128; Frank de Boer, a defender, with 112, and Phillip Cocu a defender, with 101.

### Tennis

The *Koninklijke Nederlandse Tennis Unie* (Royal Dutch Tennis Federation) was founded in 1899, and recreational tennis is very popular today. Fourteen percent of all sports clubs are devoted to the approximately 1,840 tennis clubs. Betty Stöve won 10 Grand Slam titles, six in women's doubles, and four in mixed doubles, between 1972 and 1981. With the nickname "The Flying Dutchman," Tom Okker was ranked number three in the world in 1969, and remained in the top ten for ten years. More recently, in 1996, Richard Krajicek became the first Dutch player to win Wimbledon. The ABN AMRO Bank has sponsored the World Tennis Tournament in Rotterdam every February since it began in 1972, and is currently part of the International Series Gold on the ATP Tour schedule.

### Gymnastics

The *Koninklijke Nederlandse Gymnastiek Unie* (Royal Dutch Gymnastics Federation) regulates and offers instruction for gymnastics throughout the Netherlands. Many young people take the opportunity to stretch and gain coordination through early gymnastic training. At the international level, however, the Dutch have not been able to compete at the highest levels for some time. Their 1928 Women's Olympic team (12 members) won the Gold, but since then, the Dutch have struggled. Recently, in 2002, Suzanne Harmes won a Silver medal at the European Championships; in 2005, she won the Bronze medal for the floor exercise at the Olympics and the Gold and Silver medals at the World Cup. Epke Jan Zonderland offers a new hope for men's gymnastics, having won Gold and Silver medals in 2006 at the World Cup, and a Gold medal in 2007. That same year, he won a Bronze medal at the European championships.

### Golf

Given the necessity of very restrictive land use measures in the Netherlands, planning large golf courses is challenging, but more recent elite courses, designed by recognized architects, are using the dunes or woodlands to create some variation since most of the country is so flat. Golf has become the fourth most popular sport in terms of participation due to its growing international reputation and elite status. More than 75 golf courses already exist, and many more are planned. Dutch golfers have had a difficult time of reaching the highest levels of professional play at the international tournaments. To date, only Robert-Jan Derksen and Maarten Lafeber have had any notable wins on the European Tour. Each year, the KLM Open, originally the Dutch Open in 1912, draws an international group of golfers with its substantial prize money of €1.6 million (U.S.$2,200,000).

## Field Hockey

Field hockey is played by boys, girls, men, and women at the recreation level in the Netherlands as much as *voetbal* (soccer), although it tends to be supported more by the middle and upper classes, as with tennis or golf, whereas *voetbal* remains the sport of choice for many members of the middle and urban lower classes. The *Koninklijke Nederlandse Hockey Bond* is the official organization, and it governs the field hockey leagues, as well as the national teams. The professional league, *Hoofdklasse Hockey,* was established in 1970, and consists of 12 clubs with both male and female leagues. The men's national team won the Hockey World Cup three times (1973, 1999, 1998), the Champions Trophy eight times (1981–2006), the Summer Olympics Gold medal in 1996 and 2000, and the Silver in 2004. The women's national team is ranked as the top team by the FIH. The women have been one of the most successful teams in World Cup history, having won the Gold eight times (1971–2006); the Champions League Gold five times (1987—2005); six Gold in the European Championship (1985–2007); and two Olympic Gold medals (1984, 2008), one Silver (2004), and three Bronze (1988, 1996, 2000).

## Equestrian (Hippisch)

Horseback riding is quite popular in the Netherlands, and many communities have riding facilities. The *Koninklijke Nederlandse Hippische Sportsfederatie* (Royal Dutch Equestrian Federation) regulates competition in various venues, from dressage and show horses to jumping. The Netherlands has established an international reputation for horsemanship in the Olympics. Three Dutch riders became well known: A.D.C. van der Voort van Zijp won the Gold medal in 1924 and again in 1928; Gerard de Kruijff, who won the Gold in 1924 and 1928, and the Silver in 1928; and Charles Pahud de Mortanges, who won the Gold in 1924, 1928, 1932, and 1936 (when he also won the Silver). More recently, Jan Tops won the Olympic Gold in 1992, and the Gold (1991), Silver (1997), and Bronze (1999) in the European Championship. The two most celebrated Dutch riders are Jos Lansink and Anky van Grunsven. Lansink won the Olympic Gold in 1992, a Gold (2006) and a Bronze (2002) at the world championships, and two Gold (1991, 2007), two Silver (1997, 2007), and three Bronze (1989, 1991, 1999) at the European Championships. Anky van Grunsven has won three Olympic Gold medals (2000, 2004, 2008), and has dominated the World Cup Dressage competition, having been named the champion eight times (1995–2008). Since 2006, horseback riding's popularity has grown enormously, with over 200,000 customers purchasing riding equipment, and club membership has grown by 11 percent.[3]

### Skating (Schaatsen)

Ice skating has comprised an important element of national identity in the Netherlands since the 17th century, popularized by numerous paintings that displayed the national pastime on ice at a time when there was a "mini-ice age." Since that time, the climate has not allowed the Dutch to skate very often on outdoor ice, but their identification with this sport certainly continues. In 1909, a popular endurance race, the *Elfstedentocht* (Eleven-Cities Tour), began in which racers must complete a 125-mile (200 kilometer) event. The Netherlands has long been a world leader in long-track speed skating, regularly competing at the highest levels in the Olympic Games, regulated by the *Koninklijke Nederlandsche Schaatsenrijders Bond* (Royal Dutch Skating Federation). The most distinguished skaters are Kees Verkerk, who won the Olympic Gold in 1968, and the Silver in 1964, 1968, and 1972; and Ard Schenk, who won the World Championship from 1970–1973, and went on to win the Olympic Silver in 1968, and three Gold medals in 1972. Rintje Ritsma is the most celebrated skater, and although he never won the Olympic Gold—he won Silver medals in 1994 and 1998, and several Bronze medals: one in 1994, two in 1998, and one in 2006—he won an amazing six Gold medals in the World Championships, and four Silver, four Bronze, and six Gold medals in the European Championships, followed by two Silver and two Bronze. Yvonne van Gennip won three gold medals in 1988 Calgary, as well as many Silver and Bronze medals at the European and World Championships. Marianne Timmer is the most celebrated women's speed skater in the Netherlands, winning three Gold medals in the Olympics games (two in 1998, and one in 2006), and three Gold, two Silver, and three Bronze medals in the World Championships. Ireen Wüst has emerged as the newest women's star; she recently won a Gold and a Bronze medal in the 2006 Olympic Games, and three Gold and two Silver medals in the World Championships of 2007. Dutch figure skating is also practiced at the recreational level, but few skaters have gone on to compete in international events. Sjoukje Dijkstra is the most celebrated figure skater, winning a Silver medal in the 1960 Olympics, and then a Gold in 1964, but her greatest achievement was winning the Gold in the European Championships from 1960–1964, and in the World Championship from 1962–1964.

### Swimming (Zwemmen)

Swimming has been important to the Dutch for quite some time, for obvious reasons, but in the world of competition, the Netherlands has also produced swimming champions. The *Koninklijke Nederlandse Zwembond* (Royal Dutch Swimming Federation) was established as early as 1888. Some

Double-decker commuter trains are common in the Netherlands, with one car illustrating the importance of speed skating as a national sport. Courtesy of the author.

outstanding Dutch women swimmers have been Inge de Bruijn, who won the Gold at the 1999 European Championship, three Golds and one Silver in 2000 Olympics, and one Gold, one Silver, and two Bronze in the 2004 Olympics, as well as three Golds at the 2003 World Championships. Marleen Veldhuis won a Gold medal in the 2008 Olympics and a Bronze in the 2004 Olympics; six Gold, three Silver, and four Bronze medals in the World Championships (2004–2008); and three Gold, four Silver, and four Bronze in the European Championships (2004–2008). Femke Heemskerk received the Gold in the 2008 Olympics; two Gold, one Silver, and one Bronze in the World Championships (2007–2008); and one Gold in the 2008 European Championship. Men have also recently been recognized on the international stage: Marcel Wouda won a Bronze medal in the Sydney Olympic Games in 2000; two Gold, four Silver, and one Bronze medal in the World Championships (1998–1999); and five God, one silver, and three Bronze in the European Championships (1997–2000). Pieter van den Hoogenband is the most celebrated Dutch swimmer, with an impressive list of wins: two Gold and two Bronze in the 2000 Sydney Olympics, and one Gold and two Silver in the 2004 Athens Olympics; one Gold, nine Silver, and three Bronze in the World

Championships (1998–2007), and ten Gold, five Silver, and four Bronze in the European Championships (1997–2008). Most recently, in 2008, Maarten van der Weijden won a Gold medal in the 6.2-mile (10 kilometer)/ Olympic Marathon Swim; Inge Dekker, Marleen Veldhuis, Femke Heemskerk, and Ranomi Kromowidjojo won the Olympic Gold in the 4 x 100 Freestyle Relay; and the women's water polo team won the Olympic Gold.

### Volleyball

Volleyball is very popular, with almost 130,000 participants, making it the third-largest sport in the Netherlands, regulated by the *Nederlandse Volleybal Bond*. The A-League is the highest, with eight men's and eight women's teams competing for the national championship. The national teams have done well in the Olympics, with the men winning the Silver medal in 1992 and the Gold in 1996. The women's national team won the European Championship in 1995.

### Unique Dutch Sports

*Korfbal* is a team sport with some elements of basketball, but the elevated basket (3 meters) at both ends of the court does not have a backboard, and running with the ball or dribbling is not allowed. Each team has eight players, often comprised of four males and four females, with the team split between offense and defense. The object of the game is to use creative passing, and any physical blocking or touching is strictly prohibited, thus leveling the field of play for both genders. In this way, *korfbal* functions as a popular sport for elementary-school children in the Netherlands.

*Polsstokverspringen* (pole springing) or *Fierljeppen* (far-leaping) is a traditional Frisian and Dutch sport with the object of jumping and grabbing a pole from as high up as possible and then springing across a small body of water. There is no doubt that this sport was previously a necessary part of many farmers' lives since ditches and canals often separate fields.

*Keatsen* is a traditional Frisian game of handball that is similar to American handball, while the game's scoring is similar to that of tennis. The Frisian handball tournament P.C. (Permanent Committee) claims it is the oldest regulated sport in the world, with its origins dating back to Franeker in 1854. The *keats* or *kaats* is a small block that marks where the ball has landed or the spot where a team has prevented it from going further after a rally.

*Klootschieten* (ball shooting) is a sport in which participants throw a ball as far as they can, either in a field, street, or standing mode. The intention is to reach a certain patch of grass, as in golf, and skill is required to determine the ball's trajectory. Each year, there is a European championship and teams from Belgium and Germany are also primary competitors.

*Kolven* is an original Dutch game (from the Late Middle Ages) played by three individuals with heavy curved bats (*klieks*) and a ball made from rubber or leather. The indoor court is 57.5 feet (17.5 meters) long and 16.5 feet (5 meters) wide, with two poles at either end. The aim of the game is to hit the post at the far end, and players can hit balls that come off the walls for a total of three tries, with a tournament consisting of 15 games.

## LEISURE

The Dutch are a very social people, and the roots of these important community connections certainly date back to earlier centuries, when cooperation was necessary to survive alongside the water, whether through creating dikes or sailing ships. It is common for the Dutch to form a *vergadering* (gathering) or *aktie groep* (action group) to accomplish a task. The goal of these groups is also to create spaces that are ordered, comfortable, and communal. One of the most important words used to express this concept is *gezelligheid*, which is difficult to translate, while the German equivalent, *Gemütlichkeit*, meaning cozy, is often used as a substitute in English, yet it refers as much to the interactive human qualities as to the actual physical space. For this reason, the Dutch are very fond of parks, public squares, cafes, taverns, restaurants, and also fast food stands, where one eats and interacts in a public space. According to Statistics Netherlands, about 50 percent of the Dutch participate in club activities at least once a month.

The Dutch like to travel on their vacations, and one traditionally popular means of retreating to the south of France or Spain is by packing one's household belongings into a small car and trailer (*caravan*) and driving. Often, these caravans seek out camping sites, where many other Dutch travelers set up *gezellig* camping sites, eating all of the traditional Dutch food they have brought with them. In the winter, it is very common to go to the mountains of Switzerland or Austria for ski vacations, although some prefer a short flight to the Greek or Mediterranean islands to bask in the sun.

At home, the Dutch are very fond of creating complex gardens within the postage stamp spaces that provide a small buffer zone between the front street or the rear alley way. The gardens (*tuinen*, or *tuinjes*, the diminutive that makes the garden *gezellig* indeed) are often created around a small pond (*vijfer*) or water feature that also highlights the rich variety of water plants. Numerous plant centers sell an abundance of plants for in or out of doors. In highly urban areas, it is also quite common to have municipal gardens for rent that are generally used for vegetables or flowers, and each plot often has a small house or shed that is large enough not only for tools and supplies, but for a day picnic. Fishing for recreation on the many canals and lakes is also common in the Netherlands, and many fishermen camp out for hours by the side of the water with enough equipment for rain or shine, as well as adequate food and drink supplies for the long day. All kinds of boating are very popular, too, since the Netherlands has over 2,500 miles (4,000 kilometers) of navigable waterways, with motor boats, sailboats, and sailboards are used for recreational activities.

The Social and Cultural Planning Office of the Netherlands has conducted a survey since 1975 to determine how the Dutch spend their leisure time. It has been shown that the Dutch lead very busy lives (like many Westerners); they are involved in employment, household management, advanced education, and other duties, which leaves less time for leisure than in previous years. Yet, the Dutch continue to watch television, and home computer and Internet use is on the rise. The Netherlands has one of the highest Internet usage rates in Europe, with 80 percent of households being online in 2006 (higher than Denmark's 79% and Sweden's 77%).

## HOUSING AND ARCHITECTURE

Given that the Netherlands is a country with few resources for building materials (wood, stone, or marble), architecture was simple until the 17th century. Huts on terps and, later, small towns relied on sticks and mud for walls, and reeds for roofing. With the heightened wealth of the Golden Age, however, great townhouses, fortified cities, and splendid churches arose in the highly urbanized regions of the west. Brick became the building material of choice, and it remains so to this day; it is used to construct not only buildings, but sidewalks, walls, and even secondary roads. One of the earliest architects to develop a Dutch Republic tradition was Jacob van Campen in the 17th century, and his designs stressed balanced proportions and moderate decoration. Some of his achievements included the Royal Palace in Amsterdam, the Royal Palace and the Mauritshuis in The Hague, and the New Church in Haarlem. Hendrik de Keyser set the standard for early churches with his designs for the Zuiderkerk and the Westerkerk in Amsterdam, as well as the Delft Town Hall. In most Catholic countries, Baroque architecture for large churches and public buildings became the new standard, but in the northern Protestant Netherlands, a simpler and more classic style developed. However, some southern cities in the Netherlands, where Catholic culture flourished, developed a modified Baroque style, and the architecture of the wealthy townhouses in the large northern cities followed a modified model of the great Flemish "step" façades produced earlier. But in the countryside, simple huts and farm houses attached to barns remained more primitive, with each reflecting regional standards and designs. With the exception of some grand

The town hall (*Stadhuis*) in Middelburg, Zeeland, is one of the best examples of secular Gothic architecture. It was built in 1458, with later additions and almost completely destroyed in 1940. It has now been rebuilt to its original splendor. Courtesy of the author.

city planning in the national capital of The Hague, Dutch cities lack the grandeur of other great European cities.

In a place where the threat of water inundation is ever-present, and a lack of land for large-scale farming threatens the food supply, land economy is very important. For this reason, towns and cities are highly concentrated and zoning is very strict. Each new community that develops is called a *wijk,* which represents a complete sub-division planned with uniform housing, schools, parks, and shops to ensure the best use of land and a stronger sense of community. Roads and bicycle paths are also designed to ensure the proper flow of traffic and ease of travel within the community. Almost all housing, whether in a city of suburb, tends to consist of blocks of houses with windows and doors found only on the front and rear of the house. Windows are normally very large in order to admit all of the available light due to the country's lack of bright and hot sunshine, in contrast to southern European areas, where shutters and heavy shades are needed to restrict the sun. Very thin, white lace curtains (*gordijn*) are commonly used, and numerous house plants also adorn the windows. Rooms are rather small, and the stairs leading to the second or third floors are steep. Because of the high water table that exists in most of the Netherlands, there are no basements, and houses are built on concrete slabs. What North Americans refer to as the first floor is called the ground floor, or, in Dutch, literally the "beginning ground" (*begane grond*), and what North Americans call the second floor is called the first floor in the Netherlands. In many cities and suburbs, the housing blocks offer a small rear yard, enough space to have a small garden of shrubs and plants, a patio, and a small shed to store bicycles and garden tools. Despite these small spaces, a variety of plants and flowers are very common.

With the reorganization of the Dutch Republic into the Kingdom of the Netherlands in the early 19th century, architecture began to reflect a grander style in the large cities. Three architectural styles developed in the second half of the century, creating many iconic buildings as the wealth and identity of

Behind the market square in Delft, narrow streets and canals are common. Courtesy of the author.

The first Delft town hall (*Stadhuis*) was built already in the 13th century, and although it burned in 1618, the tower ("het Nieuw Steen") remained. The current building was built in 1620. Courtesy of the author.

the nation grew. Henri Evers brought the Beaux arts style to the Netherlands, which is characterized by symmetry, designs with many details (pillars, panels, sculptures, and garlands), and the "hierarchy of spaces" that framed grand entrances and staircases, yet contributed designs to more utilitarian spaces, as well. As head of the Department of Architecture at the Academy of Fine Arts and Applied Sciences in Rotterdam, and later as a professor at the Technical College in Delft, Evers influenced a generation of architects, who developed this style in the Netherlands. Evers' great achievements were the large Remonstrants Church and the City Hall in Rotterdam.

Pierre Cuypers favored a Neo-Gothic style that gave his buildings an aura of guild craftsmanship, yet he often came under heavy criticism by those favoring modernism. He designed more than 100 new church buildings, and his original passion for architecture came out of his Catholic background in the southern province of Limburg; he believed that buildings should draw the community together. He was also awarded the commission to design the Central Train Station and the Rijksmuseum in Amsterdam, and was appointed

Chief Government Architect. The year 2007–08 became the "Cuypers Year" in the Netherlands, and the Netherlands Architecture Institute (museum) in Rotterdam and Maastricht presented the exhibition titled "Cuypers—Architecture with a Mission."

Hendrik Petrus Berlage is often called the founder of modern architecture in the Netherlands in drawing on several styles that looked to the past and being open to experimenting with the latest new ideas. He was influenced by the Neo-Romanesque brickwork of Henry Hobson Richardson, an American who had studied at the École des Beaux Arts in Paris, but whose style ("Richardson Romanesque") was far more medieval and rustic, containing elements of John Ruskin and William Morris. He designed the Amsterdam Commodities Exchange building, and in this synthesis of styles, he helped create the Dutch New Objectivity School (*Hollandse Zakelijkheid*). Following a visit to America, he came under the influence of Frank Lloyd Wright, promoting his ideas throughout Europe on many speaking tours, and incorporating them into new designs in the Netherlands. In his influential book *Principles and Evolution of Architecture,* he followed the ideas of the famous French architect Eugène Viollet-le-Duc, who combined a Gothic revival style with modern building materials, such as brick and steel, to create "an honesty" and truth in design that fit the environment and the functional needs of the space. Berlage's ability to look forward in time and accept change was also tied to his role in the European-wide CIAM (*Congrès International d'Architecture Moderne,* or International Congress of Modern Architecture) meetings about the functional city, broadening his interest in urban planning and encouraging the emerging Amsterdam School.

The Amsterdam School of architects came about in the early 20th century as a reaction to the growing problem of intense urbanization, and the rise of Socialist ideas, which had an increasing share in political and economic leadership. In 1905, Amsterdam was the first city to implement a building code and Johan van der Mey became its principal advisor. Together with Michel de Klerk and Pieter Kramer, he collaborated on a new project called the *Scheepvaarthuis* (Shipping House), which became a prototype for future brick buildings in Amsterdam, with iron work, decorative masonry and glass, and sculptures. It was their intention for buildings to carry social meaning and produce community in this expressionist manner. De Klerk and Kramer collaborated on many other projects, and soon, many new districts of Amsterdam bore their distinctive decorative turrets. Kramer became one of the most influential architects when he also became the director of the Amsterdam Public Works, and he extended his urban planning to include the city's 400 bridges, with matching landscape designs. He is still known for the distinctive *Bijenkorf* department store in The Hague.

Drawing upon Berlage as an inspiration, a younger generation of architects within the Amsterdam School developed the functional approach of the New Objectivity School, with Mart Stam and Willem Marinus Dudok serving as examples of this style. As an architect, Stam is perhaps more well known outside the Netherlands for his chair design, the "basic cantilever chair principle," in collaboration with the famous Bauhaus school in Germany. In the Netherlands, he designed Van Nelle factories (one of the largest tea and coffee producers) in Amsterdam and Rotterdam, which represent important modernists' landmarks to this day. He continued his work in Germany and Russia, as well, on large-scale housing projects after World War II. With his involvement in post-war Germany, he took a professorship in Dresden and Berlin. Dudok became the city architect for Hilversum, and he developed his own style within the New Objectivity School, adding more asymmetry and larger overhanging roof lines that were reminiscent of Frank Lloyd Wright.

Like Stam, Gerrit Rietveld was as well known for his furniture designs as his buildings, and his 1917 "Red and Blue Chair" became a new icon of the *De Stijl* movement, with its horizontal and vertical lines displaying asymmetry. He believed that the bright colors he used must follow and even accentuate the form. He contributed to the journal *De Stijl*, and exhibited his furniture together with painters and architects. His breakthrough in architecture came in 1924 with his design of the Schröder House near Utrecht, and this remains one of the finest examples of the principles of *De Stijl*; the house was given the UNESCO World Heritage Site prize in 2000. One of the key techniques used in designing the house was "Elementarism," which blurs the lines between internal and external space, using primary colors and black to highlight the orthogonal lines. He created pre-fabricated housing modules in which all of the mechanical elements, such as complete bathroom and kitchens, could be assembled on the spot for greater efficiency. Many of his commissions were individual houses, but toward the end of his career, he obtained some large-scale housing projects and factories. His last commission, just prior to his death, was to design the Van Gogh museum, with his associates completing the building after his death. Another well-known *De Stijl* architect was J.J.P. Oud, recognized in 1932 as one of the best European modernists. He became the Municipal Housing Architect in Rotterdam, and with an interest in rational, cost-effective buildings, he looked to construct functional buildings, yet he used some ornamentation that departed from strict modernist principles, as seen in his design of the Shell Headquarters in The Hague and the Dutch National War Monument in Amsterdam.

World War II brought great destruction to Dutch cities, and massive projects began in the years following the war, giving some architects the ability to put their designs into practice on a large scale. Prior to the War, Jo van

A miniature copy of the Munttoren in Amsterdam is part of the five-acre Madurodam exhibit in The Hague, which has reconstructed some of the most famous buildings, canals, airport, and farms on a 1:25 scale. Courtesy of the author.

der Broek was an experienced architect who was involved in housing projects in and around Rotterdam. In May 1940, the Germans leveled more than one-square mile (1.6 square kilometers) of the city, destroying approximately 25,000 homes, 25 churches, more than 2,000 stores, and many other civic buildings. Van den Broek was among a host of architects who planned the reconstruction, and toward the end of his life, he became a professor in Delft. After studying with Mart Stam, Jaap Bakema also helped rebuild Rotterdam, and created a company with van den Broek there, continuing to put his stamp on the city. His last major project was the Rotterdam Public Library, which was finally completed in 1983. With six levels, each story is set back, creating the look of giant stairs, and over the top of the building are very large, brightly colored exposed pipes that give it a distinctive look. Bakema, together with Aldo van Eyck, formed a splinter group (known as Team 10 for its small number) off the older CIAM group in 1954 that became known as

Structuralism. They rejected the rationalism and efficiency of CIAM Functionalism, which had left a sterile urban environment in its wake, calling rather for a return to humanism. In the journal *Forum,* van Eyck promoted the central principles of architecture, namely a sense of place, where coherence and growth are present based on the incorporation of both "high" and "low" culture in a building.

One of the best-known contemporary Dutch architects is Remment Koolhaas, who currently is a professor of architecture at Harvard University, and head of the firm Office for Metropolitan Architecture (OMA) in Rotterdam.[4] He was named in the top 100 of *Time* magazine's *The World's Most Influential People* in 2008. Koolhaas started out in scriptwriting and journalism before he turned to architecture, and this has allowed him to continue a literary career at the same time; he became known for his books *Delirious New York* (1978) and *S,M,L,XL* (1995, published with Bruce Mau and Hans Werlemann). In continuing the work performed by the Structuralists, Koolhaas sees the city as a place of "chance," where the architect must discover how to find and highlight the human element of an urban environment. His latest studies are published in *Mutations*; *The Harvard Design School Guide to Shopping* (2002); and *The Great Leap Forward* (2002). These studies have analyzed the new massive "non-city" sprawling areas in developing countries (such as Lagos, Nigeria) to discover their inner workings (the structure). One of OMA's largest recent projects was a huge redesign of Lille, France, that overnight become a main station for the speed trains through the tunnel to England. Using a new integrated method, they created a train station situated within two commercial centers, a park, and a music complex ("Congrexpo"). OMA has also moved into the lucrative China market with the creation of a new Central China Television Headquarters building in Beijing, as well as the Shenzhen Stock Exchange building (China's NASDAQ equivalent) and a large residential project in Shanghai.

Three new architectural firms have received international attention for their innovative designs: MVRDV, West 8, and UNStudio.[5] Despite the high density of urban life in the Netherlands, very few Dutch want to live in large cities, and it is this very desire for space that has pushed Dutch firms to make some radial breaks from traditional designs in urban planning. Two young architects, Winy Maas and Jacob van Rijs, who worked for OMA, left the firm in 1991 and formed their own company in Rotterdam, together with a third architect, Nathalie de Vries, and the new name reflects their initials: MVRDV. At first, they built exclusively in the Netherlands, but they have clearly gained international recognition. Their earliest projects included new offices for the Dutch TV station VPRO (1993–1997), the Wozoco housing units in Amsterdam (1994–1997), and the Dutch Pavilion at the Hannover

World Exhibition Expo 2000 (1997–2000). International projects began in pour in after their Expo 2000 designs, and today, more than 45 architects are required to keep up with new projects in South Korea, Japan, New York, Cleveland, Madrid, Paris, Berlin, and Copenhagen. The essence of their design has addressed increasing urban overcrowding, something the Netherlands has experienced for years, as it became a problem far earlier there, given that more than 16 million people live in a space only twice the size of New Jersey. MVRDV's designs utilize urban stacking (sometimes called "vertical confection") and concentration, while de-centering the space with whole glass shells over interior spaces or random window and color patterns on more traditional buildings. Within these concentrated, high-density spaces, they also constructed artificial natural spaces with ascending and descending stairs, balconies, narrow bridges, and plant designs.

Another architectural firm to gain international recognition is "West 8," founded in 1987 by Adriaan Geuze. With now over 60 staff members, West 8 has projects in New York, Toronto, London, Paris, Zurich, Vienna, Madrid, and Copenhagen. They have specialized in large-scale urban-building complexes and waterfront and landscape projects, all of which rely on large master plans to transform the urban environment and give it a unique identity. In 2007, West 8 won the contract to redesign Governor's Island in New York City, hoping to make it the "second well-known park" after central Park, and an amazing new landscape after its long history of performing different functions. Equally large is the firm UNStudio, formerly Berkel & Bos, which was founded in 1998 and is based in Amsterdam. Like the other Dutch firms, UNStudio specializes in urban master plans, large public buildings, and offices. They created the famous Erasmus Bridge in Rotterdam (1996), nicknamed "the Swan," which broke some new ground in asymmetrical pylon construction, accompanied by a second bascule bridge that opens for ships; the Swan is the largest and heaviest bridge in Western Europe.

## NOTES

1. See Sport.nl, Retrieved August 19, 2008, http://www.sport.nl/content/nieuwsartikelen/nocnsf/223198?channel=nocnsf. These figures are approximate values based on a report from July 24, 2006.

2. See Statistics Netherlands, Retrieved August 19, 2008, http://statline.cbs.nl.

3. See Statistics Netherlands, Retrieved August 19, 2008, http://statlie.cbs.nl.

4. See Office for Metropolitan Architecture, Retrieved August 19, 2008, www.oma.nl.

5. See MVRDV, Retrieved August 19, 2008, www.mvrdv.nl; West 8, www.west8.nl; and UNStudio, www.unstudio.com.

# 5

# Cuisine and Fashion

## Cuisine

With globalization, the popularity of large food franchises, and the continued mix of cultures, cuisine has become increasingly universalized and a variety of choice is expected in any larger urban area. American fast-food restaurants can be found everywhere, although one twist is that one can buy beer at McDonalds in the Netherlands and many other European countries! Today, in any large Dutch city, one can find a restaurant serving almost any major ethnic food, and while there is a distinctive traditional Dutch palette of foods and spices, it has never been attractive enough outside of the home to warrant many ethnic Dutch restaurants. In early modern Europe, however, the Dutch had the reputation of being far more interested in large amounts of food, at a lower price, than the refinements practiced by the French or Italians at that time. Even in good times, Dutch cooking had a reputation for including copious amounts of potatoes, stewed meats or sausage, all covered with heavy gravy, and slightly over-boiled local vegetables. Yet, upon closer inspection, one can find some solid recipes that do far more than fill one's carbohydrate or protein needs. The Dutch have perfected the art of deep frying foods, especially French fries and fish. Their dairy products, sausage, and breads have become well known for the great quality and variety. There are a variety of Dutch dishes or courses (*gerechten*), and it is now polite to eat almost everything with a fork and knife, rather than the fingers (a complete reversal of their early modern reputation). Just prior to the meal, people commonly say *eet smakelijk,* the equivalent to *bon appétit,* or "Eat with good taste."

### Breakfast (Ontbijt)

The typical meal eaten in the early morning is light, compared to the heartier meals eaten in the United Kingdom or Germany. *Ontbijt,* the name for this light breakfast, displays something of Dutch "dry" humor, for it means literally "not bite" in reference to the lack of substantial food, and this humor is also applied to a mixture of warm milk and coffee, similar to *café au lait,* with the name *koffieverkeerd,* meaning literally "wrong coffee" since the milk seems to replace the coffee. In addition to the love for good strong coffee after breakfast, tea (*thee*) is the beverage of choice early in the morning. The light meal often consists of bread (*brood*) or small, round, dry biscuits (*beschuit*)—sometimes called "rusks" in English—with a variety of toppings over butter. In general in Europe, bread is very distinctive to each region, and fresh bread from a local baker is still very popular. Purchasing bread from an organization of bakers with high standards is a priority for many consumers, and store owners are proud to display their membership in the window as *De Echte Bakker* ("The Real Baker"). Breads in the Netherlands consist of substantial loaves with grains and fiber. Originally, rye bread was one of the only grains, but now wheat bread varieties are the most popular kinds. Fresh bread, baked every day, is so important that clients often purchase a half-loaf to fulfill only their day's needs, and then return each day for more fresh bread.

It is very common to eat a variety of jams and honey, cold cut meats, hard- or soft-boiled eggs, and cheese. A distinctive Dutch sweet is *stroop,* a molasses-based spread, while another product combines *stroop* with apple cider to form a thick, distinctive apple syrup that is also eaten on bread. Cheese (*kaas*) is a regular part of the diet, and the most common cheese is a lightly spiced (*licht belegen*) mild cheese, such as Gouda, Edam, or Leiden, yet like bread, cheese has definitive regional characteristics, as evidenced in Leerdammer, Limburger, or Maasdam. In addition, it is also popular to add cumin, cloves, or other spices to cheese to give them specific tastes. Other cheese spreads (*schmierkaas*), such as *kwark* (yogurt-like), cottage cheeses, and yogurt, are also eaten regularly. The Netherlands is famous for its distinctive cheese markets, first established in the Middle Ages. In addition to the more commercial cheese market in Woerden, where farmers sell their own farm-made cheeses to wholesalers, four other cheese markets are far more interested in attracting tourists: Alkmaar, Gouda, Edam, and Hoorn.

The very distinctive Dutch treat for breakfast is the variety of chocolate or fruit-flavored sprinkles called *hagel,* literally hail (frozen rain), and also humorously referred to as *muisjes,* meaning little mouse (with their droppings

implied). In recent years, new varieties have been introduced, such as ani-
seed flavor, coconut flakes, and other fruit flavors. It is a ritual to serve new
mothers *beschuit* with fruit-flavored *hagel,* yet *beschuits* are quite popular for
normal breakfasts. It is also common to eat *krentenbroodjes* (currant buns),
or *ontbijtkoek* (breakfast cake), which is typically a small, dense loaf of honey
cake formed into a loaf, with the typical "Netherlandic" spices (cinnamon,
ginger, clove, or nutmeg). Hot cereal has also been popular, namely oatmeal
and wheat, and the variety of cold cereals common throughout the West has
increased the Dutch sweet tooth.

## Lunch

It is quite typical for many Dutch to pack or buy a small sandwich for
lunch. Sandwiches are called *boterhams,* which means literally "butter and
ham on bread," although this is not necessarily the case; however, ham and
cheese are among the most popular varieties. Many other ingredients are used
to make sandwiches, and in addition to the variety of breads, small buns, or
*broodjes,* are also popular. It is common to sell already prepared *broodjes* in
many shops for snacks or lunch, and seafood products are also quite common. *Pannenkoeken,* or pancakes, are very popular for brunch or lunchtime,
and it is easy to find a pancake restaurant in every city where a large variety
of pancakes are found. One orders a large pancake, and in addition to the
most common syrup, called *stroop* (made from beat-sugar and glucose), it is
common to order fruit, bacon, ginger, ham and cheese, and a variety of other
ingredients cooked into the pancake, similar to pizza varietals. The Dutch are
also fond of fast food, and French fry, or chip (*patat frite*), stands are very distinctive, and frites are typically eaten with a *frites saus,* a special mayonnaise
for fries, or spiced ketchup, peanut sauce, or piccalilli. *Kroketen* (croquets) are
also very popular, made of a deep-fried, ragout-filled, breaded roll, as well as
a variety of spiced sausages (*frikandel*), often with raw onions, and hot dogs—
one specialty is a smoked hotdog or sausage (*rookworst*) with mustard. Over
the years, American-style hamburgers have grown in popularity. One of the
most popular Dutch fast-food snack bars is called FEBO, and it consists of
an "automat" arrangement with numerous compartments filled with one hot
item of food, such as a hamburger, kroket, or chicken, and many other fried
foods.[1] In addition, many McDonald's and Wendy's restaurants abound.
Major department stores still host high-quality restaurants, and one can find
a variety of soups, sandwiches, entrees, and desserts there.

After possessing colonies in Indonesia for centuries, the Dutch acquired
a taste for spring rolls (*loempjes*) with a hot pepper sauce called *sambal.* In
places where patrons sit to eat lunch, a variety of salads are very popular,
together with soups, hot egg open-faced sandwiches (*uitsmuijters*), or grilled

cheese (*toastie*). In recent years, Middle Eastern-style pita pockets filled with meats are sold at popular chain stores, with the largest one found throughout northern Europe being "Doner." Originating in Turkey, *döners* ("to turn"), or *kebabs* ("grilled or roasted"), are the meats that fill the pita, and they are mixed up with lettuce, onions, salad, and a spicy yogurt sauce.

### Snacks and Pastry

*Koffietijd* ("coffee time") is a national ritual in the Netherlands, and most people make a point of breaking from their daily routines to drink coffee or tea, have a cookie, and create a *gezellig*, a comfortable community connection. In cafes, it is common to eat *Appeltaart* (apple cake with raisons) with whipped cream, sitting in the sun whenever possible (given the high number of rainy days), reading a newspaper, or watching people pass by. The most popular baked deserts (*gebakjes*) are *tompoes* (cream-filled and named after Marten Toonder's character, a play on Tom Thumb), *Appelflappen* (apple donuts), *Boterkoek* (thin, dense, butter cake), or *Vlaai* (Limburg pie). Some of the most popular cookies ("cookie" is originally from the Dutch word *koekje*, or little cake) are *stroopwafels* (two very thin waffles with *stroop* in between that are often served warm in a market), *speculaas* (Netherlandic-spiced, often in a windmill shape), *gevulde koek* (soft, filled with almond paste), and *krakeling* (very light, figure-eight shape). *Poffertjes* are small pancakes with powdered sugar and are a common fast-food snack. Pudding is quite popular, and comes in many varieties, displaying regional differences: *vla* (custard), *broodpap* (bread), *griesmeelpudding* (semolina), *grutjespap* (buckwheat), *Haagse bluf* (blackberry), *Hangop* (strained yogurt or buttermilk), *Jan in de zak* (buckwheat with raisin), *Karnemelksepap* (buttermilk), *Rijstebrij* (rice), *Krentjebrij* (raisin), and *Watergruwel* (pearl barley). Chocolate is taken very seriously in the Netherlands since cocoa was imported from the colonies for centuries, lending some Dutch companies international fame, such as Droste and Verkade. Chocolate and confectionary stores specialize in hundreds of small candies, and highly specialized chocolate varieties and milk chocolate bars are common. The Dutch are also obsessed with *drop*, which are black licorices that come in nearly 100 slightly different flavors, from the very salty to the sweet, and from the soft to the hard variety. Another well-known candy is *hopjes*, a small, slight coffee- and caramel-flavored hard candy named after Baron Hop, who had his baker create it.

### Drinks

In addition to tea, coffee, and milk, fruit juice (*sap*) is commonly drunk throughout the day, and the global consumption of soft drinks in modern

Netherlands is similar to that of any other developed country. The Dutch have certainly been known for their beer, and like bread and cheese, it has its regional flavors and companies. The two largest Dutch beer companies have included Heineken in Amsterdam, which opened in 1864 and today is the third-largest beer company in the world. Heineken is drunk almost exclusively in the west of the Netherlands, whereas the second-largest Dutch beer company, Grolsch, is popular in the east of the Netherlands. Grolsch was founded in 1615 and is located in Enschede, and although they were given the title "royal *Koninklijke Grolsch N.V.* in 1995, the second-largest beer conglomerate in the world, SABMiller, purchased the company in 2008. Beer consumption in the Netherlands is much lower than the top consumers per capita: Czech 42 gallons (156.9 liters), Ireland, 35 gallons (131.1 liters), Germany, 31 gallons (115.8 liters), and the United States, 22 gallons (81.6/ liters) at 21 gallons (79 liters) per year, and it has been steadily falling. But beer is not the sole alcoholic beverage of choice. The Dutch take their wine very seriously; consumption has recently been rising. Some of the Dutch specialty alcoholic drinks are *Jenever* (juniper gin), *Advocaat* (eggs, sugar, and brandy, with an Egg Nog consistency), and *brandewijn* (brandy, an English word derived from the original Dutch).

Dutch taverns or pubs are very popular for the entire family, and often serve as central meeting places where many hours are spent in conversation and relaxation. While coffee, tea, or soda is served, a variety of beers are the most popular offerings at taverns. One can also buy light snacks or pub-style food there. Some of the oldest establishments are the so-called *bruin café* or brown bar, where old, dark wood is common, and tables are often covered with old Dutch table-carpets that are specially designed for tables since, given the wet climate, carpets would not last very long on the floors, where tile is preferred to wood. It is unheard of and quite rude in Dutch taverns or cafés to suggest that a client move on when a certain time comes. Rather, it is far more common to spend a long time in a quaint and cozy (*gezellig*) setting.

## Dinner

Soups are very popular with the Dutch, and several types have been quintessentially Dutch soups, although one can often find counterparts in other cultures. Hearty winter soups include split pea (*erwtensoep* or *snert*), made with ham or smoked sausage, onions, and carrots; potato and leek; and beef stews. Other favorite soups include chicken, vegetable, and tomato. Like many northern European countries, the potato became the most stable food after bread by the 17th century, and it offered a fundamental component to the diet of the poor. Today, the consumption of potato is falling rapidly, with potatoes now mostly eaten as *frites,* but the older recipes are still important.

When the Dutch defeated the mighty Spain in the siege of Leiden, the tradition of eating *hutspot* became a national ritual, especially when this event is celebrated each October 3. It consists of mashed potatoes with onions and carrots, and is often accompanied by smoked sausage and gravy. Mashed potato dishes are also called *stamppot* (mash pot); the varieties include carrot (*wortelstamppot*), kale (*boerenkoolstampot*), endive (*andijvie stamppot*), or sauerkraut (*zuurkoolstamppot*). With its long agricultural history, the Netherlands grows many vegetables, and the commonly eaten ones include Brussels sprouts, red and white cabbage, onions and leeks, carrots, green beans, kale, spinach, celeriac, cauliflower, green and white asparagus, tomatoes, varieties of lettuce, cucumbers, and bell peppers. A popular bean (legume) dish is made with "marrowfat beans," known as *kapucijners* and named after the Capuchin monks who made them famous. Cooked with onions, bacon, and *stroop,* this dish is similar to those found in the British Isles and North America.

To round out the diet, meat and fish are also consumed during every meal. The "Dutch oven" was developed in the 1600s, and is a thick cast-iron pan with a tight lid for efficient cooking since Dutch kitchens were small and until recently, many did not have ovens. To this day, it is common to cook meats in a sauce at a low heat for long periods, often with fruit. Pork has always been popular, either fresh or cured as a variety of ham, bacon, or sausage. Beef has also become a greater part of the diet, and many recipes have developed using ground beef (*gehak*), such as large, spiced meatballs, *Slavink* (wrapped in bacon), or *blinde vink* (wrapped in veal). Meats are also spiced, and *rollade,* as the name suggests, is made by rolling spiced beef or pork, which is sometimes stuffed and cooked slowly. Sausages are also eaten regularly, and regional varieties abound, such as *rookworst* (smoked), *metworst* (pork), *bloedworst* (blood, bacon, onion, and breadcrumbs), *braadworst, knackworst, drogeworst* (dry), and other varieties based on the spices and type of meat. Sauces complement many vegetable and meat dishes, and the classic "Hollandaise sauce" has been long appreciated by the non-Dutch, as well as the Dutch.

Few Netherlanders live far from the sea or rivers, where fish or shell-fish are plentiful. Herring has a very important history for all of the North Sea regions, and the Netherlands developed the industry with their specially designed ships, called *Haring Buis,* making it possible to preserve them in a brine solution when they are already at sea. These preserved herring are called *maatjesharing,* and are eaten raw, often with onion. The *hollandse nieuwe* are the first herring catch of the season to come to port, and many communities celebrate their arrival. Herring and other fresh fish, such as cod, sole, mackerel, eel (especially smoked eel), salmon, trout, tuna, mussels, and imported shrimp, are very popular. Fast-food stands in small towns are very common in most public squares, outside train stations, or at parks and beaches, and the most typical ones are either devoted to fresh and fried fish or to French fries. Fruit is another important aspect of the diet, and native apples, pears, cherries, plums, and berries can easily be found, together with many imported fruits, especially bananas, oranges, and other citrus varieties.

While almost all cities and towns have some international food restaurants, such as Italian, French, American, etc., Indonesian food is a staple of the Dutch cuisine. In fact, the Dutch invented the *rijsttafel*, and although it literally means "rice table," there are far more delectable dishes that make up this feast, usually a dozen varieties. Some of the dishes in a classic *rijsttafel* include soup, spring rolls (*lumpia* or *kroket*), sate sticks (*satay*) of chicken or pork, *krupuk* (shrimp chips), *acar kuning* (pickles), chicken in coconut (*ayam opor*), spicy beef (*rendang daging*), salad with peanut sauce (*gado-gado*), fried rice (*nasi goreng*), roasted coconut and peanuts (*Seroendeng*), pork in sweet sauce (*babi ketjap*), mixed vegetables in spicy vinegar (*atjar timor*), spicy eggs (*opor telor*), green beans (*sambal goreng buncis*), hot fried shrimp (*udang belado*), and fried bananas (*pisang goreng*). Indonesian food is so popular that many households eat at the home, and almost all fast-food stands carry some ready-to-go varieties.

Vegetarian meals are also quite popular in the Netherlands. Nearly 5 percent of the population consider themselves completely vegetarian, and another 22 percent are part-time vegetarians, often skipping meat entirely for a meal. Many soups, salads, fruits, and a variety of vegetables abound from this small country, which has often produced an overabundance of vegetables and legumes destined for the tables of Germany or Great Britain. Given the higher-than-normal diet of dairy products, much milk, cheese, yogurt, are consumed, together with breads.

Albert Heijn is the largest supermarket chain in the Netherlands, with over 750 stores. It was founded in 1887 by Albert Heijn, and it grew in the 1970s; in 1973, it took the name "Koninklijke Ahold N.V." (Albert Heijn Holdings) and rapidly expanded to Spain, Portugal, North and South America, and Asia, buying franchise stores and retaining their local names (for example, in the United States, the "Stop and Shop" food stores). Poor management and fraud in 2003 greatly reduced the value of the company, but it still commands a large share of the food industry in the Netherlands and throughout the world. In 1932, SPAR was established, and now it is the world's largest food retailer, with stores in Europe, South Africa, Asia, and Australia. SPAR is an acronym for *Door Eendrachtig Samenwerken Profiteren Allen Regelmatig* ("Through United Cooperation, Everyone Regularly Profits"), and with its reasonably priced products, the connection between its name and its products is not lost on the Dutch since *spaar* means to "save" money. The lowest-priced

An older branch of the Rhine River flows through Leiden, and near this point, Rembrandt van Rijn was born. Courtesy of the author.

food retailer in the Netherlands, however, is Super de Boer, with over 300 stores.

## FASHION

Clothing in the Netherlands has followed general European fashion trends for, but the distinctive aspect of national identity has been traditional wooden shoes (*kloppen*), which are actually still worn by a small minority today. Some three million wooden shoes are produced each year; however, most are for tourist shops. Known in English as "clogs," the shoes were common throughout Europe for centuries, especially among the poor or agricultural workers, but by the 18th century, they were usually worn only by peasants. Yet, in the Netherlands, given the wet, boggy soil, farmers continued to wear them, and other laborers found them advantageous, as well, even after the invention of the rubber boots. They are made from willow and popular trees, and these are readily available; hence, the fashion has continued. Clog dancing has traditionally comprised another use for the *kloppen*. In the modern world, Dutch

Extensive cycling requires comfortable clothing. Courtesy of the author.

clothing has been comfortable, and with so many people commuting to work and school, fashion has had to adapt to this lifestyle. This comfortable dress also reflects directly on the Dutch idea of equality, and the feeling that no one should express some superiority through clothing. The high amount of rain in the region has also made all kinds of rain gear popular, and whether winter or summer, it is quite fashionable to wear scarves or shawls (*sjaal*). Like all European football fans, scarves are also an important symbol of one's favorite team, and team scarves with distinctive colors fill stadiums during games.

Classic Dutch folk costumes have also given different regions of the Netherlands a distinctive fashion. The older costumes, or *klederdracht,* for women consisted of a long, plain skirt (often black or red), with an apron, a shirt covered with a vest, and often a distinctive *krap lap* or stiff shoulder pads, and a distinctive hat of white lace, turned up at the corners creating small wings on each side. Each region had its own colors and fashion, together with pins and broaches. Men wore large, baggy dark pants, stripped shirts with no collars that were covered by heavy wooden coats, a small cap, and of course, a small scarf. There are still a few towns where women and some men wear these traditional costumes, particularly in Bunschoten, Spakenburg, Eemdijk, Staphorst, Volendam, and Walcheren.

Today, fashion in the Netherlands is almost indistinguishable from that of many other Western countries, where jeans, polos, T-shirts, and sweat shirts, are very common, and can be purchased in all the popular international franchises.[2] The Dutch normally dress casually and comfortably, and it is quite common for even news anchors on television to dress very casually. One can easily find very colorful clothing in large cities like Amsterdam, where an *avant garde* culture exists, whereas in many smaller cities and towns, the colors are more subdued and plain. Corporate standards still require a suit and tie for men and business attire for women. It is quite common for many Dutch companies to require dark suits and white shirts, reminiscent of the older American IBM uniforms. The Dutch have some of their own large department stores, and the largest, most successful stores, ranked by quality and price, are De Bijenkorf, Vroom, and Dressman (V&D), and M&S, all owned by Maxeda. One of the oldest companies is C&A. It was started in 1841 by the brothers Clemens and August Brenninkmeijer as a textile company, taking its name from their initials, and produces lower-priced items, with stores throughout Europe. The most reasonably priced store is HEMA, which is an acronym for *Hollandse Eenheidsprijzen Maatschappij Amsterdam* (Dutch Standard Prices Company Amsterdam), and in 2007, it was purchased by the British company Lion Capital LLP. Other more specific stores are Blokker for household items, Perry Sport, and Etos and Kruidvat drugstores, which offer an increasing variety of goods.

A successful clothing design and chain of stores originating in the Netherlands is the MEXX Company. Tattan Chadha began a wholesale clothing business in the 1970s, and by 1980, he had created "Moustache" as a men's brand and "Emanuelle" for women. In 1986, he combined the brands to form MEXX; an acronym formed from the first two brands with an XX added to signify two kisses. In 2001, the brand became a subsidiary of the American-based company Liz Claiborne. In recent years, sales have fallen off, and MEXX has not competed well with the other popular European brands, Zara and H&M, which have established a firm footing in the Dutch market. Another Dutch company, "WE," designs slightly upscale clothing for men and women and has an international market of more than 250 stores in six countries. A nationally popular clothing company based in Amsterdam is called "10Feet," and has over 250 retail stores in the Netherlands.

The Netherlands cannot compete with the fashion design capitals of France or Italy, but some recent Dutch designers and models have gained an international reputation. The recently deceased (August 2008) Aruban designer Percy Irausquin had worked for some of the best companies, such as Lacroix, Christian Dior, and Givenchy, and his work was highlighted in *Marie Claire* and *Elle* magazines. Viktor & Rolf is an Amsterdam fashion company founded in 1993 and the company has now managed to open stores in Milan, and has created products for L'Oreal and H&M stores, with their clothes being shown at important events. Warmenhoven & Venderbos is another relatively new company founded by two women in 1996; they design clothes with all the elements of haute couture and prêt-a-porter, as well as fine pieces of art. Several supermodels have come from the Netherlands, including Karen Mulder, who modeled in the 1990s for Valentino, Yves Saint Laurent, Lanvin, Versace, and Giorgio Armani; Frederique van der Wal, who is well-known for her work in *Sports Illustrated, Cosmopolitan,* and Victoria's Secret catalogs; and the most recent young model, Doutzen Kroes, who has appeared on the covers of *Time, Vogue, Harper's Bazaar,* and *Numero,* and appears regularly in the Victoria's Secret catalog. She has also been in campaigns for Gucci, Calvin Klein, Tommy Hilfiger, Escada, Dolce & Gabbana, Valentino, Versace, and Neiman Marcus.

## NOTES

1. See FEBO, Retrieved June 4, 2008, http://www.febodelekkerste.nl/catalog/.
2. See Fashion Mission, Retrieved June 4, 2008, http://www.fashionmission.nl/.

# 6

# Literature

## MEDIEVAL AND RENAISSANCE LITERATURE

One of the oldest and most illustrious stories in the Low Countries is "Ysengrimus," written in Ghent in 1148 and later known as "Reynard the Fox." The author, Master Nivardus, used satirical animal stories (*satirisch dierenverhaal*) from the Latin classics to highlight analogous human foibles. The wolf Isengrim represents the church, while Reynard the fox can often trick Isengrim since he knows his weaknesses, which is typically greed.[1] Around 1260, another version, "Van den vos Reinaerde," gave the author as William from Madocke Maecte, and in 1485, the first and famous English printer William Caxton, who produced both *Le Morte d'Arthur* and Geoffrey Chaucer's *Canterbury Tales,* printed an English translation, "The History of Reynard the Fox." The very genre of this story is characteristic of Dutch literature in two ways. First, it offers a lively critique of those in power, whether in the church, state, or other hierarchies. Political or religious power vested in the highest institutions must respect community opinion and many other local mediating powers. Second, critique is best accomplished through a playfulness whereby satire and openness allow all of the parties involved to come to a new consensus and wisdom by rehearsing and analyzing each other's actions. It is no wonder that the famous Dutch historian Johan Huizinga, who focused much of his most interesting work on the Renaissance, wrote *Homo Ludens: The Study of the Play Element of Culture* (1938).[2] Huizinga suggests that there is a constant give and take between members as society develops, and this element of play (he invented a new word in Dutch, *ludiek,* to describe this relationship) helps explain how the negotiation proceeds. In this way, freedom of individual conscience became balanced with responsibility toward the local community.

The development of Dutch as a distinctive language grew as a bridge between German and English. The Benedictine Abbey of Egmond, built in 922 in northern Holland, became a very important place where grammarians worked to create many of the rules for Dutch.[3] Therefore, Dutch language and literature is connected with the development of monastic and religious movements in the Low Countries. Specifically, Dutch prose is normally attributed to Jan van Ruusbroec, who established a community of regular canons in Groenendaal and who became a highly respected spiritual leader throughout the Low Countries, France, Germany, and England. Several of his works were widely read: *The Seven Steps of the Ladder of Spiritual Love* and *The Spiritual Espousals* show his mystical and personal theology, which encouraged spiritual growth within the Augustinian tradition; in 1908, he was beatified by Pope Pius X. The Brethren of the Common Life encouraged reading and printing, and the famous book by one of its members, Thomas á Kempis, *The Imitation of Christ,* underlined the importance of reading for personal growth and knowledge.

The earliest formal literary societies to develop were called *rederrijk-erskamers,* or chambers of rhetoric, which were, in essence, guilds. Originally these societies were formed around religious or secular brotherhoods throughout Flanders. According to Matthias Hüning "At the start of the 15th century, the members were called *gesellen van der kercke* [companions of the Church], or *gesellen van der conste* [companions of art], but they were also referred to as players and church choristers: *gesellen van den spele* [companions of the plays]. Not until the middle of the 15th century did the names *retrosijn* (corruption of the French "rhetorician"), *rhetorician,* and *cameren van rhetorike* come into prominence."[4] The chambers of rhetoric were often dominated by wealthy merchants and humanists who had gained an interest in personal achievement through new scientific and literary study. Over time, different chambers competed against each other to produce the most noteworthy plays. Although many of the plays written by amateurs were not literary masterpieces, the morality play *Elckerlijc,* written in Dutch around 1470 by Pieter van Diest, became the source for the English play *Everyman.* Another miracle play, Mary of Nijmegen, was also well known throughout Europe.

As the war between Spain and the United Provinces continued, Flemish immigrants from the south brought their chambers north. The most important chamber became the Eglantier, or Sweet Briar, in Amsterdam; the presence of some magistrates among its members underlined the position of the chambers as mediating structures between the institution and the community, where the new ideas of the Reformation were the subject of serious discussion. Erasmus of Rotterdam grew up in this environment, where chambers flourished. He successfully brought together the erudite Humanist Latin scholarship with the vernacular literature and its critique of the chambers of rhetoric. Erasmus wrote one of the best-known literary works in Western civilization, *The Praise of Folly,* published in 1511. It is a wonderfully crafted satire in which "folly" represents human weakness, and also represents the classical gods who demonstrate these foibles in their ruin. Folly is accompanied by the god of self love, Philautia, the god of pleasure, Hedone, or the god of intemperance, Komos, and in this manner, Erasmus echoes the warnings of the classical authors, as well as Augustine and the church fathers. Folly's greatest critique uncovers the apparent abuses and superstitions of the Roman Catholic Church, especially its hierarchy. Despite the fact that he remained a faithful Catholic throughout his life, the book became a touchstone for the Protestant Reformation. Erasmus also wrote some very practical works that appealed to individual conscience and piety. In his *Enchiridion militis Christiani,* the handbook of a Christian soldier, he suggests that it is necessary to follow a path of self discipline, rather than the conventions and formalism of the day, which often led one away from true piety and worship of God. Throughout his works, Erasmus called for an examination of one's life and following Christ as the only way to avoid the corruptions that are so common in human institutions and society.

The Reformation in the Low Countries was as much a political as a religious renewal. When it was clear that under William of Orange, the northern provinces could no longer negotiate peace with Spain, Philips van Marnix, Lord of Sint Aldegonde, completed a poem (c.1569–1572) that would become a powerful national anthem—the oldest in the world. Entitled "Wilhelmus," after William of Orange, the song underlined the original loyalty that he and his fellow countrymen had for the overlord, Philip II King of Spain, but that loyalty ran even deeper for their own local governing bodies, whose ultimate sovereignty rested in God alone. Therefore, the Dutch did not leave their king: the king abrogated his responsibility under God by creating a tyrannical regime. Marnix had studied with Calvin and Beza in Geneva, and he pursued the Reformation of church and society. The song became popular during many official events until the French invaded the Netherlands in the late 1780s, and it was finally officially recognized as the national anthem in 1932. The music was developed by the great Dutch poet and hymn writer Adriaen Valerius. In its entirety, the song is composed of 15 verses, and today, the first and sixth verses are normally sung at national events. In the verses below, one can see that in the face of tyranny and oppression, they expected God to deliver them.[5]

**1.** *Wilhelmus van Nassouwe*
*ben ik, van Duitsen bloed,*
*den vaderland getrouwe*
*blijf ik tot in den dood.*
*Een Prinse van Oranje*
*ben ik, vrij, onverveerd,*
*den Koning van Hispanje*
*heb ik altijd geëerd.*

**1.** William of Nassau, scion
Of a Dutch and ancient line,
Dedicate undying
Faith to this land of mine.
A prince I am, undaunted,
Of Orange, ever free,
To the king of Spain I've granted
A lifelong loyalty.

**2.** *In Godes vrees te leven*
*heb ik altijd betracht,*
*daarom ben ik verdreven,*
*om land, om luid gebracht.*
*Maar God zal mij regeren*
*als een goed instrument,*
*dat ik zal wederkeren*
*in mijnen regiment.*

**2.** I've tried to live in
The fear of God's command.
And therefore I've been driven,
From people, home, and land.
But God, I trust, will rate me
His willing instrument.
And one day reinstate me
Into my government.

**6.** *Mijn schild ende betrouwen*
*zijt Gij, o God mijn Heer,*
*op U zo wil ik bouwen,*
*Verlaat mij nimmermeer.*
*Dat ik doch vroom mag blijven,*
*uw dienaar t'aller stond,*
*de tirannie verdrijven*
*die mij mijn hart doorwondt.*

**6.** A shield and my reliance,
O God, thou ever wert.
I'll trust unto Thy guidance.
O leave me not ungirt,
That I may stay a pious,
Servant of thine for aye,
And drive the plagues that try us
And tyranny away.

Marnix was also known for his other literary works, such as the *Roman Beehive* (*De Roomsche Byen-Korf*), which was a satire of the practices of the Roman Catholic Church, his numerous educational treatises, and his biblical translations, which were used as sources at the Synod of Dordrecht to form the new States Bible in Dutch.

In addition to the national anthem, which connected the new nation with divine providence, singing Psalms was very popular, especially to rally the community or soldiers, a practice borrowed from the French tradition. Fleeing his native Ghent, Jan Utenhove traveled to Strasburg, Emden, Poland, and London. In London, he published "The Psalms of David" in 1566, and a Dutch-language translation of the New Testament directly from the Greek edition.[6] This was the first complete translation of the Bible into Dutch, and in his selection of words, Utenhove also borrowed from the low Saxon dialect of the eastern Netherlands, thereby offering a more unified national language.

In 1588, he produced the famous *een Geusen Lied Boecxken* in which he translated the Psalms to music; the *Geusen* (Sea Beggars) were the main partisans of the revolt against Spain, and their songbook (*lied boecxken*) gave them the courage and unity they needed to withstand the mighty Spanish onslaught.

Adriaen Valerius was one of the most recognized poets of the early 17th century, as he captured in word and song the earliest Dutch national identity. His *Nederlansche Gedenck-clanck* (*Netherlands Commemorative Songs*) was a collection of folk poetry and songs that illustrated God's protection and deliverance from the usurping powers. Known in the Netherlands for his development of the music for *Wilhelmus*, his hymn "We Gather Together," written in 1597, is certainly better known in America as one of the most recognized hymns for Thanksgiving.

Dirck Volckertszoon Coornhert was one of the founders of Renaissance scholarship in the Netherlands. Although he earned a living as a cooper engraver, like many merchants, he pursued the study of Latin and the classics. Eventually, he translated the works of Cicero, Seneca, and Boethius, and his greatest achievement was his translation of the first 12 books of Homer's *Odyssey* in 1562. Like William of Orange, he had a strong desire for tolerance and individual freedom, but like Erasmus, he never left the Catholic Church; instead, he labored to reform society through personal piety and humanist scholarship. Together with the Spiritualists Sebastian Franck and Caspar Schwenckfeld, he insisted on tolerance based on the belief in human perfectibility (the ability to completely obey God), rather than on doctrinal debates that appeared to divide. Likewise, Anna Bijns was a Catholic nun who ran a school in Antwerp with her brother, and she became recognized by Renaissance humanists as a writer of note. She fought the new ideas of Martin Luther, and in her polemics, spearheaded the Counter-Reformation in Antwerp, yet at the same time, she was critical of the Catholic Church for its abuses and its role in the status quo, especially the great subservience of women in marriage. She vigorously defended the rights of women in her moralizing poems, and suggested that women would be better off single, for freedom to act according to their own conscience is the ideal.

## GOLDEN AGE LITERATURE

The chambers of rhetoric continually developed throughout the 17th century, and they became an integral part of emerging communities, where a devotion to literature served to bind people together. With competition between chambers, they experimented with poetry and verse in their quest for new forms. This was also true in the visual arts, where experiments with perspective, color, technique, and content pushed Dutch art to the forefront of expression. In literature, the chambers could zero in on very selective techniques, such as the "palindrome," a line that was identical whether one read it from left to right or from right to left: "ons leven sy een snee ijs nevel sno" (Our life is snow, ice, mist of little value), and a form that they called *aldicht* (all-poem) in which the lines rhymed word for word. The most complicated tour de force was the chess-board: each of the 64 squares contained a line and if one made the right moves, 38 different poems could be produced.[7] The best-known rhetoricians of the 17th century belonged to the Eglantier chamber in Amsterdam, where moral and didactic lessons were far more important than technical achievement. As a Low German language, Dutch was still emerging and struggled to establish itself among the well-known European vernacular languages of Italian, French, High German, and English. Roemer Visscher was among the rhetoricians in the Amsterdam Eglantier circles who actively supported the development of the Dutch. His house was constantly filled with guests who marveled at the community he supported. He became known for his work with the epigram, which was a short poem with a clever twist, and also for his many *emblemata,* which are composed of one or two rhyming sentences accompanied by didactic pictures. A parallel genre can be found in the art of Brueghel, especially in his famous painting "Netherlandic Proverbs." In 1614, Visscher produced *Sinnepoppen,* meaning emblems, which was full of illustrations of everyday life and reality with a clear moralistic tone.

Another Eglantier was Samuel Coster, who wrote the first classical tragedy in Dutch, *Ithys* (1615), following the theme of the bloody drama of *Metamorphoses* of Ovid. Coster and several other rhetoricians, such as Gerbrand Bredero and Pieter Corneliszoon Hooft, became increasingly unhappy with exclusive use of Latin at the universities in Leiden, Franeker, Hardewijk, and Groningen. They formed a new *Nederduytsche Academy,* where scientific discussions could occur. While Bredero was known for his painting as well as his writing, his *De Spaansche Brabander* of 1618 became one of the most famous plays in 17th-century Dutch literature. In this play, Bredero warns of the capitulation to the Spanish that split the older region of Brabant in two, with the southern areas accommodating the Spanish, and the northern Brabanters remaining faithful to the new Republic. The play served to create a unity among the country's religious diversity by suggesting that what united the Dutch was the rejection of the tyranny of Spanish rule, not adherence to either the Catholic or Protestant churches. Hooft was praised as the most historical writer of his day, and like his fellow companions, he introduced classical tragedy into Dutch literature with his first play of Achilles and Polyxena, performed in 1597; in 1612, he began his historical works: the national tragedy *Geeraerdt van Velzen,* an account of Count Floris V, followed in 1616 by another tragedy, *Baeto, or The Origin of the Dutch*. Inspired by the works of the Roman historian Tacitus, Hooft wrote a *History of Henry the Great* (*Henri IV of France*) in 1626, and in 1638, branched out to include the *Miseries of the Princes of the House of Medici*. His crowning achievement was his *Dutch History*, a contemporary account of the struggle with the Spanish (1555–1585), in which he demonstrated the best use to date of the Dutch language.

Like many of his companions in the Eglantier, Joost van den Vondel was a merchant first who came under the influence of the literary circle in Amsterdam and took up this study of Latin and the classics. In 1641, he converted to Roman Catholicism, which shocked his companions since Calvinism had become the heart of the Dutch Republic, even though many Catholics resided in Amsterdam. He felt more at home in a new Brabant-based chamber *het Wit Lavendal* (white lavender) founded by Flemish Catholic refugees. Living in the northern Dutch Republic, which was dominated by Calvinists, Vondel called for great tolerance, while at the same time, he used satire to criticize the prominent radical Calvinist leadership, which pitted Prince Maurice of Nassau against Johan van Oldenbarnevelt. He protested with a political drama *Palamdes* (*Murdered Innocence*) in 1619, but he had to go into hiding. He then developed a close friendship with Hugo Grotius. Given Oldenbarnevelt's arrest and execution, Vondel did not have a large following in his day and was embittered until the end of his life. Yet, his command of language in his poetry makes him one of the greatest Dutch writers. He was later honored by having the largest park in Amsterdam named after him, and by having his portrait placed on the Dutch guilder.

The central themes in Vondel's writings represent those of the Dutch writers in general. First, they work very closely with the classical authors, a common element of Renaissance literature. Secondly, beyond the Greek and Roman writers, they also concentrated on the Bible, and in particular, the Hebrew patriarchs of the Old Testament. It was already a common element of the Low Countries and France to sing the Psalms in public meetings and for soldiers marching to battle: the Renaissance had not only discovered the classical pagan authors, but the stories and heroes of the Old Testament, like that of the young shepherd boy David who had become king, gave them courage. The great sculptors, such as Michelangelo and Donatello, had certainly recreated their glory for the wealthy merchants, princes, and church. But it was the French Reformed theologians who had pushed even further to discover the unique position of the Hebrew people as a small tribe chosen by God to act as a moral compass for the rest of the world.

John Calvin, through his unique combination of Christian Renaissance humanism, which supplied him with the tools and methods of inquiry, his biblical study, the more fully developed language learning available to scholars of the mid-16th century, and his careful reading of the early church fathers, especially Augustine, had opened up an important new direction for him in terms of understanding the history of God's providential activity. A central component of this new tradition was that the Dutch theologians and scholars, literary authors, painters, political theorists, and historians understood their world in direct connection to the story of ancient Israel. An element of their national identity was connected with God's providential activity with ancient Israel, which continued in the new Dutch Republic. Modern scholars refer to this as Dutch Hebraism, for the moral lessons embedded in the Old Testament had a direct bearing on life in contemporary Netherlands. It is not difficult to see these themes in Vondel's works, as the titles are replete with these Old Testament images. Prior to his conversion to Catholicism, *Het Pascha* (*The Passover*), his first play, was performed in 1610 and published in 1612, and in it, he dramatized the Jewish Exodus from Egypt that served as an allegorical representation of the plight of the Calvinists who had fled Spanish tyranny in the Low Countries.[8] Vondel also wrote about the Dutch in reference to the classical authors, and provided translations of the tragedies of Seneca, Euripides, and Sophocles.[9] Some scholars have claimed that John Milton's *Paradise Lost* (1667) drew some of its inspiration from some of Vondel's works, especially *Lucifer* and *Adam in Ballingschap*. Yet, we can be certain that both authors were influenced by the biblical stories, and possibly by Grotius' *Adamus Exil* (1601), as well.

A more conservative literary direction is evident in the poetry of Jacob Cats (1577–1660)—not to be confused with the well-known painter Jacob Cats, who lived a century later (1741–1799). After a career in law, Cats became the Grand Pensionary in 1636 and the keeper of the seal in 1648, and as an active promoter of Orange power and a more orthodox Calvinism, he was known as "Father Cats." He is most remembered for his *emblemata* book *Proteus Ofte Minne-Beelden Verandert In Sinne-Beelde* (*Proteus,* or *From Love Emblems to Moral Emblems*, 1618). Johan van Heemkerk was another Dutch poet who had first studied law and started in that practice. He went to England and tried to settle disputes for the VOC (East India Company). His own literary pursuits brought him to publish several love poems on the art of love, *Minnekunst* (1622), on the duty of love, *Minnepligt* (1625), and on the science of love, *Minnekunde* (1628). His most famous work, the *Batavische Arcadia* (1637), was the first original Dutch romance.

Constantin Huygens was an advisor for three generations of stadholders, a passionate lover of the English language, and a supporter of the arts and sciences. He brokered art and literature, especially English, for the house of Orange and personally supported all of the arts in the Dutch Republic.

But just when France and England began to experience very fruitful literary achievements in the 18th century, Dutch literature on the whole declined, which paralleled the decline of the Dutch Republic; one of the wealthiest states of the 17th century now began to lose many wars to the English and French. Illustrative of this decline was the poetry of Rhijnvis Feith. Although he had a very comfortable life as mayor of Zwolle and built himself a magnificent house, his poetry embodied tragedies, despair, and melancholy, as seen in his novels *Julia* (1783), *Thirsci* (1784), *Fredinand and Constantia* (1785), and *The Patriots* (1784).

Very few women were recognized in literature before the 18th century, and Elisabeth (Betje) Wolff and Aagje Deken were two of the most well known of their day. Betje Wolff found herself alone after her elderly husband died and she embarked on a literary career with *Reflections on Pleasure* (*Bespiegelingen over Het Genoegen*) in 1763. She formed an acquaintance with another writer, Aagie Deken, and the two soon became great companions, eventually publishing novels together, such as *Historie van mejuffrouw Sara Burgerhart* (1782) and *Historie van den heer Willem Leevend* (1784–1785), which became quite popular. In 1788, on the eve of the French Revolution, their growing Patriot sympathies made it too difficult for them to remain in the Netherlands, so they sojourned in Burgundy for seven years, and returned in 1795 when the Patriots had overtaken the older government. They went on to publish more novels together.

## 19TH-CENTURY LITERATURE

In the same year that Wolff and Deken were returning to the Netherlands because of the Patriot victory, Willem Bilderdijk was departing his beloved land, just as the House of Orange was forced to do. He was a lawyer, and when the French began to occupy the Netherlands, he refused to take an oath and fled to Hamburg and London, where he pursued an active life of learning and writing, and tutored. When Louis Bonaparte was appointed King of Holland, Bilderdijk was convinced to return to the Netherlands and serve the new king in several capacities, creating a royal library and becoming president of the Royal Institute. He also taught the new king Dutch. A legendary humorous event occurred when King Louis (Lodewijk in Dutch) announced in his new-found language at a great public event that he was the *konijn van 'Olland*, which was rather close to the truth, but missing a few letters. In essence, he meant to say *Koning*, which means king, but instead said *konijn*, which means rabbit, a point not lost in the press, even though Louis was well liked by his subjects.[10] One of Bilderdijk's best biographers, Joris van Eijnatten, has underlined his importance as the Goethe of the Netherlands.[11]

Indeed, he is responsible for more than 300,000 lines of poetry, in almost every genre, plus a host of important writings, leading many to call him "an indefatigable *versifex*" (*een onvermoeibare versifex*), referring to his ability to produce so much literature. He is the first Romantic poet in the Netherlands, and his historical writings of the "fatherland" (*Geschiedenis des Vaderlands*) constituted 13 volumes. He published on many more subjects: natural law, science and botany, geology, architecture, perspective, philosophy, and theology. In the 1820s, he became part of the *Réveil* movement in the Netherlands, and in this religious renewal, he tutored a new generation of poets who were equally influenced by a return to a deeper personal faith based on the *Nadere reformatie* of orthodox Calvinism and the Romantic movement. Isaac da Costa, Willem de Clercq, and Abraham Capadose all became popular poets and writers in the 19th century. Bilderdijk's legacy has often been met with either great admiration or derision and hatred.

After the founding of the new monarchy, a contest was held for a national anthem. The original *Wilhelmus* had fallen out of usage by then because the Patriots and French had forbidden it. In addition, specific verses had glorified orthodox Calvinism, thus it had less applicability to Catholics, Liberals, and Jews, who had taken up prominent positions. In 1815, the poetry of Hendrik Tollens, together with the music of J. W. Wilms, was selected; the new anthem was titled *Wien Neêrlands bloed* ("Whose Dutch Blood"), and it was sung until 1932, when the *Wilhelmus* returned. As a writer, Tollens stood more for the German Biedermeier tradition than Romanticism. He focused on the petit bourgeois' comfortable domestic life by constructing poems demonstrating virtues, choosing to avoid controversy and politics.

Official spelling was also a matter of debate as the Dutch entered the 19th century. The Dutch language had slowly developed through the years, although Dutch scholars continually relied on Latin for scholarship, and either French, English, or German for diplomacy. In 1804, Matthias Siegenbeek created the first official spelling of the Dutch language in his book *Verhandeling over de Nederduitsche Spelling ter Bevordering van de Eenparigheid in Dezelve* (*Treatise on Lower Dutch Spelling to Promote Uniformity Herein*), and a priest, Petrus Weiland, was asked to create a book of grammar. Siegenbeek also wrote the *Woordenboek voor de Nederduitsche Spelling* (*Dictionary for the Low German—i.e., Dutch—Spelling*) in 1805. Not all scholars were pleased with his new spelling, as witnessed by Bilderdijk's reliance on some quaint words he popularized, and until the 1850s, three systems existed. In 1851, a new congress met in Brussels, the *Taal- en Letterkundig Congress*, to determine the correct Dutch spelling for the Netherlands and Flemish Belgium. Matthias De Vries and Lammert Allard Te Winkel's *Woordenlijst voor de Spelling der Nederlandsche Taal* (*Vocabulary for the Spelling of the*

*Dutch Language,* 1866) became the official system, yet discussion of the issue continued for another century. As late as 1994, the Committee of Ministers of the *Nederlandse Taalunie* (Language Union) produced the *Groene Boekje* (*Green Booklet*), which became official in 1996.

The Romantic movement offered the Dutch a rich genre within which they could recover a sense of national identity after the French occupation, and the influence of English writers was enormous. Romantic literature was dominated by the old patrician class and monarchists, for it gave them a way to demonstrate the historical importance of royalty and church in their new world. Lord Byron was translated into Dutch by many literary scholars in the early 19th century. Many of the poets and literary scholars had also studied theology, and sought a pastorate in the Reformed Church, while at the same time publishing their literature. Romanticism allowed them to create an idealistic world in which Christian moral values were demonstrated in daily life and where attention to hard work, patriotism, family, and community were clearly evident. Katharina Schweickhardt, the wife of Bilderdijk, translated Byron's *Childe Harold's Pilgrimage* in 1819, a year after it was written. Likewise, Isaac da Costa translated *Cain* in 1822 only a year after it was published. Jacob van Lennep was one of the most prolific translators of Byron, with versions of *Marino Faliero,* the *Bride of Abydes,* and parts of *Don Juan* and *Manfred.* In his own right, he gained considerable popularity for his *Nederlandsche Legenden* (*Legends of the Netherlands,* 2 vols., 1828), reminiscent of Sir Walter Scott.[12]

Nicolaas Beets became one of the best-known pastors who wrote in the Romantic style. Despite the church being an institution, it was a host of local pastors who worked closely with local leaders to monitor community morals, and it is common to call this influence a *domineescultuur* (pastor's culture); many wrote poetry as *domineesdichters* (pastor poets). Beets was also a member of the *Réveil* movement to restore a proper balance between individual faith and orthodox doctrines, and he actively wrote for the theological journal *Ernst en Vrede* (*Ernestness and Peace*). He wrote both prose and poetry extensively, and used the pseudonym "Hildebrand" after 1837. Beets translated many of Byron's works into Dutch, including *Hebrew Melodies, Childe Harold's Pilgrimage, The Prisoner of Chillon, Parisina, Mazeppa, The Lament of Tasso,* and excerpts from *Don Juan.* In 1837, he wrote *Vooruitgang* (*Progress*), and wrote for the literary journal *De Gids,* which is still published today. Beets is best known for his series of short stories in *Camera Obscura,* published in 1839 and expanded in 1851. Like Charles Dickens, he presented a series of stories that had a keen eye on the society of the times, and suggested moralistic solutions to contemporary problems. In many ways, François Haverschmidt followed in the path of Beets as a pastor. He used the pen-name "Piet Paaltjes" for his poetry, which led to his substantial popularity. Haverschmidt is best known for his reflections on his student days in *Snikken en grimlachjes* (*Sobs and Smiles*,1867). Unfortunately, after the death of his wife, a deep depression overtook Haverschmidt and he committed suicide in 1894.

Conrad Busken Huet was also trained for the pastorate, but his ministry did not last long. In 1863, he embarked on a critical journalistic path, editing several newspapers and cultural magazines, such as the *De Gids, the Opregte Haarlemsche Courant, Algemeen Dagblad,* and the *Nederlandsch Indi & euml.* He went to Java, Indonesia, in 1868 as editor of a newspaper. It was there that he discovered a much bigger world and developed a critical distance from what he found to be a very provincial Dutch world. In his later life, he became more critical of his colleagues and wondered whether Dutch literature had really contributed much to Europe. He stated in his book *The Land of Rembrandt:* "Who of us would seriously consider a modern Dutch history of literature to have been composed, as one can analyze the novels of Walter Scott and the poems of Lord Byron, which since 1825 or 1830 were translated into Dutch?"[13] He continued to publish, and his critical remarks about the Bible, the poetry of Vondel, and later Bilderdijk shocked his contemporaries.

By far, the most celebrated Dutch writer of the 19th century is known by his pen name "Multatuli." His real name was Eduard Douwes Dekker, and with his novel *Max Havelaar,* written in 1860, he became the Dutch equivalent to the United States' Harriet Beecher Stowe. With Multatuli, Dutch literature turned from reflections on national identity and the moral compass of the church and state to a sustained critique of Dutch society and its involvement in its colonies, especially Indonesia; the moral compass turned against the church and state for the first time. Born in Amsterdam, Dekker spent his early years in Indonesia, rather than following in his father's profession as a ship's captain. After working for the Dutch bureaucracy in Java and the Moluccas in the years 1838–1857, he became incensed over Dutch policies, which he believed were very unfair. Arriving back in the Netherlands, he took the pen name "Multatuli," which means "I have suffered much," and began a literary career that would greatly challenge Dutch colonial possessions. He published several writings that used satire to uncover the abuses of the colonial government, such as *Love Letters* (1861), and his seven volumes of *Ideas* (1862–1877). But his earliest novel *Max Havelaar, of de koffij-veilingen der Nederlandsche Handel-Maatschappij* (*Max Havelaar: Or the Coffee Auctions of the Dutch Trading Company*), written in 1861, remains his best-known work, and many critics see it as the most important Dutch literature of all time. Max Havelaar, the protagonist, battles the Dutch government's "cultivation system" (*cultuurstelsel*) and the abuse of power. Dekker's account of the abuses was very effective because he had had an inside look at the Dutch policies in action. The novel had the effect of raising awareness among Europeans of the ethical dimensions of colonialism, and this led to the alteration of Dutch strategy in Indonesia. Dekker is highly praised in Indonesia for starting the country on the road toward independence, and influencing Sukarno and nationalism.

By the end of the 19th century, many had reacted to the Romantic genre that was so prevalent in the first half of the century. The *Tachtigers* (Eightiers) denoting the literary movement between the late 1870s and 1894 rejected the *domineedichters* for ignoring the reality of injustice, individual experience, and art for art's sake. With a concentration on naturalism and subjectivism, a new generation of poets formed a new magazine in 1885, *The New Guide* (*De Nieuwe Gids*), in marked contrast to the earlier *The Guide* (*De Gids*). It became a forum for their new aesthetic ideals: rather than seeking to use poetry to teach morality, the *Tachtigers* wrote to discover nature and the individual soul. Willem Kloos, founder and editor, explored the individual's deep and unique emotions. Yet, the irony of this new group, which included Frederik van Eeden, Frank van der Goes, Willem Paap, and Albert Verwey, is that slowly a deep personal rift developed, and one by one, they quit as editors until only Kloos remained. His collection of poems, *Het Boek van Kind en God* (*The Book of Child and God*), published in *The New Guide*, met with instant success. Kloos began to need psychiatric treatment, and he turned to his friend Frederik van Eeden, a well-known psychiatrist and fellow member of *The New Guide*. But Kloos' condition deteriorated as alcoholism and his attempt to hide his homosexuality added to his difficulties, and his life ended in mental illness and tragedy.

Frederik van Eeden used his scientific studies of the human personality to explore the effects of modern society on the individual. He wrote extensively, producing novels, plays, poetry, and essays in which these themes are evident. For example, *De Kleine Johannes* (*Little John*, 1887), is the story of a man who endures the harsh realities of his world without much hope, but despite this, learns to find himself in serving those around him. The *Tachtigers* were heavily influenced by the American transcendental movement, and van Eeden often took the pen-name "Mark Twain." He also established a commune called "Walden" where, inspired by Thoreau, he believed living a simple life in nature was the answer to the alienation of modern society. The *Tachtigers* were also supporters of the growing Socialist movement, yet not all were as radical as Herman Gorter, who became the founding member of the Dutch Social-Democrat Party in 1909, espousing Communist ideology. His series of epic poems represented the highest form of Dutch impressionist writing: *Mei* (*May*, 1889), and a sequel *Juni* (*June*). Frank van der Goes, another *Tachtiger*, was heavily involved in socialist politics, as well.

Jacques Perk was another early member of the *Tachtigers,* and he wrote more than a 100 sonnets in *Mathilde,* edited by Kloos, which set the stage for the new style. While vacationing in the Ardennes, Perk had the good fortune to meet Oscar Wilde and the French beauty Mathilde Thomas. It only took a few days for Perk to idealize her, and as soon as he returned to Amsterdam, he wrote love sonnets that bordered on divine worship. Perks' mastery of verse seemed to flow freely from his pen (unlike the more careful work that Kloos needed to do). Inspired by Shelley, Perks turned his attention to another woman who caught his attention but eluded him, Johanna Blancke, and in 1881, he published a great work with her in mind in *Iris.* This explores unrequited love and, borrowing from Shelley's *The Cloud,* whenever Iris, the rainbow, tries to kiss Zephyr, the west wind, he disappears. After a boating party on the Amstel, Perk contracted a horrible illness in the form of an abscess on his lung, which could not be operated on; within weeks, he was dead at the young age of 22. In this rich environment of writers, Kloos thought that Hélène Swarth was the greatest poet of the *Tachtigers.* Kloos saw her poetry in *Snow Grains* (1888), and a life-long friendship developed. Yet, Swarth's literary achievement was like Perk's: built on unrequited love. In her youth, she had been in love with Max Waller, a Belgian poet, but he had an untimely death in 1889, and shortly after this, she wrote *Rouwviolen* (*Mourning Violin*).

One should not mistake the famous American story of Hans Brinker, the boy who put his finger in the dike and saved a village, for an original Dutch tale. Yet, in time, this powerful symbol of Dutch determination and courage, as well as its touristic value, became embedded in Dutch culture. Mary Elizabeth Mapes Dodge, an American who had never visited the Netherlands, published *Hans Brinker* or *The Silver Skates* in New York in 1865. Although the story centers on a skating race, the famous image of Hans putting his finger in the dike remains a powerful cultural icon. In 1950, the Dutch Bureau of Tourism erected a statute of Hans Brinker in Spaandam and the inscription reads: "Dedicated to our youth, to honor the boy who symbolizes the perpetual struggle of Holland against the water."[14]

## 20TH-CENTURY LITERATURE

Albert Verwey was one of the most productive writers of the late 19th and early 20th century. Together with the other *Tachtigers,* he believed that poetry should serve as a social force, and he published in the *Amsterdammer* from 1882–1889, and then *The New Guide* until 1894 when he founded, with Lodewijk van Deyssel, the journal *Tweemaandelijks* (*Two Months*), which eventually changed its name to *The Twentieth Century.* From 1905–1919,

Verwey wrote in his own periodical *Beweging* (*The Movement*, a monthly magazine for literature, art, science, and state). *The Movement* studied Vondel, Potgieter, Bilderdijk, or Spieghel, and Verwey also translated works by Shelley, Hofmannsthal and others in *Poetry in Europe* (1920). His essays on people and movements in the first decades of the 20th century are grouped in ten parts in his *Prose* (1921–23). Lodewijk van Deyssel, the pen-name of Karel Joan Lodewijk Thijm, was another *Tachtiger* who was initially attracted to French naturalism, but later, he turned toward a more mystical life. His best-known works are *A Love* (1887), *The Small Republic* (1902), and *The Life of Frank Rozelaar* (1911).

Louis Couperus seems to have been the beneficiary of a century of Dutch literature that slowly broke away from a concentration on its own history and culture. If Multatuli had accused the Dutch government of abuse in the colonies, his works were still read by the Dutch in great numbers, even though he gained international interest. Couperus' first novel in 1888, *Eline Vere,* was influenced by Emile Zola and Gustave Flaubert, and was a psychological work set in The Hague. Oscar Wilde greatly praised his 1891 novel *Noodlot* (*Footsteps of Fate*), which one can easily compare to Wilde's *The Picture of Dorian Gray.* His historical novels were very popular throughout the English-speaking world, as well as in Germany. *De Stille Nacht* (*The Hidden Force,* 1900) is a psychological thriller set in Java. After a series of unexplained events, the story shows that humans are not in control of their destiny nor of the elusive forces present in nature. Martinus Nijhoff also explored the mystical side of life. He came from a family publishing business begun in 1853 that remains a prominent publisher today under the E. J. Brill company (itself established in 1683 in Leiden). After studying law and literature in Utrecht, Nijhoff began his career in 1916 with *De wandelaar* (*The Wanderer*) using traditional sonnets and rhymed verse. He is known for his works *Awater* (1934), which explores the need for travel with a companion, and *Het Uur U* (*The Hour You*, 1936), which presents life during wartime. He is also known for his biblical plays, such as *Holy Wood* (1950).[15]

The critical analysis of Dutch colonial experience did not end with Multatuli; indeed, the growing nationalism and decolonization of the 20th century brought a new generation of writers. After Multatuli, Edgar du Perron was the most important writer in the Indies. In addition to his debt to Multatuli, he was influenced by his friendship with the Nobel Laureate Andre Malraux from France. He is best known for his novel *Het land van Herkomst* (*Country of Origin,* 1935). Likewise, Hella Haase became another influential colonial writer. She was born in Batavia in the Dutch East Indies, and *Krassen op een rots* (1970) is an autobiography of her first 20 years there. She has had a very long career, gaining fame for her first novel in 1948, *Oeroeg*, the last lines of which summarize her feelings: "Am I forever a stronger in the land of my birth, on the ground where I do not want to be transplanted."[16] Throughout her career, she has written over 50 separate titles. Continuing the theme of life in Indonesia, in 1992, she wrote *Heren van de Thee* (*The Tea Merchants*), and in 2000, she published another novel, *Sleuteloog* (*Eye of the Key*) in which she questions whether the friendship between a Dutch and an Indonesian can last since they come from such different worlds.[17]

Herman Heijermans is best known for his work, *Op Hoop van Zegen* (*The Good Hope*, 1910). Under the pen-name "Samuel Falkland," he published stories of Jewish life in the Amsterdam *Handelsblad* newspaper long before the World Wars. He wrote a number of novels, such as *Trinette* (1892), *Fles* (1893), *Kamerertjeszonde* (1896), *Interieurs* (1897), and *Diamanstad* (1903). His play, *Op Hoop van Zegen* (1900), achieved great success when it was performed in Paris and England by the Stage Society under the name *The Good Hope*. Jacob Israël de Haan was also a very colorful Jewish writer early in the century. His controversial 1904 novel *Pijpelijntjes* (*Lines from De Pijp*, a working-class Amsterdam district), displayed a shocking homo-eroticism that was scandalous. In 1919, he went to Jerusalem filled with zeal for the Zionist cause he had written about for the previous nine years, and he adopted Haredi (very orthodox) Judaism. He was assassinated in 1924 for his political intrigue with Arabs amid the fight to control Zionism.

Simon Vestdijk was one of the most productive Dutch writers of all times, with over 100 books, including 38 novels, over 20 volumes of poetry, and other studies ranging from music and astrology to religion. One of the few novels translated into English, *The Garden Where the Brass Band Played* (*De Koperen Tuin*) chronicles the life of his chief character, Anton Wachter, in eight volumes (1939–1960). This complex story is autobiographical, and uses a psychoanalytical approach, especially that of Freud and Jung, to explore empty provincial lives and tragic love affairs. During World War II, Vestdijk was interned by the Germans, and this experience led to novels dealing with occupation and resistance; *The Waiter and the Living* (1949) is a Kafkaesque novel about persecution. Yet, Vestdijk also loved music and wrote books on Mahler, Sibelius, and Bruckner. His poetry was written in definitive blocks of time, between 1930–1932, 1942–1943, 1945–1946, and 1955–1956. He wanted his poetry to develop a more lyrical quality, and he showed the tension between mind and matter, and reason and feeling.[18] Piet Bakker wrote one of the most popular children's novels in the form of the trilogy of *Ciske the Rat (1941–1946)*, the story of a street urchin named Ciske Vrijmoeth, who gets a second chance to redeem his life. The story has been filmed twice (in 1955 and again in1984).

Willem Frederik Hermans was also deeply affected by the German occupation and the horrors of war. He is considered to be among the best post-war authors in the Dutch language, along with Harry Mulisch and Gerard Reve. Jan Wolkers is often added to this list. These authors represent a new generation greatly affected by World War II and the older pillarized society, and they express a great need for freedom in politics, religion, community, gender, and sexual relationships. Hermans' suspense novel *De donkere kamer van Damokles* (*The Dark Room from Damokles*), written in 1958, reflects on his own disillusionment over World War II and is framed in an existential manner. He fought the establishment constantly: in 1973, he resigned his professorship at the University of Groningen in favor of spending his time writing literature instead of teaching physical geography, and in 1986, Amsterdam's Mayor and City Council declared him persona non grata when he defied the boycott of apartheid and visited South Africa. He later received an honorary doctorate from the University of Pretoria.

Born of an Austrian father and a Jewish mother, Harry Mulisch's reaction to World War II can be found in his own personal history. His family was saved only through the collaboration his father was able to accomplish, yet his father was incarcerated for three years following the war. His well-known novels about the war years are *De Aanslag* (*The Assault,* 1986), which received an Oscar and a Golden Globe for best foreign movie; *Het stenen bruidsbed* (*The Stone Bridal Bed.* 1959), and *Siegfried* (2001). Mulisch has been highly praised, as well, for his philosophical and historical knowledge, seen in *De toekomst van gisteren* (*Yesterday's Future,* 1972), *De Elementen* (1988), *De ontdekking van de Hemel* (*The Discovery of Heaven,* 1992), and *De Procedure* (1999). Like Hermans, he was clearly on the left wing of politics; he even defended Castro and the Cuban revolution. His novel *De ontdekking van de Hemel* (1992) was filmed in 2001 as *The Discovery of Heaven* by Jeroen Krabbé. He received the coveted *Prijs der Nederlandse Letteren* in 1995.

Gerard Reve was also heavily influenced by the great changes that occurred in the Netherlands after the wars and in the 1960s. He was the best-known writer to first explore the sexual revolution as it was underway, and wrote explicitly and shockingly about homosexual acts between men. He also wrote extensively about religion and tried to break the taboos established by a strict confessional society, yet the two were often interrelated, as he claimed that salvation was needed from the world of matter and from older mores of love. He had been raised in a Communist family and came to hate its ideology with a passion, choosing rather to seek a personal religious understanding that denied any historical dimension; rather, he saw the rituals as a means to his own salvation. Reve acquired many enemies, however, when he connected erotic sexuality with a religious quest, despite his conversion to Roman Catholicism. His own quest, *Revism* as he called it, combined homosexuality with religious ritual and sadomasochism, as evidenced in the novels that made him famous: *De avonden (The Evenings,* 1947), *Op weg naar het einde (Towards the End,* 1963) and *Nader tot U (Nearer to Thee,* 1966). He became the most prominent gay celebrity with his publications and his editorial work on the *Dialoog (Dialogue),* a liberationist gay and lesbian magazine (1965–1967). Paul Verhoeven's film "The Fourth Man" (1983) was based on Reve's novel *De Vierde Man* (1981).

Jan Wolkers is as controversial as Reve, but explored the sexual revolution between heterosexuals, with many harsh things to say about his conservative Reformed upbringing. In addition to achieving fame as a writer, Wolkers considered himself a sculptor. His 1969 novel *Turks Fruit* was made into a very popular film by Paul Verhoeven in 1973. It was based on his failed relationship with his second wife, and in the novel, the main character seeks out sexual freedom as salvation. His books are filled with guilt and punishment, as well as sex and death. *Terug naar Oegstgeest (Return to Oegstgees,* 1965), often considered his best book, is strongly autobiographical. He wrote passionately about the great doubts he had about the historical authenticity of the Bible and about the received morals in the Christian tradition, mixed with hatred of his own childhood yet envy of his parents' certainty. He refused to accept the Constantin Huygens Prize and the P. C. Hooft Prize in 1988 and 1989. Like Wolkers, Jan Cremer also shocked the Dutch public with his 1964 book *Ik Jan Cremer (I Jan Cremer),* which was filled with sex, violence, and blood. It sold over 5,000 copies and demonstrated an underlying public need for freedom; the sexual revolution was well underway.[19]

A bold break with traditional poetry is clearly seen in a group known as the *Vijftigers,* or the Fifties, by the late 1950s. They strongly opposed the aesthetic principles and rules of their predecessors, who they felt were locked into a rigid system and wrote in isolation to what was happening in post-World War II Europe. The *Vijftigers* were linked with an international artistic group called CoBrA, combining Copenhagen, Brussels, and Amsterdam into a new literary guild. Freedom was foremost, and they worked toward spontaneity, directness, and an exploration of the senses. Remco Campert helped found this movement with his role in the magazine *Braak,* together with Rudy Kousbroek, Lucebert, and Bert Schierbeek in 1950. In 1951, the group expanded with the publication of an anthology *Atonal,* edited by Simon Vinkenoog, and featuring Gerrit Kouwenaar, Jan Elburg, and the Belgian Hugo Claus. Campert was the most comprehensible *Vijftiger* since he combined the new expressions with some older traditions, making poetry accessible to the general public. Campert has over 60 publications, and has mastered the short story and novella. Of late he has been known by the Dutch public for his writing in many popular newspapers with the ex-footballer and author Jan Mulder, often signed "CaMu."

Bert Schierbeek has also contributed some very significant literature, and his first novel in 1951, *Het Boek IK* (*The Book I*), became the first experimental Dutch prose writing. The book ends with, "We go forth moved into other names," and this launched him into an autobiographical trilogy known as *De andere namen* (*The Other Names*) and *De derde persoon* (*The Third Person*). Schierbeek called his prose-poetry "compositional novels," for they have a musical form and content, with words as notes, as seen in *De gestalte der stem* (1957), which was translated as *The Shape of the Voice* in 1977.[20]

Several post-war Jewish writers have continued to study and reflect on the Holocaust and the place of Dutch Jews in World War II. Recognized globally, the letters and diary of Anne Frank have been studied, increasing the historical record in recent years. Renate Ida Rubenstein is part of the generation of Jewish writers reflecting back on this period. Her father was arrested by the Nazis in Amsterdam in 1940, after emigrating from Berlin, and killed at Auschwitz, and this would have a lasting effect on her entire life and on her writing. After her formal education and some work in Amsterdam, she worked on a kibbutz in Israel, and then studied at the Hebrew University of Jerusalem, returning to the University of Amsterdam to finish her studies in social in 1955. She embarked on a busy journalism career, writing for the *New Israelite Weekbald*, the *Propria Cures, Free Netherlands, Het Parool, NRC Handelbald, Hollands Weekblad, Hollands Monthly*, and the *Tirade*. Rubenstein was famous for her deep polemical battles, and she even had conflict with some "radical" writers, such as W.F. Hermans. Contemporary Dutch Jewish writers are still reflecting on the meaning of the Holocaust and its implications for the future of Judaism in the Netherlands and Europe. Frans Pointl lived with his mother through World War II after his parents divorced; she never recovered from the ravages of war. After his mother's death, Pointl began to write in a more directed manner, and in 1989, he gained considerable fame with his novel *De Kip Die over de Soep Vloog* (*The Chicken that Flew over the Soup*), and has continued to offer reflections on the Holocaust.

Like many Jewish authors, Marcel Möring has roots in Eastern Europe and his novels reflect a sense of longing; his characters try to reconstruct their own history to make sense of their journey. These themes reverberate with many readers, and his books have been translated into more than 15 languages, bringing him international recognition. His first novel, *Mendel's erfenis* (*Mendel's Legacy*, 1990), shows the main character struggling in the midst of a deep depression to reconstruct his Jewish family's past. In 1993, he published *Het Grote Verlangen* (*The Great Longing*) and received the Literature Prize AKO, and in 1997, *In Babylon* brought him the highest recognition as one of the best contemporary Dutch writers.[21]

Leon de Winter is another Jewish writer whose stories are filled with reflections on war, life, and death, but he has appeals to a wide audience in writing with humor while penning thrillers.[22] These works feature protagonists searching for a Jewish identity, and they try to bring order out of chaos and are, as a result, discontent with their seemingly empty and aimless lives. De Winter became involved in political writing in newspapers and magazines, and appearances on television, perhaps the most recognizable of these being his utterances of support for the invasion of Iraq, which alienated him from many radical Dutch writers.

Contemporary Dutch literature continues to develop in many directions. Cees Nooteboom has traveled widely and uses his experiences to construct his books, which incorporate history, art, psychology, and geography. His novels include *Rituelen* (*Rituals*, 1980), *Een Lied van Schijn en Wezen* (*A Song of Truth and Semblance*, 1981), *Berlijnse Notities* (*Berlin Notes*, 1990), *Het Volgende Verhaal* (*The Following Story*, 1991), *Allerzielen* (*All Souls' Day*, 1998), *Paradijs Verloren* (*Paradise Lost*, 2004), and *De Slapende Goden* (*The Sleeping Gods*).[23] Nine of his novels have been translated into English, giving him a wider audience. A. F. Th. van der Heijden is another prize-winning contemporary author who, in 1983, published one of the most controversial books in contemporary Dutch and European literature, *De slag om de Blauwbrug* (*Battle at the Blue Bridge*). It questioned the fundamental presence and role of monarchy in the Netherlands and throughout Europe. The book was set during the riots caused by Queen Beatrix's coronation in 1980, and one gets a very different impression of the royal event through the eyes of a social deviant who witnesses only the violence and anarchy of the day. He continued this attack with *De Tandeloze Tijd* (*The Toothless Time*), a seven-volume saga about Amsterdam in the 1970s and 1980s that won him international fame.

Connie Palmen has some of the most extensive lists of publications in recent times, beginning with her 1991 literary novel, *The Laws,* which gave her instant success. The real substance behind her work was forged in her academic study of writers and philosophy. In 1986, she completed a dissertation of a critical study of Cees Nooteboom and the place of the writer in a novel. She produced another dissertation in 1988 on Socrates and the relationship between language and reality, where she worked through the ideas of Sartre, Foucault, and Derrida. Behind all of this is a very gripping autobiographical story of her own tragedy when the love of her life, the well-known journalist Ischa Meijer, died at the age of 25 only two weeks before the publication of *Friendship* in 1995. In 1998, Palmen reflected on friendship, life, and death again in *IM: Ischa Meijer, In Margine, In Memoriam,* and then again in *Whole Yours* in 2002. In essence, her message is that people find their fulfillment in relationship to one another. Her novels push the limits between fiction and reality.[24] Her fame is also the result of intense media coverage each time she emerges with another piece of work.

Geert Mak spans the gap between journalist, social critic, story teller, and historian very successfully. He grew up in a small Frisian village that he later memorialized in a popular book *Hoe God Verdween uit Jorwerd* (literally, *How God Disappeared from Jorwerd*, but translated as *Jorwerd: The Death of the Village in the Late 20th Century*). Certainly, despite secularization, religion is still of interest in the Netherlands. Hailing from the smallest village, Mak turned his attention to a much wider field in his well-known book *In Europa: Travels Through the Twentieth Century*, which became the best-selling book by a Dutch author in 2004. Professional historians are reluctant to review his work since its content does not follow the usual path of analysis, yet Mak's factual accuracy and ability to tell a good story is second to none, and he won the Leipzig Book Award for European Understanding in 2008. Other books of note are his histories of the city of Amsterdam, *De engel van Amsterdam* (*The Angel of Amsterdam*, 1992), *Een kleine geschiedenis van Amsterdam* (1994), and *Het Stadspaleis: De Geschiedenis Van Het Paleis Op De Dam* (*The City Palace*, 1997); and *De Eeuw van Mijn Vader* (*The Century of my Father*, 2001), *De Mord van Theo van Gogh* (*The Death of Theo van Gogh*, 2005), and *De Brug* (about the Galata bridge in Istanbul, 2008).

Maarten 't Hart was a zoologist at the University of Leiden before he decided to embark on a career as a writer. He is best known for his novels, including *de Kroongetuige* (*The Novel Witness*, 1983) and *Het Woeden der Gehele Wereld* (*The Raging Throughout the World*, 1993), and three short stories that have been translated into English: *Een Vlucht Regenwulpen* (*A Flight of Curlews*, 1978, trans. 1986), *De aansprekers* (*Bearers of Bad Tidings*, 1979, trans. 1983), and *De Zonnewijzer* (*The Sundial*, 2002, trans. 2004). Typical of many Dutch citizens, 't Hart grew up in a conservative Reformed family, and later rebelled. Many of his novels and essays reflect his uneasy position and his lack of trust in the truth of organized religion, which can be seen in *Wie God Verlaat Heeft Niets te Vrezen, De Schrift betwist Essays* (*Who Leaves God has Nothing to Fear, De Schrift betwist Essay*, the Scripture-disputed essays, 1997) and *De bril van God, De Schrift betwist II essays* (*The Glasses of God, De Schrift betwist II essays*, the Scripture-disputed essays II, 2002). He has also written about classical music, and he claims that Bach has taken the place of God in his life. Jan Siebelink also grew up in a conservative Reformed family, and it appears that while he often sees the deep anxiety and problems in traditional religion, he is not so ready to leave it all behind. His literary debut, *Nachtschade* (*Nightshade*, 1975), attracted attention because of the dark-romantic obsession with decay, death, and religion. His other important novels include *De Herfst zal Schitterend Zijn* (*Autumn Will Be Magnificent*), *De overkant van de rivier* (*Across the River*), and

*Vera, and Margaret.* By far his most famous work has become *Knielen op een Bed Violen* (*Kneeling on Bed Violins*).[25] Willem Jan Otten converted to Roman Catholicism in 1999. As a poet, novelist, playwright, and essayist, he has always written about the larger questions, such as the meaning and purpose of life, but also the very personal experiences of desire, lust, guilt, and jealousy. His novel *Paviljoenen* (*Pavilions*, 1991) shows a woman's love for a man in completely realistic ways, yet is also symbolic of the metaphysical dimensions that are present. His quest is a soul searching whereby the mind cannot always comprehend the inner-most parts, but in the end, he discovers freedom.[26]

Comics have also played a distinctive role in Dutch literature. They have acted to portray human foibles and heroism, good and bad deeds, and worthy goals and detours to avoid, with politics, religions, or economics in mind. In the early modern period, when the literary rate was lower, broadsides, emblematic literature, and cartoons communicated valuable information. In the modern world, the Netherlands has continued its interest in comics, or "strips." They share a broad European and American tradition, as well as some distinctive stories and literary-type comics.[27] Two European-wide comic series have been extremely popular in the Netherlands: *Kuifje,* or its original name *Tintin,* published by the Belgian artist Hergé, the pen-name of Georges Remi, which first appeared in 1929, debuting in Dutch after World War II. Kuifje, a reporter, is the main character (a "kuifje" is a hair cowlick in English, characteristic of his hair), and he is always accompanied by his faithful dog, Snowy. The second is *Asterix and Obleix,* the first book published in 1961 by the French team René Goscinny (stories) and Albert Uderzo (illustrations), displays humorous ancient Gallic characters battling their Roman overlords.

The first popular modern national Dutch comic strip to appear in 1922 was *Bulletje en Boonestaak,* the creation of writer A.M. de Jong and the illustrator George van Raemdonck. It was a critique of Dutch society from a Socialist standpoint, published in the newspaper *Het Volk.* One of the most successful Dutch comic has been the series *Tom Poes* by Marten Toonder, a small white cat, and Heer (Mister) Oliver B. Bommel, an anthropomorphic bear. The first publication in the newspaper *De Telegraaf* was meant to replace Mickey Mouse in 1941. Tom Poes is a word play on the Dutch pastry *tompouce,* and Bommel's constant phrases have become household references in Dutch, such as *Als je begrijpt wat ik bedoel* (if you know what I mean). The most popular recent comic strip is *Fokke & Sukke,* featuring a canary and a duck who give their opinions on every subject. It is published by the writers John Reid and Bastiaan Geleijnse, and illustrated by Jean-Marc van Tol, first appearing in 1994 in the student newspaper *Propria Cures* and then in the national *NRC Handelsblad.* The comics often express politically incorrect statements, differences between genders, or other social conditions.

## Notes

1. Additional characters include King Noble the lion, Brun the bear, and Tybalt the cat. The Latin text contains 14 tales, with over 6,000 lines of elegiac couplets. Similar tales can be found in France in *Le Roman de Renart,* written by Perrout de Saint Cloude around 1175, where the fox signifies the church, the lion the king, and the wolf the barons.

2. See Johan Huizinga, *Homo Ludens: The Play Element in Culture* (New York: Beacon Press, 1971). Huizinga's original title was in Dutch, and his intention was to say "The Play Element *of* Culture," which changes the meaning.

3. It is interesting that the very name "Egmond" may be derived from "eg," derived from "egin," meaning to create; "mo," derived from "moldez," meaning skillfully; and "ond," derived from "ondorekigego," meaning common inheritance and therefore suggesting a skillfully created common inheritance. See "Dutch Language Development," University of California, Riverside, Retrieved July 9, 2008, http://www.faculty.ucr.edu/~legneref/bronze/dutch.htm.

4. See Matthias Hüning, "The Rhetoricians ('*Rederijkers*') and their influence on Dutch," Retrieved June 24, 2008, http://www.ned.univie.ac.at/publicaties/taal geschiedenis/en/rederijkers.htm.

5. Lyrics and translation found on Dutch Ministry of Foreign Affairs Web site, http://www.minbuza.nl/en/welcome/History,national_anthem___the_wilhelmus. html#a6.

6. *De Psalmen Davids* (1566); His New Testament, *Het Nieuwe Testament na der Griekscher waerheyt in Nederlandsche sprake grondlick end trauwelick overghezett* ("The New Testament Translated Thoroughly and Faithfully into the Dutch Tongue According to the Original Greek") was also published in 1566, after the Church of Emden requested that he do so.

7. Reinder P. Meijer, *Literature of the Low Countries: A Short History of Dutch Literature in the Netherlands and Belgium* (Dbnl: 2006), 52–53.

8. He continued with *Hierusalem Verwoest* (*Jerusalem Laid Desolate,*1620); *De Gebroeders* (*The Ruin of the Sons of Saul,* 1640); *Joseph in Egypten* (1640); Lucifer (1654); Salmoneus (*Solomon,* 1657); *Jephtha* (1659); *Koning David in ballingschap* (*King David in Banishment,* 1660), *Koning David Hersteld* (*King David Restored,* 1660); and Samson (1660); *Adam in Ballingschap* (*Adam in Exile,*1664), after the Latin tragedy of Hugo Grotius.

9. *Palamedes, of Vermoorde onnooselheyd* (*Palamedes, or Murdered Innocence,*1625); *Gijsbreght van Aemstel* (1637); *Maria Stuart, of Gemartelde Majesteit* (1646); *The Pastoral of De Leeuwendalers* (1648); and *Batavische Gebroeders,* the subject of which *is* the story of Claudius Civilis (1663).

10. See "5 juni 1806: Koninkrijk Holland," Koninkrijk Biblioteek (Royal Dutch Library), Retrieved June 25, 2008, http://www.kb.nl/dossiers/koninkrijk/konink rijk.html.

11. See Joris van Eijnatten, *Hogere Sferen: de ideeënwereld van Willem Bilderdijk (1756–1831),* (Hilversum: Verloren, 1998). See also "Bilderdijk Profiel," Koninkrijk

Biblioteek, Retrieved June 27, 2008, http://www.kb.nl/dichters/bilderdijk/bilderdi jk-03.html.

12. He continued his historical series with *De Pleegzoon* (Amsterdam: P. Meijer Warnars, 1833; *The Adopted Son*, trans. into English in 1847), *De Roos van Dekama*, 2 vols (Amsterdam: P. Meijer Warnars, 1836), *The Rose of Dekama*, (trans. into French and German, 1847), *Onze Voorouders*, 5 vols. (Amsterdam: P. Meijer Warnars, 1838); *Our Ancestors*), *De Lotgevallen van Ferdinand Huyck*, 2 vols. (Amsterdam: P. Meijer Warnars, 1840; *The Adventures of Ferdinand Huyck*, 2 vols. (Amsterdam: P. Meijer Warnars, 1840), *Elizabeth Musch* (3 vols.('s Gravenhage: Nijhoff, 1850), and *De Lotgevallen van Klaasje Zevenster*, 5 vols. ('s Gravenhage: Nijhoff, 1865; *The Adventures of Klaasje Zevenster*). He also produced several pieces of Dutch history intended for young readers.

13. Conrad Busken Huet, *Het Land van Rembrandt: Studiën over de Noord-Nederlandse beschaving in de zeventiende eeuw*, Eerste Deel, Zesde Hoofdstuk, II, ed. Laurens Janszoon Coster, Nederlandstalige Klassieke Literatuur in Elektronische Edities, Retrieved June 30, 2008, http://cf.hum.uva.nl/dsp/ljc/huet/.

14. See Theo Meder, "Hans Brinker," http://members.chello.nl/m.jong9/map12/hansbrinker.html and; Theo Meder, *The Flying Dutchman and Other Folktales from the Netherlands*, Illustrations by Minke Priester (Westport, CT: Greenwood Press, 2007).

15. He is also known for many fine translations, and in 1953, the Prince Bernard Fund established a Martinus Nijhoff Prize to honor translations between Dutch and other languages.

16. See "Dossier Hella Haasse," Koninklijk Biblioteek, Retrieved July 2, 2008, http://www.kb.nl/dossiers/haasse/haasse.html.

17. Haasse has been recognized at home and abroad: she is the only author who has been awarded the prestigious annual National Book Week Present three times (1948, 1959, and 1994). In 1981, she received the Constantijn Huygens Prize, and in 1984, she was granted the P. C. Hooft Award. She also won the Annie Romein Prize and the Dirk Martens Prize. Queen Beatrix distinguished her with the prestigious Medal of Honour for Art and Science of the House of Orange. In 1988, Haasse received an honorary doctorate in literature from the University of Utrecht in 1988, and she is an officer in the Order of the Legion of Honor in France.

18. Vestdijk received numerous awards, including the CW van der Hoogt prize (1938), Wijnand Francken Prize (1941), the Prose and Novel Prize of Amsterdam (1946, 1960), the PC Hooft Prize (1951), Jan Campert Foundation Prize (1953, 1955), Prize for Dutch Letters (1971), and an honorary doctorate from the University of Groningen (1964). Since 1957, he has been a candidate for the Nobel Peace Prize.

19. Other writers of note are Anna Blaman, *Op leven en dood*, (Amsterdam, J. M. Meulenhoff, 1954, *A Matter of Life and Death*), which represents a struggle with verzuiling; Marga Minco, *De Glazen Brug* (Amsterdam: CPNB, Collectieve Propaganda van het Nederlandse Boek, 1986, *The Glass Bridge*), a reflection of life 40 years after World War II; Koos van Zomeren, *Otto's Oorlog* (Amsterdam: Arbeiderspers, 1983, *Otto's War*), which explores the feelings of a man who cannot separate himself from

the war; Dirk Ayelt Kooiman, *Montijn* (Amsterdam: De Harmonie, 1982, *A Lamb to Slaughter*); Armando, *Voorvallen in de Wildernis* (Amsterdam: Bezige Bij, 1994); and Tessa de Loo, *De Tweeling* (Amsterdam: Arbeiderspers, 2003, *The Twins*).

20. He received many awards, including the Vijverberg Prize in 1971 for Novel Participation (1970), the Herman Gorter Prize in 1978 for his poetry in Weerwerk (1977), and the Constantin Huygens Prize in 1991 for his complete works.

21. Other books translated into English include *The Great Longing* (1995), *The Dream Room* (2002), and *In Dark Wood* (2007).

22. He is known for his novels *De Verwording van de Jonge Durer* (Apeldoorn: Walva-Boek/Van Walraven, 1978), which received the Reina Prinsen Geerligs Prize; *La Place de la Bastille* (Haarlem: In de Knipscheer, 1981); *Zoeken naar Eileen W* (Amsterdam: Knipscheer, 1981*Search for Eileen W*); *Vertraagde Roman* (Amsterdam: Knipscheer, 1982); *Kaplan* (Amsterdam: Bezige Bij1986); *Hoffman's Honger* (Amsterdam: De Bezige Bij, 1990*Hoffman's Hunger*); *Supertex* (Amsterdam: De Bezige Bij, 1991); *De Ruimte van Sokolov* (Amsterdam: De Bezige Bij, 1992 *Sokolov's Space*); *Zionoco* (Amsterdam: De Bezige Bij, 1995); *De Hemel van Hollywood* (Amsterdam: De Bezige Bij, 1997, *The Heaven of Hollywood*), which was later filmed with Rod Steiger, Burt Reynolds, and Tom Berenger; *God's Gym* (2002); and *Het Recht op Terugkeer* (*The Right 2008*). In 2005, he received the Buber-Rosenzweig-Medaille Prize.

23. He has won many prizes: the Aristeion Prize, the P.C. Hooft Prize, the Pegasus Prize, the Constantin Huygens Prize, and the Austrian State Prize for European Literature.

24. She has received the AKO Literature Prize, the Humo's Golden Bookmark, and the Trouw Public Prize.

25. In 2002, Siebelink received the Ferdinand Bordewijk Prize, and in the AKO Literature Prize in 2005. He also became interested in "decadent" literature, and he translated J.K. Huysmans' novel, *À rebours*.

26. He has received many prizes for his work: the Herman Gorter, Jan Campert, Busken Huet, Constantin Hygens, and Libris Literature prizes.

27. See "Lambiek: History of Dutch Comics," Retrieved July 9, 2008, http://lambiek.net/dutchcomics/index.htm.

# 7

# Performing Arts and Media

## THEATER

The tradition of *rederijerkamers,* or "chambers of rhetoric," in the Netherlands promoted literature and public dramas, building on the medieval tradition of mystery plays.[1] This indicates an early tradition of public discourse that included many levels of society in a discussion of social issues. The chambers regularly challenged contemporary authority, and included a larger number of people that were more directly involved in public opinion than many other states of the time, reflecting their development into a republic. The Dutch Republic spent its early years at war with Spain, and when the struggle carried over into religious matters, the dominant Calvinist pastors discouraged drama for its connections with Catholic practices. Then, in the early 17th century, cities began to recover and attention turned once again to the arts. In 1617, the Eerst Nederduytsche Academie (First Low-German Academy) was established primarily to support the sciences, but also to help support and train future writers and actors, and promote drama. Samuel Coster was the founder, and received support from the well-known writers Bredero and Hooft, and despite continued protest from the Reformed Church, some of its supporters were also Mennonite professors: Sibrant Hanses Cardinael, a professor of arithmetic and Jan Thonis, a professor of Hebrew. In 1637, the architect Jacob van Campen built the first theater in Amsterdam, and called it the *Schouwburg* (which became the Dutch word for theater). The building replaced the *Nederduytsche Academie,* and by the end of the year, Vondel's *Gijsbrecht van Aemstel* was performed. Reminiscent of Shakespeare, Vondel inscribed a motto above the doors: "The world is a theater; each man plays his role and learns his part." In 1665, a new building twice the size of the original structure replaced the older theater.

In 1774, a new city theater was built on the Leidseplein (Leiden Square), where it remained until a fire consumed it in 1892, and by 1894, a new, much larger building replaced it and is in use to this day.[2] The theater is home to the *Toneelgroep Amsterdam,* the largest Dutch repertory company, and internationally recognized directors have regularly contributed performances, such as Krzysztof Warlikowski (Polish), Christoph Marthaler (Swiss), Wim Vandekeybus (Belgian), and Emio Greco (an Italian-born resident of Amsterdam). Currently, the Flemish director Ivo van Hove, known for his innovative and often iconoclastic performances, is the artistic director of the *Toneelgroep Amsterdam,* directing works such as *More Stately Mansions* (which won the OBIE award for direction), Tennessee Williams' *A Streetcar Named Desire,* Susan Sontag's *Alice in Bed,* and Hendrik Ibsen's *Hedda Gabler.* In addition to the tradition of established theater, which was patronized mainly by the elite prior to the 20th century, by the 1980s, some smaller companies were established that performed in public and "on spot," and opened up the theater to the general audience. One of the best examples of this is the *Theatregroep Hollandia* under the direction of Johan Simons and Paul Koek. Established in 1985, this group performed many Greek tragedies, and then, in the 1990s, turned to current social and political issues with productions of *Voices, The Fall of the Gods, Quick Lime,* and *GEN.* In 2000, the company received the European Prize for Theatrical Innovation, and Simons has become a guest director throughout Europe, helming ancient Greek tragedies, modern productions, and operas.

## DANCE

In early modern Netherlands, dance was largely a social phenomenon that was quite popular at town and city festivals. Several names describe traditional folk dancing: *Folkloristisch* indicates folk-lore dancing, also known as *Boerendansen* or "farmer-dancing," and more specifically, *Klompendansen* refers to clog dancing. Clogs were the most popular form of foot wear for almost every level of society throughout the history of the Netherlands, offering a practical solution to wet soil, and they made an impressive noise when used for dancing. Clog dancing became popular in many other European countries since in early modern Europe, the use of wooden shoes was also common in many regions, especially among the poor. Professional dancing was not very common in the Netherlands until the 19th century.

In 1642–1645, Amsterdam experienced the first ballet performances with the arrival of the "Ballet of the Five Senses." Few Dutch choreographers gained international recognition until Pietro Nieri, who was based in Amsterdam, performed the "Peasant Life" in 1762. The 19th century was filled with Romantic ballets, and the choreographer Piet Grieve preformed "The Golden Magic Rose or Harlequin Freed from Slavery" in 1819. Andries Voitus van Hamme (1828–68) was the most prolific director and choreographer of the 19th century, and he brought a *commedia della'arte* style to the Netherlands. In all, he performed 115 three-act ballets with his own company.

Few Dutch dancers have received the same level of international recognition as Mata Hari, the stage name of Margaretha Geertruida Zelle, who one of the best-known exotic dancers in the later 19th century. After an early marriage to a Dutch officer in Indonesia, she moved to Paris, pretending to have royal Indian roots as a princess of Java. She was flirtatious, and shocked many audiences with her nude or nearly-nude dance during a time when dancers were always fully covered. As a courtesan of many wealthy and powerful men, including the German Crown Prince, she was accused of being a double-agent by the French during World War I, and was subsequently executed by a firing squad in 1917. To this day, she remains the model of the femme fatale. The Dutch National Ballet (*Het Nationale Ballet*) was established in 1961 from the amalgamation of the Amsterdam Ballet, founded in 1954 by Sonia Gaskell, and the *Nederlands Ballet*. It is the largest dance company in the Netherlands and is based in The Hague, although it often performs in the *Muziektheater* in Amsterdam. The choreographers Rudi van Dantzig, Toer van Schayk, Hans van Manen, Maguy Marin, and Edouard Lock have attempted to bring new material to the company. Of the nearly 80 members, one of the most celebrated Dutch members of the company is Igone de Jongh, who was a finalist at the Prix de Lausanne in 1995. The Dutch Dance Theater (*Nederlands Dans Theater*) was founded by Benjamin Harkarvy, Aart Verstegen, and Carel Birnie in 1959 in order to pursue contemporary dance. Currently, Jiri Kylián, a Czech choreographer, is the artistic director, and his most well-known work is "Symphony of Psalms" (1978). Some of the dancers, such as Gérard Lemaître, Charles Czarny, and Martinette Janmaat, have contributed significantly to contemporary dance and are recognized throughout Europe.

The Holland Festival has become the largest performing arts festival in the Netherlands since its establishment in 1947, encompassing music, opera, theater, and modern dance, with performances in many Amsterdam venues. The Dutch government has actively supported the arts through the "Performing Arts in the Netherlands" policy. There are approximately 400 companies involved in dance, drama, mime, and puppetry, and they are evaluated every four years under the *Kunstenplan* (Arts Plan). Once qualified, they can receive subsidies to encourage and fund performances.

## MUSIC

The Netherlands boasts world-renowned symphony orchestras, the Royal Concertgebouw Orchestra (*Koninklijk Concertgebouworkest,* where *gebouw* means hall or building). The *Concertgebouw* in Amsterdam has some of the best acoustics in the world, and has become an important place to record music, featuring approximately 800 concerts a year in three halls: the *Grote Zaal, Kleine Zaal,* and *Spiegelzaal* (large, small, and mirror halls). The *Concertgebouw* opened in 1888, and in 1988, Queen Beatrix conferred the title of "royal" in honor of its great achievement. Willem Mengelberg served as its first conductor and continued for 50 years. Amsterdam has another well-known orchestra, the *Nederlands Philharmonisch Orkest* (Netherlands Philharmonic Orchestra), which is located in the *Beurs van Berlage* (Berlage Stock Exchange) concert hall, but it occasionally performs in the *Concertgebouw,* as well. Other important orchestras in the Netherlands are the *Residentie Orchestra* in The Hague, the Rotterdam Philharmonic, and the *Radio Filharmonisch Orkest Holland* (Netherlands Radio Philharmonic Orchestra), which has its headquarters in Hilversum. Other chamber groups include the Netherlands Chamber Orchestra, the Amsterdam Baroque Orchestra, and the Orchestra of the 18th Century, supported by the Netherlands Chamber Choir. Willem Pijper became one of the best known Dutch composers in the first half of the 20th century, and influenced a future generation through his teaching and his direction of the Rotterdam Conservatoire. After World War II, Louis Andriessen experimented with many forms of music, reflecting the European trend toward dissonance.

Organized and supported by the Reformed Church in the Netherlands, which had a dominant position in Dutch society until the 1960s, choirs and organ music have held a very important place in Dutch culture. The Protestant Reformation had removed stained-glass windows, paintings, and statues, and often white-washed the churches since all of these adornments had become bitter reminders of external oppression and inquisition. Only the great pipe organs remained, and a decidedly oral liturgical tradition replaced the visual one. Reformed cathedrals and churches prided themselves on the size and sound of their organs, and the technological developments dove-tailed with the Dutch love of engineering. In the Baroque period, Catholic churches also favored organs and choirs. Jan Pieterszoon Sweelinck, a 17th-century composer, was known throughout Europe, and helped establish the Dutch organ tradition that is still popular today.

St. Laurens Church in Alkmaar has the oldest organ (Van Covelens) in the Netherlands, dating from 1511, and it also possesses one of the most impressive large organs built by Van Hagerbeer and Schnitger in 1639–1646. Today, Ton Koopmans is one of the country's most famous organists, and he is the founder of the Amsterdam Baroque Orchestra & Choir. He concentrates on Baroque music, and his recordings include the complete Bach cantatas and organ works, St. Matthew (twice) and St. John Passions, Mass in B minor, Christmas Oratorio, the lost St. Mark Passion, Mozart's Coronation Mass and Vespers, Requiem, a cycle of Mozart symphonies, Vivaldi's Four Seasons, Handel's Messiah, and Organ Concertos.

The Dutch street organ (*draaiorgel*) became very popular in the early 20th century. Leon Warnies starting a thriving organ rental business in Amsterdam, and soon, street markets and fairs had organs playing throughout the day. Today, few street organs remain, but in some towns, it is still common to hear that distinctive organ music and the owner shaking his can of coins to the music, trying to encourage passers-by to contribute. Some would like to continue the tradition, and the *Kring van Draaiorgelvrienden* (Circle of Street Organ Friends) has grown to about 1,500 persons, the largest in the world.

The leading opera company in the Netherlands is *De Nederlandse Opera,* located in Amsterdam. In 1986, a new musical theater was built on the Amstel called the *Stopera,* a combination of *stadhuis* (city hall) and opera.[3] Since 2005, the chief conductor has been Ingo Metzmacher. Cabaret has held an important place in Dutch performance, as well. Similar to German cabaret, comedy is mixed with theater, and it often offers a critique of social and political life. New Year's Eve performances on the television have become quite popular. Toon Hermans was one of the most famous comedians of the cabaret in the 1950s and 1960s, together with Wim Sonneveld and Wim Kan. Hermans told long stories, filled with characterizations of family, friends, neighbors, and pets, and interspersed with French-style chansons and simple jazz, and was typical of the humor found in the southern Netherlands. André van Duin came into the public eye in the mid-1960s and has continued to offer comedy and song, helping to define Dutch humor for years. He has also acted in several films, expanding his repertoire to reveal a serious side, and he continues to act.

By far, the most internationally recognized arts festival in the Netherlands is the annual North Sea Jazz festival held during the second week of July. This festival was established in 1975 by the businessman Paul Acket, and it has since grown to 15 stages with over 1,200 artists and 23,000 concert goers each day. Many of the world's most famous jazz musicians have played at the festival, including Tony Bennett, Herbie Hancock, Miles Davis, Count

Basie, Dizzy Gillespie, and Oscar Peterson. Apart from the growth of many forms of music, such as folk, pop, rock, and rap, a unique form of Dutch rock, *Boerenrock* (farmer's rock), mixes regional culture and dialect with rock music.

## CINEMA

The Dutch film industry is small since the market for Dutch-language productions is not large, but it has been an important part of the larger culture. Many well-known directors have begun by producing documentaries, which are very popular. Dutch films began to be made in the 1930s and production boomed until World War II. Following the war, the luxury of making films was not feasible, given the widespread reconstruction, and it was not until Bert Haanstra made his first film, *Fanfare,* in 1958, with the help of the newly organized Dutch Film Fund, that the industry began to develop again. This film remains one of the most popular Dutch films ever. Also in 1958, Fons Rademakers studied in Rome and Paris and debuted his first Dutch film, *Dorp aan de rivier* (*Village on the River*), for which he became the first Dutch film director to receive an Oscar nomination. He produced many important films based on famous Dutch novels: *When Two Drops of Water* (1963, W.F. Hermans), *Mira* (1971, Stijn Streuvels), *Max Havelaar* (1976, Multatuli), and *The Attack* (1987, Harry Mulisch), for which he was awarded an Oscar.

Paul Verhoeven has dominated the Dutch film industry with his characteristic productions that explore science fiction, violence, and sex. His Dutch film *Wat Zien ik?* (*Business Is Business,* 1971) received the award of Best Film of the Century from the Netherlands Film Festival.[4] In 1973, he directed *Turks Fruit* (*Turkish Delight*) that became one of the most successful Dutch films, with approximately 27 percent of the population attending a showing. He is well known internationally for several films: *Robo Cop* (1987), *Total Recall* (1990), *Basic Instinct* (1992), *Showgirls* (1995), *Starship Troopers* (1997), and *Hollow Man* (2000).

Other acclaimed directors include Marleen Gorris, Dick Maas, and Theo Van Gogh. Gorris is known for her active support of gay and lesbian issues and her film *Antonia's Line* won an Oscar in 1995. She has also gained recognition for the film *Mrs. Dalloway* (1997), based on the Virginia Woolf novel of the same name. Maas started out as a comic artist and created the characters Mug and Zifter, but turned to film and produced *De Lift* (*"The Elevator,* 1983), *Flodder* (which is a family name, but means "blank cartridge" in Dutch, pointing to their asocial humorous side, 1986), and *Amsterdamned* (1988), and he is the only Dutch director to receive the famed Grand Prix at the Festival of Avoriaz (France). Although Theo van Gogh had been known to the Dutch for his outrageous commentaries in print and television, his high-profile political murder in 2004, touched off by his film *Submission* (2004), brought him to the forefront of radical films and literature against Islam, which was a component of his flamboyant criticism of all religions. His previous film *Blind Date* (1996) was recognized with the Dutch equivalent of the Oscar, the Golden Calf Award.

Several Dutch actors have been distinguished in the international arena. Rutger Oelsen Hauer played a role in Verhoeven's film "Turkish Delight," and went on to act in many other Verhoeven productions. He also established an English-language film career, acting in "The Wilby Conspiracy" with Michael Caine and Sidney Poitier. He collaborated with another famous Dutch actor, Jeroen Krabbé, on *Nighthawks* (1981), with Sylvester Stallone, and on *Blade Runner* (1982). Hauer also continued his career with *Eureka* (1983) with Gene Hackman; *Ladyhawke* (1985) with Michelle Pfeiffer; *The Hitcher* (1986); and *Wanted: Dead or Alive* (1987). The most famous Dutch female actor is Famke Janssen, who came to international prominence with her role in the Bond film *GoldenEye* (1995), and also starred in *X-Men* (2000) and *Nip/Tuck* (2003).

## MEDIA

### Broadcasting: Radio and Television

Any discussion of media in the Netherlands prior to the 1970s must take into consideration the "pillarization" model that had developed by the opening of the 20th century. As already discussed in Chapter Three, pillarization (*verzuiling*) refers to the social division of the Netherlands into four distinctive pillars, or social, political interest groups: Protestant, Catholic, Liberal, and Socialist workers. While the characteristics of each group varies—the first two groups have far more prominent religious orientations—each group developed its own political, economic and labor, educational, and media institutions. Within the pillarized model, the government organized all radio and television channels to ensure public service and equal opportunity, and commercial stations were banned until the 1980s. Three national television channels were established: Nederland 1, Nederland 2, and Nederland 3; and five radio channels: Radio 1, Radio 2, Radio 3, Radio 4, and Radio 5. Each channel provides different coverage and is in turn used by various independent stations, or broadcast associations, based on the size of their constituency. In this way, all stations utilize common facilities. Nederland 1 covers news, sports, and family programming; Nederland 2 highlights culture, arts, politics, and religion; and Nederland 3 focuses on youth and progressive programming. Private stations receive funding from three sources: dues paid through membership, the smallest percentage, income from advertising, and grants-in-aid directly from the government. Once the pillarized model broke down in the 1970s, new stations developed, although some of the first stations established still remain popular with loyal members.

The oldest stations are organized as both radio and television institutions. The NCRV (*Nederlandse Christelijke Radio Vereniging*) Dutch Christian Radio Association opened in 1924 and has represented a broad and moderate Protestant constituency. The Association broadcasts television shows on Nederland 1 and 2. In 1925, the KRO (*Katholieke Radio Omroep*) Catholic Radio Broadcasting was established and almost exclusively uses Nederland 1. Since 2005, the show "Farmer Seeks Wife" (*Boer zoekt vrouw*) has been their highest-rated TV program, with an average of 4.5 million weekly viewers. In 1926, liberal Protestants were unhappy with NCRV's broadcasting and started their own VPRO, an acronym for Liberal Protestant Radio Broadcasting Company (*Vrijzinnig Protestantse Radio Omroep*). By the 1960s, it remained liberal but lost its religious platform, yet the name VPRO was kept. It was the first station to show a nude woman, Phil Bloom, on Dutch television in 1967. By 1967, a more conservative Protestant faction was also unhappy with the NCRV and established EO (*Evangelische Omroep*) Evangelical Broadcast station, with the goal of remaining faithful to a more conservative (often called "Orthodox Protestant") religious mission. In addition to the original religious pillars, VARA (*Vereeniging van Arbeiders Radio Amateurs*), the Association of Worker Radio Amateurs, was founded in 1925, and supported the concerns of labor and socialism, with close ties to the Social Democratic Workers Party and the Labor Party that followed. In 1957, the name was changed to *Omroepvereniging VARA* (Broadcasting Association VARA).

The Dutch government also established a national public broadcasting system to offer news, and in 1923, the AVRO (*Algemene Vereniging Radio Omroep*) opened within the larger Netherlands Public Broadcasting (*Nederlandse Publieke Omroep*) system. In 1969, the Dutch Parliament established another public broadcasting company, NOS (*Nederlandse Omroep Stichting*) Netherlands Broadcasting Foundation, to coordinate and complete the shows operating on the three established television networks. They provide approximately 25 percent of television programming and 15 percent of radio content. In 1995, NOS divided its programming and the NPS (*Nederlandse Programma Stichting*) Dutch Program Foundation took over the culture, information, minorities, and youth programming, while the NOS provides impartial news coverage.

New organizations began once the pillars broke down in the 1970s. Originally established as a pirate broadcasting station beamed from an off-shore oil platform in the North Sea, TROS (*Televisie Radio Omroep Stichting*) finally gained government recognition in 1964, and had wide appeal for its largely entertainment- and news-oriented shows. Since this time, new broadcasting organizations have narrowed the focus. The BNN, a pun on CNN using its founder's first name, Bart de Graaff, began in 1997 and it targets the young adult market with programs and feature films. On the other end of the spectrum, MAX was founded in 2002 to develop programs for people over 50. The Humanists Alliance established HUMAN (*Humanistische Omroep*) Humanist Broadcasting in 2001, and in 2005, LliNK combined two former organizations involved in environmental and global issues.

New religious groups have also established broadcasting associations: the Buddhist BOS (*Boeddhistische Omroep Stichting*), Jewish JO (*Joodse Omroep*), Islamic NIO (*Nederlandse Islamitische Omroep*), Muslim NMO (*Nederlandse Moslim Omroep*), and the Hindu OHM (*Organisatie Hindoe Media*). In addition, some associations have the very specific purposes of televising meetings and information: the ZvK (*Zendtijd voor Kerken*) and the IKON (*Interkerkelijke Omroep Nederland*) were recently organized to broadcast Protestant church services and activities; the PP (*Zendtijd voor Politieke partijen*) was established to transmit news and presentations for political parties; the TELEAC/NOT (*Televisie-academie/Nederlandse Onderwijs Televisie*) was created broadcast educational programming; and OF (*Omrop Fryslân*) is devoted to Frisian-language broadcasting.

Today, there are four television channels: Nederland 1, Nederland 2, Nederland 3, and the newer, digital Nederland 4; and seven national radio networks: Radio 1, Radio 2, 3FM, Radio 4, Radio 5, and Radio 6, as well as "Concertzender" (for concerts), FunX, 24News, top 2000, Radiocast, and RNW. With increasing broadcast bands, the largest foreign station is the RTL (*Radio Télévision Luxembourg*), which was founded in Luxembourg and is currently owned by the German company Bertelsmann. It has 43 television and 32 radio stations broadcasting in 10 countries. The newest international networks are MTV Europe, Discovery Communications, and Time Warner Incorporated.

## NEWSPAPERS

Newspapers were originally linked to the different pillars, yet, today, most organizations are privately owned and commercial with no explicit association; however, some political and ideological orientations still exist. The most important national newspapers include *De Telegraaf* ("Telegraph"), which represents a "conservative-liberal" constituency served by one of the largest newspaper companies. The Amsterdam-based Telegraaf Media Group is the largest publisher of national newspapers in the Netherlands, and also owns the daily, free tabloid paper the *Sp!ts* ("Rush-Hour"), which one finds distributed at all public transportation facilities. The other national papers are all owned by the second largest Netherlands publisher, PCM Uitgevers (PCM Publishers), which prints several newspaper with different social-political stances: the more "progressive liberal" newspaper, the *NRC Handelsblad* ("Trade Journal"), the left-wing *De Volkskrant* ("People's Paper," which was originally a Roman Catholic newspaper), and the traditional Protestant *Trouw* ("Fidelity," which was established as a Protestant resistance paper during World War II). *Het Parool* is an Amsterdam-based newspaper that was also founded during World War II as a resistance paper, and its name means "the password." Until 2003, it was also owned by PCM Publishers, but it was purchased by the Belgian Vlaamse Persgroep and in 2004, shifted into more of a tabloid format.

The largest publisher of regional newspapers is the Royal Wegener N.V. company, which prints seven papers in east and central Netherlands. There has also been cooperation over time with the Rotterdam-based A D Nieuws-Media, which prints the *Algemeen Dagblad,* a regional paper in the west that inserts specific news sections to replace the smaller city newspapers in Rotterdam, The Hague, and other cities. In 2007, the large London-based Mecom Group purchased a 87 percent share of the company, connecting it to many other European national-regional papers. Newspapers catering to more specific religious groups, traditionally the pillarized groups, continue, albeit in smaller numbers, including the Protestant *Nederlands Dagblad* ("Netherlands Daily Paper"), the *Reformatorisch Dagblad,* and the Roman Catholic *Katholiek Nieuwsblad.*

The newspaper *Het Financiële Dagblad* is specifically aimed at the financial and business community. By the 1990s, the newest popular newspapers became the smaller tabloids, such as the *Sp!ts,* the *Metro, De Pers,* and the *ncr.next.* Many news blogs have also appeared on the Internet, as with many other language groups in the world.

## Magazines

By far, the largest and most important magazine in circulation is the weekly *Elsevier*—the Dutch *Time* and *Newsweek.* It is published by Elsevier Publishing Company NV (NV Uitgeversmaatschappij Elsevier). In 1880, Jacobus George Robbers had already established a small publishing house to print literary classics and the best-known Dutch encyclopedia *Winkler Prins.* But the name has its roots in the 16th century when the Elzevir family published the works of Erasmus in 1587. Robbers also began to publish a monthly magazine, the *Elsevier's Geïllustreerd Maandschrift* (*Elsevier's Illustrated Monthly*).

After World War II, the magazine was revised to become a weekly, and it attempted to adopt a neutral position, yet soon became embroiled in the Indonesian call for independence in clearly promoting a position against their freedom, and since that time, it has maintained a more conservative position. Soon, international offices were established in Houston, Texas (1951) and in New York and London (1962). In subsequent years, Elsevier became the world's largest publisher of scientific and medical literature, and by 1979, its name, Elsevier Scientific Publishers, reflected this change. In 1991, the English publisher Reed was acquired and its name was again changed to Reed Elsevier. With the acquisition of Reed Elsevier, the publisher moved into business publications: Reed Business Information and LexisNexis.

In addition to *Elsevier*, the other conservative national magazine is the *HP/de Tijd*, the product of a 1990 merger of the *Haagsche Post* and *De Tijd* (*The Times*), owned by Audax Publishing. More liberal and left-wing magazines of note are the *Vrij Nederland*, with an intellectual audience, and *De Groene Amsterdammer*. The latter was originally founded in 1877 as simply *De Amsterdammer*, but in 1925, due to its distinctive green ink, it was renamed *De Groene Amsterdammer*. It has established a reputation for covering a wide range of subjects, and although it was initially left-wing, it has developed a much more centrist position over time.

Other popular national magazines include *Privé* and *Weekend*. *Privé* is published by the large newspaper company, Telegraaf Magazine Group (TTG), part of Telegraaf Media Group. Telegraaf also publishes niche magazines, such as the women's publication *Vrouw in Beeld, Voetbal Magazine,* and *Tennis Magazine*. One of the largest European publishers is the Sanoma Oyj company, based in Helsinki, Finland, with over 300 titles in 20 European countries. In addition to many popular women's magazines, such as *Libelle, Margriet, Yes, Viva, Cosmopolitan,* and *Flair,* they also publish home magazines, such as *VT Wonen,* and the Dutch language versions of *National Geographic, Playboy,* and a Disney magazine for children, among others. The oldest and largest football (soccer) magazine in the Netherlands is *Voetbal International*.[5]

## NOTES

1. See Gary Waite, *Reformers on Stage: Popular Drama and Religious Propaganda in the Low Countries of Charles V, 1515–1556* (Toronto: University of Toronto Press, 2000).

2. See George W. Brandt, ed., *German and Dutch Theatre, 1600–1848* (Theatre in Europe: A Documentary History) (Cambridge: Cambridge University Press, 1993).

3. Another origin of the name Stopera is a humorous byword for literally "Stop the opera," since the destruction of many older houses in the area to make way for the opera building launched a large protest to "Stop the opera.".

4. Other Dutch feature films include: *Turks Fruit* (*Turkish Delight,* 1973), *Keetje Tippel* (*Katie Tippel,* 1975), *Soldaat van Oranje* (*Soldier of Orange,* 1977), *Spetters* (1980), *Costa!* (2001), *Volle Maan* (*Full Moon,* 2002), *Shouf Shouf Habibi* (*Hush, Hush, Baby,* 2004), *Het Schnitzelparadijs* (*Schnitzel Paradise,* 2005), and *Zwartboek* (*Black Book,* 2006). Verhoeven has a PhD in mathematics and physics from the University of Leiden. See "Film in the Netherlands from 1896: an Encyclopedia of Film Culture," http://www.cinemacontext.nl/.

5. See a list of media services in the Netherlands at ABYZ News Links, *Netherlands Newspapers and Media Guide,* http://www.abyznewslinks.com/nethe.htm.

# 8

## The Visual Arts

### EARLY NETHERLANDISH ART AND THE RENAISSANCE

The Netherlands is well known for its contribution to Western art, dating from the Renaissance to the modern world, and certain artists have achieved international distinction, such as Rembrandt and Vincent Van Gogh. When the Low Countries began to develop as commercial centers in the 14th century, art began to reflect a distinctive northern style. Whereas most art in the Middle Ages was patronized by the Church alone, the Renaissance movement was led by princes and merchants who had a great interest in displaying their wealth and emulating the ancient world. The Burgundian court actively supported the arts in its urban centers, and the counts and dukes favored elaborate courtly pageantry, and wanted to have their achievements memorialized in churches and chapels. The medieval illuminated manuscript trade had been very active in the Low Countries and was supported by the Burgundian and French rulers. The Limburg brothers began to produce miniatures in several illuminated manuscripts, and their most famous, commissioned around 1410, was the *Très Riches Heures du Duc de Berry,* seasonal calendars with depictions of landscapes and farms. By the middle of the 15th century, Brussels had the largest court, and the Flemish towns of Bruges, Gent, and Tournai (Doornik) emerged as the centers of painting and printed works, where artists such as Jan van Eyck, Rogier van der Weyden, Hans Memling, and Gerard David took on many commissions. Later, Leuven, Mechelen, and Antwerp developed their own centers of art. This first period is called the Early Netherlandish, and it began in the early 1400s with Robert of Campin, also known as the Master of Flémalle, and ended around 1500 with the works of Gerard David.[1]

There are several characteristics of this period that introduced some new elements to painting. First, a strong realism was reflected in art; this was established in a religious piety developed in the monastic houses of the Dominicans, Carthusians, and the Augustinians, which then spread to the laity. New depictions of Jesus stressed his humanity; he was painted into scenes from daily life, and in his passion, his suffering could be clearly seen. This is a contrast to the medieval depictions where only Jesus' divine nature was shown; he is often sitting with the Trinity or judging human kind from above. Rogier van der Weyden's painting of the *Descent of Christ from the Cross* (c.1435) shows a very human Jesus who is clearly dead, supported by the disciples and Mary who are in great distress, with eyes closed and tears streaming down. In this way, Jesus is more real; he can be touched and his actions can be emulated, a point made in the many "enchiridions" or hand-books for religious instruction that were common in the Modern Devotion movement, as illustrated in Thomas á Kempis' famous book *The Imitation of Christ*. Secondly, this realism was not only evident in the subject matter and the emphasis on human elements, but was achieved through new painting techniques that highlighted the fine details in nature.

The most important new technique was a refined way to use oil painting to achieve a deeper and richer surface. The use of oil in painting was already prevalent in the ancient world, but traditional oil paints had only been applied after a base coat of egg tempura sketched out the scene; dried natural materials with particular colors were ground and mixed with eggs, and these needed to be applied in thin, short brush strokes. The new oil paint technique allowed an artist to apply much thicker layers directly to a surface, producing more three-dimensional pictures with much brighter colors and translucent surfaces where needed. The oil dried very slowly, allowing the artist to apply new colors over the old and achieve new shades and depth that were not previously possible.[2] Jan van Eyck's *The Madonna with Canon van der Paele* (1436) is able to show exquisite detail not only in facial expressions, but in jewels embedded in the head attire, and to highlight the rich fabrics in robes, drapery, and carpets. Robert Campin's "Merode Altarpiece" displays a very rich, three-dimensional painting of Mary's annunciation, and the brilliance and multiple tones of the cloth are astounding.

Doubtless, the attention to the details of the fine textiles manufactured in the Flemish towns was fully appreciated by the new patrons of the arts: the wealthy merchant patricians. The new and expanded patronage of the arts constitutes the third characteristic of early Netherlandish painting. In

Jan Van Eyck, *Betrothal of the Arnolfini,* 1434.
© National Gallery, London/Art Resource, NY.

Campin's altarpiece, the triptych is devoted to the central scene of Mary's Annunciation, but the left panel depicts the merchant couple who commissioned the art. Unlike medieval art, which was commissioned by the Church, neither patron nor artist is present; the realism of art in the Low Countries placed the biblical scene in a contemporary setting, collapsing the temporal difference between the ancient story and the Renaissance time period. In essence, the event was so real that it was occurring "now," while the story and the characters were from the ancient world; they were painted in a contemporary Flemish setting with the attire of the day.

While a lot of art reflected religious subjects, it was wealthy merchants who often commissioned the art for use in monasteries, chapels, and churches, as well as for use in their homes, where they displayed their family portraits, and in their shops. Jan van Eyck's portrait of Giovanni Arnolfini and his wife is a good example of the new art. The painting was realistic, but also highly symbolic, with each detail representing signs of fidelity, honor, piety, and devotion. The convex mirror on the wall in the center of the painting depicts small scenes from the passion of the Christ, which are embedded in the frame and represent God's promise, while in the background, two figures can be seen; they are there to witness the wedding or engagement (depending upon the interpretation). Among the many other symbols, the small dog represents faithfulness and love; the oranges represent innocence; and the green dress on the woman represents hope. This focus on symbols represents the growing sense in the Low Countries that the spiritual world and God's design for the natural world were made manifest in the details of ordinary life, as depicted in the religious art of the Middle Ages, which created unrealistic scenes that pointed only to otherworldly concerns.

Many northern Flemish artists traveled to Rome to study and admire the artistic achievements of the famous southern artists. The Renaissance artists were most interested in capturing techniques and scenes from the ancient classical world, and stories and characters from Greek and Roman history became subjects for Italian art. A fourth characteristic of early Netherlandic art was the incorporation of these "Roman" elements into painting, which makes them classic Renaissance subjects with their own northern interpretation. Gerard David's painting of the *Judgment of Cambyses* in 1498 shows the story from Herodotus of the Persian King Cambyses, who ordered the wicked judge Sisamnes to be skinned alive for his crimes. While the story acts as a warning, the entire scene is framed by contemporary garb and scenery. Romanism, however, was not fully developed until another generation of artists arose in the 16th century, and even then, it became transformed as it was interpreted within the context of northern Europe and the Low Countries.

A final characteristic of early Netherlandish art was its connection with the social commentary strongly present in growing urban societies, where the *rederijkerskamers,* or chambers of rhetoric, actively monitored the community through drama and writing. The variety of crafts and skills in Renaissance Europe were already organized in guilds that regulated trade, quality, quantity, education, and membership; they also established their own showrooms to sell art. Typically, one became an apprentice for a period of three to five years and after a successful education, one became a journeyman, which allowed the young artist to work for any member of the guild. A successful journeyman could make a payment to the guild after a few years and become a full-fledged free master. The earliest art guilds included painters, sculptures, manuscript illuminators, and many other artists with a connection to embroidery. City and town governments often gave a guild exclusive control of the craft, and many of these guilds had connections with other guilds throughout the land. The patron saint of artists was St. Luke, who was said to have painted a portrait of the Virgin Mary, and thus, the Guilds of St. Luke began to form in the Flemish cities; many of them were also connected with the local chambers of rhetoric. Antwerp had one of the oldest guilds (mentioned as early as

1382) and it became one of the most important during the Renaissance. In Antwerp, the Guild of St. Luke was connected with the *Violieren* chamber, and in Haarlem, the guild was connected with the *Liefde boven al* ("love above all") chambers of rhetoric.

In a thriving urban economy, the artist reminded the public that the pursuit of wealth as a singular goal had many dangers, and that it was far more important to pay attention to family, friends, community, and one's religious commitments. The Hundred Years War, the Bubonic Plague, and numerous natural disasters could be seen as eternal warnings that needed to be heeded. This social commentary can be divided into three inter-related parts: warnings about the excesses of earthly wealth and power; the impartation of wisdom about how to proceed through life; and direct religious instruction. Quentin Matsys' *De goudweger en zijn vrouw* ("The Moneylender and His Wife," 1514) is a good example of a commentary on ordinary life, with warnings about deflecting one's attention away from the fundamental religious values toward the pursuit of wealth alone. The picture depicts a man counting his money with great concentration; his wife, who sits by his side, is distracted from the devotional book she is reading in glancing at the money, as well. Matsys' audience would recognize the many symbols that act as warnings: the snuffed-out candle represented original sin, whereas the carafe of water and the rosary hanging from the rear shelf represent purity. One must choose between the two, and perhaps the wrong choice has been made by the inclusion of the small wooden box, where their faith is believed to have retired.

Pieter Breugel the Elder offered the contemporary wisdom of the day in his painting *Nederlandse Spreekwoorden* ("Netherlandic Proverbs," 1559), something Erasmus had done in his *Collecteana Adagiorum,* which was published in Paris in 1500 (it contained around 800 proverbs). Traditional proverbs had been a common way to offer wisdom, and Breugel combined many of them in one mise en scene displaying almost 100 different physical acts or situations that clearly demonstrated the sayings. Most of the proverbs turn reason on its head, showing the absurdity of human desires and actions, which points to the other title of the painting, *The Topsy Turvy World,* shown, for example, in a phrase that is still common today that it is folly to "bang one's head against the wall." The second types have deeper moral lessons, even if they are lighthearted; for example, "Where the gate is open, the pigs will run into the corn" means that disaster ensues from carelessness, or "Horse droppings are not figs" means do not be fooled by appearances.

A third means to provide social commentary can be seen in Hieronymus Bosch's direct religious instruction, which can easily be seen in a great wheel paralleling the wheel of fortune. His painting of the *Seven Deadly Sins* (1480) displays a great circle with Christ in the center and God's all-watchful eye,

Pieter Brueghel, *Peasant Dancers,* 1568. Courtesy of Corel.

and in a pie-chart surrounding the center are lively examples of each sin; each scene is constructed from popular proverbs common to the times.

## MANNERISM AND THE REFORMATION

The 16th century brought many changes to the Netherlands in terms of political, social, and religious ideas, which became primary themes in art. The Renaissance movement had already undergone some major changes by the 16th century, and the next generation of scholars and artists reacted to the instability that war, disease, and the complexity of life had wrought over two centuries. The new style is known as "Mannerism" (a term that was not coined until the 19th century) to describe a new manner of depicting reality. These artists reacted to the earlier Renaissance emulation of the classical forms as naive, for life was neither balanced nor regular. Mannerist painting borrowed some earlier Netherlandic compositions, with their late Gothic style, and combined them with a fervent critique of contemporary life. They protested against the earlier Renaissance concentration on exterior beauty and form alone, and in their new Mannerist style, probed the interior and psychological aspects of humanity instead. By nature, they were more didactic in their goals. Craig Harbison has pointed to the "authority of the artist's pictorial purpose" to show how artists manipulated the scene to tell a story.[3] In order to draw attention to the interior life and to the vicissitudes of life, they clad their subjects in lavish costumes with imaginative colors, the figures were often elongated and in twisted poses, as in medieval art, and they were placed in dramatic settings to draw attention to symbols and devotional themes. Several examples demonstrate the Mannerist style. Hieronymus Bosch is difficult to interpret indeed, for he clearly went the furthest in highlighting the folly of humanity through grotesque and surrealistic scenes. His *Ecce Homo,* painted sometime in the years 1475–1480, reflects the words used by Pilate in the Latin Vulgate version of John 19:5: "Behold the man." Painted in a Flemish city setting, a Turkish flag symbolizes that the so-called enemies of Christ had control, and the fools surrounding Jesus are grotesque with evil symbols, the owl and giant toad, contained in the scene. Later, Matsys also offered a good example in his painting *Ecce Homo,* where he has highlighted the eyes as a window to the soul: Pilate turns his eyes away and Jesus lowers his gaze, while the old man to the left is an old fool with sarcastic eyes, and the madman to the right has eyes of violence and rage. These Mannerist figures surrounding Jesus are grotesque and pathetic, yet they appear unaware of the presence of Jesus, the Son of God.

Another example of the Mannerist style can be seen in Bosch's painting the *Ship of Fools* (c.1490–1500). A small boat contains a symbol of all humanity, including a nun and monk, all of whom are unaware of the foolish nature of their lives. They are eating, drinking, and making merriment, trying to reach for unattainable things. Bosch highlights their foolishness by turning their internal evil desires inside out, and we can see their external ugliness exposed. Cornelius Engelbrechtszoon's triptych *Crucifixion Altarpiece,* painted sometime in the years 1500–1525, is yet another example, and shows a thin, elongated Jesus surrounded by mourning disciples in a surrealistic landscape and locked into a Gothic framework.

A second major change in the 16th century was the challenge of the Protestant Reformation, and although it started as a protest against widespread abuses in the Church in general, art became one of the touchstones to express a variety of opinions about daily life, heaven, and hell. The first major impact of the Reformation on the visual arts began with the iconoclastic events of August 1566, when religious riots led to the wholesale destruction of Church property. Frans Hogenberg captured this moment in his print called *The Calvinist Iconoclastic Riot.* One can point to at least two different phenomena occurring simultaneously during the iconoclastic controversy. On the one hand, the art that filled the churches—the many stained-glass windows, and the statues of saints and Madonna and child—had come to represent the power of the Roman Catholic Church. Until the early

16th century, this power was indirect and mediated through the practical work in which the monastic orders were engaged. In an even more indirect way, several organizations emerged with quite specific goals, such as the Brethren of the Common Life, which connected the religious with laity in childhood education, printing devotional literature and acts of service, and the Beguine movement for the care of women. By and large, the Church hierarchy in the Low Countries worked extensively with the local religious leadership and respected a practical piety established in the Modern Devotion movement. The Inquisition became firmly established under King Philip II of Spain, who reorganized the Church in the Low Countries and imposed a stricter interpretation of Roman piety that was not in sync with the sensibilities of the local population. The wholesale destruction of many of the religious works of art by a hostile crowd must be seen in light of its symbolism of this imposition of authority, rather than as a direct aesthetic reaction.

On the other hand, a far more important phenomenon was occurring based on a change in religious imagination and view of the world. According to William Dyrness, "In place of previous practices, the reformers promoted an internalized faith that privileged the ear over the eye, but that nevertheless embodied structures that were in themselves visual."[4] The roots of this movement from eye to ear were already firmly established in the history of Christianity in what Dyrness calls a "tradition of suspicion" dating back to Plato, who saw images as illusory shadows. This tradition was largely accepted by Augustine. The iconoclastic controversy that rocked the early Eastern and Western Churches between the sixth and eight centuries, based on the Second Commandment (fear of idolatry), temporarily defined the limits of visual representations, but throughout the Middle Ages, the suspicion continued. The reintroduction of Augustinian monasteries, the aesthetic movement of Mannerism as a reaction to earlier Renaissance emulation of classicism, and the simple practical piety of the Low Countries certainly led to this controversy. One might also add that the Low Countries in particular developed a highly literate culture, and the printing and book trade led to a taste for the written word and criticism of older visual means of education (for example, the well-known adage that the stained-glass windows were books for the illiterate).

In the place of elaborate and highly decorated churches, the new Reformed churches were white washed, with clear or opaque windows, and the new technology of organ music became their signature. By the 17th century, Pieter Janzoon Saenredam had captured the serenity of these churches in his detailed paintings. The older cathedrals had been resacralized as Protestant churches, and where there had been a plethora of images, a more singular focus was brought both to the place where the word of God was preached (in Dutch, a *preekstoel,* or pulpit, has become a powerful symbol and is prominent in churches) and to the massive pipes of the organ that accompanied the responsive songs of praise. Before the Reformation, the laity did not sing in church; that was done exclusively by monks and nuns. The Reformed Church drew from the French popular tradition of singing Psalms, and gained further support from direct biblical injunctions, such as James 5:13, which prescribe singing songs of praise. Together with the original Genevan Psalter, the Dutch Reformed joined other churches, such as the Scottish Presbyterian Church, in constructing Psalters for use in the churches. Petrus Datheen produced a metrical Psalter in 1566 that became the new standard, but he also included the Decalogue, three canticles from the gospel of Luke, two versions of the Apostles' Creed, and five hymns of prayer already established in the Low Countries. While the Lutherans and Anabaptists included many hymns in worship, the Reformed limited themselves to the Psalter, although from region to region, some additional hymns were also included.

Another way the Reformation directly affected the arts was through new depictions of the struggle to persuade the laity to either accept the different Protestant churches or remain with the Roman Catholic Church. One of the most famous paintings showing this struggle is Adriaen van de Venne's "Fishing for Souls" (1614), no doubt a powerful symbol for a seagoing culture, as well as Jesus' statement that "I will make you fishers of men." Several boats are filled with either Roman Catholic priests or Protestant pastors, each rescuing as many sinking faithful as possible. The depiction clearly favors the Reformed, who attract people with the virtues of hope, faith, and charity inscribed in the Bible, whereas the Catholic boats are nearly sinking and only music and incense attempt to lure their captives. Yet, while the Reformed became more powerful, this painting acknowledged the pluralistic nature of new Dutch society, where persuasion, not power, was responsible for converts.

The Reformation was not merely a matter of theological or intellectual questions, but politics and questions of authority were at its center. When the seven northern provinces broke from Spain in 1579, they desperately needed to establish a new national identity, and the art that flourished after this time supplied pregnant images for the new republic. Artists were inspired to search for symbols and heroic deeds to forge a new identity. In 1565, Breugel painted a classic Renaissance scene of the infanticide of Herod the Great recorded in Matthew 2:16–18, yet it was understood to represent the present-day brutality and injustice of the Spanish overlords in the feared Inquisition, which had increased by 1561. This painting served to place their own struggle in a historical context, justifying their own cause for proper justice. The murder of William of Orange in 1584 almost eliminated the solidarity and organization the north had had and that was necessary to fight the Spanish, but his tomb in the Nieuwe Kerk in Delft, captured in several of Gerard Houckgeest's paintings, gave the Dutch the resolve they needed to endure until they were internationally recognized in 1648. One of the most important events that captured this sense of victory over a powerful opponent was the success of Leiden in resisting the Spanish siege of 1573–1574. Otto van Veen's painting of the *De Uitdeling van de Haring en Wittebrood na de Opheffing can het Beleg van Leiden* ("Distribution of Herring and White Bread during the Siege of Leiden") reminded the Dutch for years to come that they could overcome great adversity if they worked together.

## GOLDEN AGE ART AND PAINTING

The arts flourished in the 17th century as the Dutch Republic gained recognition as an independent state and as wealth grew rapidly.[5] The market for art was unprecedented, and while the quality greatly varied, almost all burghers could afford some type of art, especially the popular ink prints. In the seven northern provinces, new centers arose in the cities of Middelburg, Rotterdam, Delft, Gouda, The Hague, Leiden, Haarlem, Amsterdam, and Utrecht. Like the earlier Flemish centers, the guilds of St. Luke, often connected with local chamber of rhetoric, became the exclusive entry to the art market. The Golden Age is characterized as the Baroque period, and at its core, the goal was to present life as it could be in a simple yet dramatic appeal to the senses. It relied on a counterpoise between figures, creating tension and movement. The Roman Catholic Church relied on Baroque art to promote the Counter-Reformation, and the Flemish artist Peter Paul Rubens became well-known in Europe for his mixture of the style of the great Roman artists, such as Titian, with the naturalistic work of Caravaggio. He is the perfect example of Baroque religious art that gave an evocative rendition of biblical stories and reflected the didactic nature of Jesuit education. In the Netherlands, Utrecht became the home for the Dutch Caravaggists, such as Gerard van Honthorst and Hendrick ter Brugghen; the Italianate style, especially the dramatic use of light and dark (chiaroscuro), became firmly established.[6]

The most popular form of art in this Baroque era can be described under the general classification of genre painting. "Genre" is a French word for type or sort, and refers to scenes from daily life. The common term used in the Netherlands was *beeldeken,* meaning little painted figures, referring to numerous scenes with people performing their daily tasks like actors on a stage. The production of art in painting, sculpture, and architecture flourished with the new found wealth in the Golden Age of the Dutch Republic, just as the Republic of Florence had experienced in the 14th and 15th centuries.

We can identify a variety of painting types: landscape (*landschap*), city views (*stadgezicht*), history (*historiestuk*), portraits (*portret*), daily life (*genrestuk*), and still lifes (*stilleven*). In addition, many new techniques developed throughout the 17th century, such as great attention to fine detail (*fijnschilder*), the use of new brush strokes by Frans Hals, and the new "photographic" viewpoint of camera obscura. The Golden Age also produced some celebrated sculptors, such as Hendrik de Keyser and Artus Quellen. In general, Dutch art was asking the observer to take another look at nature and man-made objects to discover things they had not previously seen. In a society that had supported technological inventions, such as the new hydraulics and windmills of Leeghwater, the microscopes of van Leeuwenhoek, and the discovery of the rings of Saturn by Huygens, the message is that the world is not always as it appears. In many ways, the Golden Age may be seen as the science of art.

## Landscape

The term "landscape" is very common in the English language. It derives its concept from the original Dutch word *landschap,* which has a rich meaning, since *schap* had the same meaning as "ship" in English, as in craftsmanship. Literally, the land has been ordered in such a way that humans can utilize and enjoy its beauty to the fullest extent. Landscapes were measured with the eye, and controlled and cultivated to some extent in celebration of nature. Several artists with a variety of specialties emerged in landscape painting. The earlier landscapes of Bosch or Joachim Patenier envisioned a world of nature behind the main scene, which was largely unrealistic and fanciful, whereas Breugel had created much more realistic scenes. The new landscape painters of the Golden Age recorded nature in very fine detail, and often set the study of nature on par with humanity. Hendrick Avercamp specialized in winter scenes, and his vision of numerous skaters on frozen rivers and lakes depicts a society thriving in what has been called the "Little Ice Age" since the average temperature had dropped between the years 1550–1800. His paintings were active and colorful, showing people working, relaxing, playing a primitive form of golf, and displaying numerous personalities reminiscent of Breugel. Aelbert Cuyp was one of the most famous landscape painters, showing the cultivation of the Dutch countryside from the rising to the setting of the sun, displaying a rich diversity of light and shadow, boats on the water, and cattle in the fields. In gazing at Cuyp's landscapes, one experienced nature in an ideal setting, yet challenged the public to cultivate and enjoy nature for all that it offered. Jacob van Ruisdael, who had studied landscape painting with his father Isaak and his uncle Salomon, emerged as one of the greatest Dutch landscapists. He recorded the variety of trees with great precision, and his views of towns and villages placed them in the expanse of nature. He is noted for his great cloudscapes that were a regular feature of the Low Countries, forever blowing freely from inland coastal areas. Unlike later landscapists, Ruisdael had a very poetic sense of nature, rather than a scientific sense, and one of his most famous pictures was the *Castle of Bentheim in Lower Saxony* (1645), creating a romantic vision of the castle in harmony with nature.

### City Views

Other painters turned their attention to urban landscapes, architecture, and city views (*stadsgezicht*). This demonstrated art for the citizens (*burgerlich*) of the Republic; rather than private castles, the city views show public life. Pieter Janzoon Saenredam's interiors of the great churches of the Netherlands highlighted the resacralized places of worship in their serenity and simplicity, whitewashed after the changes in the Reformation, yet filled with new sound from dominating pipe organs. Gerard Houckgeest was also an innovator from Delft whose more diagonal perspectives created far more dramatic scenes of the interior of churches. But the more common views of the urban landscape were topographical views of cities and towns from a far. The most famous city view is *The View of Delft* by Johannes Vermeer (1659–60). Vermeer has used a particular perspective to interpret the actual city of Delft in a way that both simplifies its skyline and highlights certain buildings and towers to tell a story, and to show great pride in the achievements of Delft. The city is protected by its walls, but allows great commerce and trade through its gates and river. The central tower, painted with a golden hue and glow, highlights the Nieuwe Kerk, making it appear much larger and prominent than it actually was. The city is backlit with light to give depth to the painting and to show the power of the community within the walls. The sky is filled with clouds, both heavy dark rain clouds and billowy white ones. Vermeer was part of the Delft School of painting, and Delft was the city where he spent his entire life. The great achievement in technique came from new optical effects, often associated with the camera obscura, that measured the scene in a new way through a pin hole in a box; the reflected light could be focused on a white background to produce a new effect of perspective, which was no doubt influenced by the work of the Dutch microscopist van Leeuwenhoek, who resided in Delft and sometimes worked for the city council. The Delft School was known for its city views, church interiors, and domestic and daily life depictions, and it reflected the popular image of Delft as one of the cleanest places in the Netherlands.

### Historical Themes

Since the Renaissance era, history has played a key role in the development of new states and churches. The proper recounting of history legitimized

Johannes Vermeer, *View of Delft.* Courtesy of Corel.

the place of the new state or church in time and in terms of God's perceived purposes for history. Protestants were especially cognizant of the need to use the historical method to show that Rome had indeed erred, and that reformers had recovered the original sources (*ad fontes*) through their use of the new humanistic methods. By the 17th century, the polemical nature of the theological debate had subsided and a deeper interest in the lessons to be learned from biblical stories gripped the public. Historical paintings (*historiestuk*) had three basic themes: biblical (or the history of ancient Israel); the history of the Low Countries; and the history of the classical world. These stories stood as reminders to the religious and civic community, and to family and friends, to remain faithful to God.

One cannot say too much about the work of Rembrandt Harmenszoon van Rijn. He is one of the most important European artists in history, and is well known for his historical paintings, portraits, and etchings.[7] One of the few artists known primarily by his first name alone, Rembrandt was born in Leiden, near the old Rhine River (hence his family name), but made and lost his fortune in Amsterdam. By the time he died, he had completed about 300 paintings, almost 300 etchings, and more than 2,000 sketches. His historical art was drawn from the Old and New Testaments, from the classical world, and from the history of the Low Countries.

Living near the Jewish section of Amsterdam, he often used his neighbors as models to reconstruct scenes from the Old Testament, rendering a realistic historical record of an important event. One of Rembrandt's powerful depictions is the classic story of Abraham and Isaac in his *The Sacrifice of Abraham* (1635); as in the work of Brunelleschi (1401) and Caravaggio (1601), the power of human actions is present, with the angel needing to restrain the hand of Abraham, who was filled with conviction and faith. In the same year, Rembrandt painted a careful study of his Jewish neighbors in the excitement-filled scene of *Belshazzar's Feast,* where Belshazzar is utterly surprised by the hand of God writing on the wall. These paintings demonstrate the necessity of faith and serve as a warning about turning against God, a poignant message in the midst of the great wealth of the Golden Age. This also shows that the new Republic identified God's covenant with Israel as it now pertained to them: they were God's chosen people, and they had been given a new land.

But if the warning about turning away from God was overwhelming, Rembrandt's painting of "The Return of the Prodigal Son" (1669) inspired hope. In this painting, we can see the how he developed a very rich lighting known as chiaroscuro, borrowed from Carravaggio, in which the significant aspects of the pictures are highlighted in soft tones of ochre, olive green, and even red, with a dark background that frames the scene. He also expressed deep emotions in his paintings, especially the many faces he found to relay different moods and characters. But the use of chiaroscuro did not require paint, for Rembrandt also became a master at etching, and in his famous *Hundred Guilder Print,* which he worked to improve throughout the 1640s, he developed the technique of hatching (small lines) to create dark areas; his *Three Crosses* (1653) is considered one of the most dramatic depictions of Christ on the cross at Golgotha.

Rembrandt also painted classical historical pictures, such as *Aristotle with a Bust of Homer* (1635) for a wealthy Sicilian, Don Antonio Ruffo. In his characteristic manner, he used models from his Jewish neighborhood to capture the look of Aristotle and his portrayal of Homer resembles several Hellenistic busts he had in his possession; in the painting, Rembrandt has captured the great philosopher in deep thought. Finally, Rembrandt reflected on his own national history, capturing the moment when the brave Celts stood up to the colonizing Romans in 69 AD in the painting *De Samenzwering van Claudius Civilis* ("The Conspiracy of Claudius Civilis," 1661), which was intended for the new building for the City Council of Amsterdam. However, it never hung in the gallery since the members could not accept his portrayal of the barbarians, as they expected something far more majestic; instead they found uncontrollable, primitive liberty. Unfortunately, the surviving copy has been severely trimmed to its bare minimum, but it still carries a powerful message about the tenacity of the northern tribes. Likewise, Otto van Veen had

Rembrandt, in *The Return of the Prodigal Son* (c.1669), shows the father's sympathy for the delinquent son and demonstrates mercy, which underlined a vibrant sense of community. Courtesy of Corel.

depicted a similar theme in his 1613 work *De Bataven Verstaan de Romeinen bij de Rijn* ("The Batavians Defeating the Romans on the Rhine"), underlining the long and tenacious history of the Dutch, which served to legitimate the Netherlands' own sovereignty as a nation.

## Portraits

Dutch artists in the Golden Age experimented with paint, techniques, and various poses and costumes in their quest to understand human emotions and character. There was a fine distinction between a *tronie* (a Dutch translation of the French word *trogne,* which means an expressive facial shot) that was an experimental portrait, highlighting a particular facial type or foreign clothing, and a true portrait that was meant to be a realistic copy of a particular individual who commissioned the art. Portraits gave the sitter a personal identity, recording important moments and demonstrating qualities befitting their social status.

Rembrandt was immensely popular for his many portraits and *tronies,* and this popularity brought in the commissions that were necessary for him to continue his lavish lifestyle in his middle years. One of his most well-known paintings is the *Nachtwacht* ("Nightwatch," 1642), although its real title is "The Company of Frans Banning Cocq and Willem van Ruytenburch," which was commissioned for the Amsterdam "Kloveniersdoelen," a civic militia company. In the center of this very large painting, Cocq is dressed in black, with a red sash, and Ruytenburch is dressed in yellow. In addition to these central figures, which are surrounded by many men whose individual character is captured in their poses, a small young girl, also in yellow, has a chicken tied to her belt, and this symbolizes the militia's name since the prominent claws are a pun in Dutch for "Kloveniers" (*klauw* in Dutch). This painting is famous for its movement, and this is achieved through an impressive use of chiaroscuro, which creates an action-packed procession. Rembrandt's many other portraits are unique for their realism, their ability to capture the uniqueness of each individual, and for the artist's techniques, especially his shadowing on faces, where the eyes are sometimes not visible, so that one has to read the lips instead.

The other great innovator in portraits was Frans Hals, who lived and worked in Haarlem and who was embarking on new techniques in portraiture 25 years before Rembrandt. His *Banket van de Officieren van de St. Joris-doelen* or *Banquet of the Officers of the St. George Civic Guard* (1616), the first monumental civic guard painting, shows the officers ordered according to rank, but each is a full character sketched in a casual pose of his own. The painting represents the Dutch Baroque style of the 17th century, which demonstrates pride in achievement and protection of the Republic. Hals drew on the rich tradition of Dutch painting, filling portraits with numerous symbols. In 1622, he painted the *Married Couple in a Garden,* and he placed them in a very natural and casual pose; the entwining ivy and the women's hand on the man's shoulder show permanence in marriage, whereas the thistle near the man reminds us of the cursed ground in Genesis 3, where work becomes a necessary struggle to maintain life, but in the Republic, a strong work ethic had become preeminent. Baroque sought to capture human emotions in all their manifestations, from sadness to joy, and Hals' *tronie* paintings are masterful studies. The greatest technique of Hals can be seen in his 1615 painting of the *De Vrolijke Drinker* ("The Merry Drinker," c. 1628–30), where his short brushwork makes the paint flicker and dance, lending movement to the piece. In *Malle Babbe* (1633–35), an old woman with a scowl on her face shows great emotion in an instance of having drunk too much.

Perhaps the most intriguing set of eyes, after the famous *Mona Lisa* by Leonardo da Vinci, are those of the girl in *Het Meisje Met de Parel* ("Girl With a Pearl Earring," 1665) by Jan Vermeer. He seems to apply the same technique of using a very dark background to create a three-dimensional effect. The unnamed girl is full of mystery as her head turns away from some other activity, and she appears to be looking at the viewer rather than merely at the subject. Her eyes and the pearl earring are painted with exquisite depth of color, and her gaze is fresh, pure, and even sensuous. Vermeer painted many other women, such as *Het Melkmeisje* ("The Milkmaid,"1658), which displayed a careful study of light and color with new pigments, and showed the strength and dignity of ordinary work in the home.

### Daily Life

While historical pictures taught lessons from the past, art that studied contemporary Dutch society taught social and moral lessons necessary for successful citizenship and life. Jan Steen is a good example of how an artist could offer moral lessons through humor, which is certainly far more amenable than other, harsher means. He warned of the ill effects of an unruly household, and too much alcohol, idleness, and sexuality; indeed, it became commonplace in the Netherlands to refer to a dysfunctional family as a "Jan Steen household" (*een Huishouden van Jan Steen*). A good example of this is seen in *Soo d'oude Songen, Soo Pypen de Jonge* ("The Way you Hear it is the Way you Sing it," also known as "As the Old Sing, So Twitter the Young," c. 1665) in which the elders in the household have all had too much to drink, while chaos abounds and parental abandon is obvious. The point is underlined that children will learn these bad habits from their parents. Steen also used humor to uncover real human motives and feeling, and his painting *De Kwakzalver* ("The Quack," c. 1650–1659) was one of many studies of the real motives of quack doctors and patients. In the painting *Het Dokterbezoek* ("The Doctor's Visit," c. 1658–1662), it is clear that the younger doctor is far more interested in the young lady he is treating than her illness, and one suspects that her illness is really romantic love-sickness rather than medical, although to the medical community of the time, a disequilibrium of the four humors caused melancholy and the cure was marriage.[8] Steen also painted scenes depicting exemplary behavior, such as several paintings titled *Grace Before Meat*.

One of the characteristic elements of genre painting was to show how the private is connected to the public and how what is done in secret will eventually be revealed. Painters constructed their interior scenes using *doorzicht* or *doorkijk* (literally to see through) techniques; that is, they crafted interior paintings featuring open doors, windows, and reflections of the outside world. The purpose was often to make the point that all citizens must care for the moral community, and that the strength of the Republic was dependent on order and hard work. Pieter de Hooch is one of the best genre painters to use this technique. He was an astute observer of ordinary life, recorded the smallest details, and used light very well, like Vermeer. He did many scenes of inside courtyards, with doors and passages open where the street is visible, such as in *Een Gezelschap op de Plaats Achter een Huis* ("A Company in the Courtyard

Behind a House," c. 1663–1665). Unlike Steen, all of Hooch's images are positive renditions of proper bourgeois social relationships, as demonstrated in his *Kaartspelers* ("Card Players," 1658), which shows a very civil card game in progress between several men and a woman; the sun streams through the window, and through the open door, another woman appears to be headed for the same room, with all of the figures evoking a quiet domestic contentment. One of his more private scenes is *Binnenhuis met Vrouwen bij een Linnenkast* ("Inside the House with Women by a Linen Closet," 1665) showing the matron and maid carefully stacking fresh linens in a cabinet (*kast*), and a little girl playing with her *kolf* stick (like hockey or golf) and small ball. Some have interpreted this as a deep moral lesson whereby Godliness and cleanliness go hand in hand, and where the role of the mother as protector of the household was a necessary part of life in cities that sent many men away as sailors and merchants for long periods of time.

While many of the artists of the Baroque age developed similar techniques in the use of light and color, some artists have been particularly renowned for their very detailed brush work, which lends almost a photographic appeal to their work. They constructed portraits of daily life and still lifes using these techniques, and their brush work came to be known as *fijnschilder,* literally fine painting. Gerrit Dou's *Lezende Oude Vrouw* ("Old Woman Reading a Bible," 1660) is one of the best examples of how soft the brush strokes could become, as he captures the fine fur on her shoulders and head, her soft yet aging skin, and the Bible opened to St. Luke's Gospel, which offers great hope for eternal rest. Likewise, *De Arts* ("The Physican," 1653) seems so real; viewed from the outside, one can see the doctor looking at his glass beeker, and the brass bowl, vase, and open book of anatomy are lined up at the window, with a curtain pulled to one side—all tricks to create multi-dimensionality. Gabriel Metsu must also be mentioned as a *fijnschilder* who used his highly refined techniques to capture human emotions, and displayed the use of light and dark he had learned from Rembrandt. His *Het Zieke Kind* ("Sick Child," 1660) is a very touching moment when the child has lost all energy, yet sits restfully in her mother's arms, and one can see the incredibly fine brush strokes and colors that allow one to glimpse the child's illness through the skin tones. Metsu painted a pair of pictures called *Briefschrijvende Jongeman bij Geopend Venster* ("Young Man Writing a Letter by a Window," c. 1662–1665) and *Brief Lezende Vrouw* ("Woman Reading a Letter," c. 1662–65) with a masterful display of silvery light that display two wealthy burghers in love.

### Still Life

Similar to the *tronie* studies of human faces, some Dutch artists turned to the study of the objects that are sold in the market, including food and game, dinnerware, elaborate tables, linens, musical instruments, tobacco, and writing utensils. Although the exact meaning of many still life paintings are disputed, in general, they represent a new republican society conversing about the meaning of life and the objects that surround them, made possible by new-found wealth. The English words "still life" come directly from the Dutch characterization of these paintings as *stilleven,* which refers to their inanimate state, for they represent but a moment of time, yet serve as a constant reminder that time will change the very things that one is viewing. While many enjoyed the virtuosity and incredible detail of these works, they often had a didactic and moral message. Still life depictions go beyond the real, and in their hyper-realism, force the viewer to decide what is deceptive about what they perceive about the world, and what is, in fact, reality.[9]

One of the most common still life depictions is the *banketjes* (little banquets), also called *ontbijt* (breakfast), which is a display of common foods that were eaten during the day that are normally set out in great splendor. Willem Claesz. Heda painted some of the most memorable *banketjes,* such as *Ontbijt met Krab* ("Breakfast with Crabs," 1648), which displays a wonderfully laid out table, suggesting the end of a meal, with crabs in the shell, shiny silver goblets, a lemon with the peel hanging off the table, and a left-over bun. In this case, Heda chose a rather rough brush stroke, yet still managed to capture the delicate shine in the silver objects. Floris Claesz van Dijck painted classic small Dutch meals, shown in his *Stilleven* (1613), which depicts a finely embroidered table cloth with several wheels of cheese, grapes, nuts, apples, olives, and bread.

Another type of still life, known as *pronk,* meaning a "rich display," featured expensive objects not readily available in the Netherlands, such as Chinese porcelain, Venetian glass, figs and prunes, all of which point to a delicate abundance bordering on ostentation. Jan Davidsz de Heem produced by far the most lavish *pronk* still lifes, which especially appealed to the Flemish Baroque imagination. His *Pronkstilleven* (1650) features a richly displayed table with lemons and oranges, cooked ham, exquisite and ornate goblets that reflect their surroundings, and a recorder and music on the table, all in a classical Mediterranean setting, including a parrot. Heem also produced many paintings of flower arrangements, another specialty within still lifes, and this displayed both an interest in the collection and aesthetic enjoyment of flowers, as well as the botanical interest in discovering new types. It is well known that during the 17th century, the tulip, originally imported from Turkey, became a very thriving business and was soon the symbol of Dutch enterprise.

Another interesting development was combining the skills of still lifes with the perspectives of house interiors and camera obscura in the creation of "peep shows." Samuel van Hoogstraten painted a very interesting view of a house interior, with the illusion of a three-dimensional space in his *Kijk-dozen* ("Box With Peep Show," 1663) in which he painted certain objects on the bottom horizontal plane and continued to paint them on the side vertical plane, changing the correct angles to fool the eye. He also worked at this *Tromp l'oeil* (French, meaning to deceive the eye) in his still life paintings, such as *Tromp-l'oeil Stilleven* (1664), which shows scissors, pearls, bows, and pen and paper pinned to a board. What is striking is that there is absolutely no natural depth to the painting, yet the eye views the objects as having volume.

Still life paintings reflected reality, but warned of how quickly the "shelf life" of objects might vanish, a concept that was easily conveyed with food and flowers, but suggested as well for human life. The word *vanitas* was used to point to the vanity of specific human endeavors when compared with life in general. Pieter Claesz' "Vanitas Stilleven" (1630) is an example of a painting that has all the elements of the shortness of life; the candle has gone out, the pocket watch is opened, the goblet is turned over, and a human skull sits on top of pages that contain the last of the writing. In some ways, still life *vanitas* paintings signal the end of the Baroque goal to heighten reality in its extravagance. A new consciousness of the inability to separate vision and perception from the reality of nature has dawned on this science of art.

By the 18th century, many artists had turned away from the Baroque style, and instead came under the influence of the Rococo style (the word combines the French *rocaille,* decorative rockwork, and *coquillage,* shell-fish) that had transformed the art and architecture of France. The Enlightenment brought a new skepticism about previous ideas of nature and reality, and the new art reflected this vision of capturing nature in art. It also turned toward worldly enjoyment, rather than toward heroes and pious martyrs. Although Rococo art continued some of the ornamentation of Baroque art, it used muted colors and more whimsical lines. Unlike the fame of numerous Dutch Baroque painters, no 18th-century painters in the Netherlands achieved much fame beyond their borders. Cornelius Troost is sometimes called the Dutch Hogarth, his English contemporary, for his depictions of the wantonness of drunkenness, yet he did not moralize in his art like Hogarth, but used satire as an indirect way to make a point. His *Rumor Erat in Casa* ("There was a Commotion in the House," 1740) shows what happens at a reunion of gentlemen who end up drinking too much. This type of art was often called a conversation piece. Rachel Ruysch continued the still life tradition of painting flowers, but often placed them in more natural settings, such as in her *Flowers on a Tree Trunk.* Present in the painting with flowers are rocks, insects, snakes, and toads, all competing for their share of the flowers. One can also interpret this painting symbolically; the butterfly over the lily represents the Holy Spirit coming to

Mary, the lily, whereas the insects are interpreted in a negative manner. Jan van Huysum was another well-known floral painter, and like Ruysch, his flowers are placed in a very natural setting, displaying more subdued colors, such as in his *Fruit and Flowers* (1720). The 18th century also turned once again to classicism, and Gerard de Lairesse became an important painter in Amsterdam with a new opulence that followed the classical French style. He found many commissions for the wealthy Amsterdam merchants and new government buildings. In addition, his work as an art critic influenced a host of artists in the 18th century.[10]

## 19TH-CENTURY ART AND PAINTING

The new Kingdom of the Netherlands needed artists to record and display its new identity, and the Romantic Movement was the predominant style of the day in the early 19th century. Jan Willem Pieneman was trained in the Romantic style, and his painting *The Triumvirate Assuming Power on behalf of the Prince of Orange, 21 November 1813* in 1828 recalled the historic moment when the house of Orange-Nassau was raised to monarchy. Romanticism was a reaction to the classical ideal of order and harmony, and given the recent experiences of the great changes wrought by the French Revolution, artists and poets welcomed deeper emotions that so-called Rationalism could neither probe nor understand. The view of nature had also changed from a mechanistic understanding to a new appreciation for unbridled power, mystery, and awe.

A search for the real people (*volk*) and their elevation to the essence of the nation became the focus of many Romantic artists. Andreas Schelfhout was a student of the 17th-century landscape artists, and Romanticism allowed him to resurrect an interest in the Dutch countryside, which went hand-in-hand with the sense of the recovery of old Holland after the French occupation. His "Passage of Winter by a Windmill" (1835) showed ordinary people by several old windmills going about their daily tasks. Another example is his painting *The Palace at Het Loo* (1838), which was the summer royal residence near Apeldoorn, and in addition to its Baroque architecture, designed by André Le Nôtre, it boasted a large garden, reminiscent of Versailles. The painting by Schelfhout downplayed the extravagance and cast the residence in a more natural setting. Adrianus Eversen, another Romantic artist, concentrated on daily life in Dutch cities and towns. His paintings showed ordinary houses, many of which were in need of repair, and also cluttered places of business: men pushing heavy loads, women cleaning, and dogs barking. These views depicted an honest day's work in a community setting.

By the mid-19th century, many artists were greatly influenced by the new Romantic developments in France, especially the so-called Barbizon School. During the Revolutions of 1848, artists congregated at Barbizon to follow John Constable's ideas, and artists such as Jean-François Millet concentrated on nature, and on peasants who worked and lived close to nature. In the Netherlands, a school copying the Barbizon style developed in The Hague; it used pastel and subdued colors, which some interpreted as washed out, giving it the reputation as the "Gray School." Willem Roelofs was one of the founders of the new school, and he popularized rural scenes of the Netherlands with an attention to the details of nature, including plants, insects, and larger animals. His interests also turned to the scientific study of beetles. Many of his paintings in oil and watercolor depict cows drinking and eating by rivers, or sunsets or cloudy skies over cities and towns. They display a peaceful setting, and life in harmony with nature. Roelofs trained Willem Mesdag, who went on to produce many nautical scenes. A commission by the Belgian company to paint a very large scene of the coast of The Hague led to the specialty of panorama paintings, yet the vogue for such enormous works came to an end by the late 19th century. In this way, The Hague school continued the general trend of Realism, although this term was not coined until 1855 by the French painter Gustave Courbet.

The Hague School had led to new innovations, as artists worked to describe the experience of ordinary people in their daily lives. The youngest artists followed trends in France, and found that the new Impressionism fit their needs. The new style had been coined from Monet's painting "Impression, Sunrise," and while Romanticism had furnished basic goals, Impressionists used bold, solid, color over lines, and they painted in short, visible brush strokes, capturing the play of light. They were also unconventional since they believed that one must paint out of doors, or *en plein air*. Amsterdam became the center of Dutch Impressionism, and George Hendrik Breitner began to offer city views that captured the movement of daily life. His "A View of the Dam Square in Amsterdam" is a good example of the impression he had of the thriving city, and one can see the continuation of The Hague School's gray colors, while at the same time, the new play of light. With the photography advances that had transpired by the 1880s, Breitner began to explore the connections between painting and photography, and he traveled throughout Europe and the United States, developing his style.

Isaac Israëls, the son of the famous Hague School artist Jozef Israëls, was a collaborator with Breitner in developing Impressionism in Amsterdam. Their interest in capturing ordinary life was enhanced by their close connection to the *Tachtiger* (Movement of the Eighties) writers, who sought to understand individual emotions. Isaac Israëls' "Donkey Ride on the Beach" (1898–1900)

Vincent Van Gogh, *Starry Night*. Courtesy of Corel.

shows three girls riding on donkeys, and captures their individual experiences as they ride in tandem on the beach. In the same way that Romanticism led to The Hague School and Impressionism, by the end of the 19th century, artists like Jan Toorop progressed through these styles until he began to work with Post-Impressionism, even connecting with Symbolism and Art Nouveau. In 1905, Toorop converted to Catholicism and had yet another career: producing religious art.

Next to Rembrandt, Vincent van Gogh has achieved equal international recognition for the quality of his art. At a young age, he worked for a French art dealer where his older brother Theo had a position, but his religious interests turned his attention to evangelizing and working with the poor miners in Borinage, Belgium (1879–80). Van Gogh was deeply affected by the tradition of Dutch piety in Thomas á Kempis' *Imitation of Christ* and in Erasmus, and despite the new techniques he learned from the contemporary French artists, he remained quintessentially Dutch in his vision of the world. This experience of living with the miners remained with him throughout his life, and he identified with their lives and families; his later depictions of peasant scenes continued to comprise an important theme throughout his life. After a few years of studying art, in 1885, he produced *De Aardappeleters* ("The Potato Eaters"), which was not readily received by his brother and other art critics, but was recognized much later as an important work.

Reminiscent of Jozef Israel's dark scenes of peasant life, such as "All Alone in the World" (1878), the *Potato Eaters* captures hard and simple lives with coarse and ugly faces. Van Gogh achieved his goal of showing movement in the painting, and the peasants display an honesty and deep spirituality as they gather around the oil lamp to eat the potatoes they have painstakingly gathered. The main theme in most of his paintings was, in the words of Kathleen Powers Erikson, the " . . . expression of the infinite in the mundane. . . ."[11]

Van Gogh greatly admired Rembrandt's use of chiaroscuro to capture the play of light, and his early paintings attempted to copy this style. His early paintings reflect the darker monochrome of the Dutch school. In 1886, Van Gogh went to Paris, where his brother Theo managed an art gallery; there, he was heavily influenced by Impressionism and Post-Impressionism. He met Claude Monet, Edgar Degas, Camille Pissarro, Henri Toulouse-Lautrec, and Paul Signac. He was most influenced by Paul Gauguin, who showed him paintings he had done in Martinique, and this sparked Van Gogh's interest in several sunflower studies. He also experimented with the new Pointillist style, clearly seen in several self portraits in 1887. The real breakthrough that would determine his mature, Post-Impressionist style began when he moved to Arles in the south of France in 1888.[12] In total, he produced approximately 2,000 works (900 paintings and 1,100 drawings), with most done in the last two years of his life.

## 20TH-CENTURY ART AND PAINTING

Developments in the art world of France continued to influence Dutch artists. Luminism was a movement that devoted great attention to the effects of light, and can be seen in the early works of Piet Mondrian and Jan Sluijters. The journal *De Stijl* (*The Style*), published by critic and painter Theo van Doesburg, supported a new Dutch "neoplasticism" (*Nieuwe Beelding*), and gave its name to the new school where Piet Mondrian emerged as its most famous representative.[13] Several characteristics of the movement were the use of only three primary colors—red, yellow, and blue—and three primary values—black, white, and grey. The works avoided any symmetry and used opposition to achieve balance, with crossing vertical and horizontal lines; this came out of the early 20th-century Cubist movement that searched for ideal geometric and spiritual forms promoted by the Theosophical movement. Although his earlier works were Impressionist landscapes, Mondrian experimented with these elements in many non-representational, minimalist works (1919–1944) incorporating the name "composition" in the titles of his works, and these grid-based works had white backgrounds with black vertical and horizontal lines, as well as small patches of blue, yellow, or red.

Jan Sluijters experimented with different approaches to Post-Impressionism, and developed a clear Expressionist style. This style distorts reality in order to achieve a subjective, emotional effect, reminiscent of the older Mannerist style, which challenged former rules of painting and graphics (first raised by Friedrich Nietzsche). Sluijters painted the *Staphorster Family* in 1915, which shows a flare of colors over a dark brown and olive background, serving to demonstrate his interpretation of how their very conservative and religious villagers (likened to an Amish village) conducted their lives. On the other hand, he painted many female nudes, and his voluptuous figures caused a great commotion in the art world. His *Two Women Embracing* (1905), which he painted while in Paris, cost him the bursary of the prestigious Prix de Rome prize he had won earlier to study there.

Several young artists in Groningen reacted to what they felt were the very strict rules of painting and in 1918, formed a society called "De Ploeg," meaning the plow. Although anyone could join and use various techniques, the strength of this group in the twenties was the development of an Expressionist school, which had roots in Van Gogh, yet focused on the region of Groningen. They key members were Jan Altink (who named the society), Jan Wiegers, Johan Dijkstra, and George Mertens; soon, many of its members moved toward an Impressionist art and were later joined by Nicolaas Werkman, Jan Jordens, Jan van der Zee, and Job Hansen.

Although it never became a prominent school, several Dutch painters found their style in the French Surrealist School of painting. Willem Wagenaar became acquainted with the French movement and attracted many artists to his store in Utrecht, which became the center of Dutch Surrealism, and soon, Jopie Moesman, Louis Wijmans and Willem Van Leusden had developed their art in a Surrealist direction. In a slightly different direction, Albert Carel Willink called his new Surrealist style "imaginary realism," which adhered to the metaphysical paintings of the Italian artist Girogio de Chirico. Today, several artists, such as Rik Lina and Willem den Broeder, have continued the Surrealist tradition.

After World War II, Piet Ouberg influenced a younger generation of artists with his colorful abstract composition. In 1948, a new group of artists in Amsterdam began to follow the new trends of American Abstract Expressionism, characteristic of Jackson Pollock and known as the Experimental Group, which included Constant and Jan Nieuwenhuys, Corneille, Karel Appel, Theo Wolvecamp, Anton Rooskens, and Eugene Brands. By 1949, they joined a wider group called "CoBrA" after the collection of artists and poets from Copenhagen, Brussels, and Amsterdam, who collaborated on various projects. This diverse group of painters reacted to all of the rules and conventions of the art academies in Europe, and experiments with forms, colors, and medium; they incorporated animals and imaginary creatures as part of mythological art. They also had political motives that generally followed Marxist ideology, and envisioned art for everyone. Their ideas for art included traditional compositions on canvas, as well as sculpture, and they began to include architecture or any household object in their path. They began a journal called *CoBrA,* as well, and theorized about the place of art in society. The Amsterdam Stedelijk Museum featured their first international exhibition in 1949, and when the journal wrote about this show, the cover displayed a large tongue sticking out of a mouth, which no doubt represented their response to traditional bourgeois society.

Under the CoBrA umbrella, Constant Nieuwenhuys developed a new movement called "Unitary Urbanism" that rejected the functional value of urban architecture and the detachment of art from daily life. In the years 1956–1974, he developed a visionary new utopian city with his series of paintings called "New Babylon," where people are able to constantly interact with their environment and drift through a labyrinthine network. In this way, he contributed to the Situationist International activist group of architects, artists, and political anarchists. In 1949, Karel Appel created a work of art called "Questioning Children" that was comprised of old pieces of wood nailed onto an old window shutter, and he covered this with bright colors representing several children. The composition is typical of how young children might construct a picture, but the overall message is a deep social critique. The picture was to hang in the Amsterdam Town Hall, but it was covered up for ten years since the public was not yet ready to reconsider the events of World War II. Anton Rooskens is also a good example of the experimental art of CoBrA. His paintings reflected the simple, clean lines of folk art, and he traveled to Asia, where he found new styles to incorporate into his work. He was one of the only artists in the group that had a permanent job teaching art, and he used the classrooms and school building to paint large murals with fantastic colors and shapes. Cornelis van Beverloo, known as Corneille, has created imaginative works and been influenced by African art. Many of his paintings incorporate either birds or women into a composition with bold colors and heavy black lines. He has also collaborated with artists in Israel, and has worked with galleries there.

Several Dutch illustrators and graphic designers have made a huge impact on 20th-century Dutch culture. In the early part of the century, Dutch graphic artists began to make a name for themselves outside the Netherlands. One of the most clever and world famous artists was Maurits Cornelis Escher, who created impossible pictures of his own creation that, while mathematically correct, played directly on the problems of perception and were reminiscent of the earlier Dutch Still Life tradition. Typical of his work was the construction of a set of stairs that appeared to be descending and ascending at the same time, and he titled a picture using this technique "Ascending and Descending" in 1960. Many other pictures explored the manner in which one form is transformed into another form, and he used a unique tiling effect, also known as tessellations, to subtlety change black birds into white birds, birds into fish, angels into devils, and many other transformations.

The most significant typographic designer was Sjoerd Henry Roos, who grew up with strong Social-Democratic beliefs; he turned his artistic talents to industrial design and applied arts in order to create better consumer goods, such as furniture, containers for goods, etc. He was influenced by F.D. Morris in England, and in 1903, wrote a book, *Art and Society,* with many of Morris' essays included in the book. He is also well known for creating several new type-faces, such as the "Holland Medieval."

Dick Bruna is one of the most well-known children's book illustrators in the Netherlands, with over 200 books, many of which were translated into more than 40 languages. His style is very simple, with bold, primary colors and black lines, and was not unlike the palette of Mondrian, although Bruna's depictions created a number of animal characters. Miffy, the English name for a small rabbit named Nijntje (a play on the Dutch word for rabbit, *konijn*), has become a recognized trademark of his art; there are shops in nearly all the major cities of the Netherland that highlight this character. Other characters include Boris and Barbara the bears, Poppy the pig, Snuffy

*Day and Night* by M.C. Escher. M.C. Escher's *Day and Night* © 2009. The M.C. Escher Company-Holland. All rights reserved. www.mcescher.com.

the dog, Hettie the Hedgehog, and farmer John. In addition, Bruna has illustrated more than 2,000 book covers for his family's publishing company, A.W. Bruna & Zoon, which publishes many Dutch and translated works through their "Zwarte Beertjes" (little black bears) series (in many ways, they are the Netherlands' equivalent to the English-language Penguin paperback publisher).

Rien Poortvliet carved out a type of literature of his own with fascinating illustrations. As a painter and draftsman, he is most famous for his collaboration with Wil Huygen in the creation of the fantasy world of *The Gnomes* and *The Secret Book of Gnomes* (*Leven en Werken van de Kabouter*). Poortvliet loved nature and animals, and he made them very popular through his detailed descriptions of every aspect of their lives. Other books explored the lives of animals in nature, domesticated dogs, farm animals, and nature itself. He was particularly known for explaining daily life through his illustrations of how farm equipment works, how woman dress in many layers of traditional costumes, or how to care for pigs. He was a master at capturing the character of humans and animals in their many different moods, emotions, and duties. Most of his books were first published in Dutch by van Holkema & Warendorf of Weesp in the Netherlands, and later found a wider audience after being translated and published in New York by Harry Abrams.

Jan Dibbets is a good example of recent trends in Conceptual Art in the Netherlands. He uses the medium of photography to force a new perspective by creating a "destablized gaze" by placing rope or string into certain shapes located on the viewing plane, but the position of the shapes placed into nature or architecture forces the eye to doubt its correct vision. Dibbets received international attention in 1994 for his monument in tribute to François Arago, a French scientist and politician. There is a central monument on the island in the Seine, with a small bronze medallion with the name "Arago" placed on a massive stone structure. Another 134 medallions were also systematically placed throughout Paris on the route of the meridian; each medallion has notches to also mark north and south.

Ger van Elk is another Conceptual artist who uses photography techniques to alter perceptions of reality. In 1971, he took two photographs of a blacktop road, one of the wider road with an automobile passing by and the other, which was more detailed, being of a crack in the roadway, with a crushed aluminum can halfway in the crack; he titled the latter *The Discovery of the Sardines*. Using techniques similar to those of Escher, another van Elk work displayed a painted scene of a lake, but the painting is cut horizontally in half and framed by an optical illusionary border whereby it is twisted diagonally in a manner that gives the appearance of greater depth. In another Escheresque display, titled *Little Man Behind the Door* (1999), a door is propped up in a free-standing frame, and projected onto the door is a small child who appears to be behind the door, but the child's hand is also reaching out of the door to pull the handle.

Despite the transition in the late 19th century and 20th century from Realism to Impressionism and many other forms of abstract art, there are a small number of Dutch artists who have returned to a much older Realism and still life style made famous in the 17th century; currently, this broad group of painters are often referred to as conveying New Dutch Realism. Some in this late 20th- and early-21st-century group call themselves *Realistisch Fijn-schilders* (Realistic Fine Painters), and they take ordinary objects from nature or man-made objects and paint them in fine detail, using a variety of brush strokes. While not meant to be photographic in their quality, they display an appreciation for the textures and colors in nature. Aad Hofman painted *Rust* in 2000, and in this still life, he depicts discarded pieces of metal and a soft drink can beginning to rust, but rather than lament the previous usefulness of the objects, a beautiful natural rust tone frames the composition. Joke Frima offers another good example of a careful and detailed interpretation of nature in her still life *Painters Mussels* (2004), and in her *In the Shadow of the Plum Tree* (2001), she displays a pumpkin patch with large succulent leaves, wherein filtered light shines on the pumpkins.

Rob Møhlmann has also established a strong realistic style and, reminiscent of the use of the convex mirror employed by Quentin Matsys and Jan van Eyck in the 15th century, Jan Vermeer in the 17th century, and Escher in the early 20th century, he uses a convex mirror in several paintings that serve to absorb and reflect the world outside the painting. In his *Holland, Detail* (1985), one views a silver ball with breaks on the top and the reflection of the artist painting in his studio. Møhlmann has also perfected the very fine brush work of the 17th-century *fijnschilders*; in his still life painting *Cut for the Still Life* (1995), he has displayed in near photographic quality two bunches of pears with leaves laying on a wood structure with a pair of red clippers. Likewise, Hans Deuss picks up on the playfulness of Dutch still lifes with his *Box Spring* (2003), which turns the normal meaning of box spring from a picture of a bed to the literal vision of a small tree with rocks that serves as the origin of a water spring, set in a cardboard box.

The Netherlands is quite unique in its active support of the arts, and the Work and Artist Income Act (WWIK) has created supplemental incomes for any artist who qualifies, under certain regulations. Artists must have finished their education in a recognized art school, their income must be below €5,325 (U.S.$7,500) for a single person, and €10,650 (U.S.$15,000) for a family, they must demonstrate that they have earned some income from art, and their net worth must be below a certain level. In 2008, the allowance per month for a single person was €694.12 (U.S.$975) and, for a married couple, €1,014.28 (U.S.$1,400).

## NOTES

1. Several Web sites have excellent collections of Dutch art. See The Web Gallery of Art: http://www.wga.hu/index1.html; the Rijksmuseum Amsterdam: http://www.rijksmuseum.nl/index.jsp; the Maurits Huis Museum http://www.mauritshuis.nl/index; the Flemish Collection at the Louvre: http://www.louvre.fr/llv/commun/home.jsp; the Web Museum, Paris, http://www.ibiblio.org/wm/paint/; and Olga's Gallery, http://www.abcgallery.com. See also Hans Koning, *Modern Dutch Painting: An Introduction* (New York: Netherlands Information Service, 1950), http://online books.library.upenn.edu/webbin/book/lookupid?key=olbp43076.

2. See Paul Arblaster, *A History of the Low Countries* (New York: Palgrave Macmillan, 2006), 105: "The Flemish 'secret' was eagerly sought after by French and Italian artists, who traveled to Flanders to learn the techniques of such vibrant color. Depth was suggested not by a geometrical calculation of perspective (an Italian trick), but by the gradation of hues, achieved by the painstaking application of multiple layers of paint and gloss."

3. Craig Harbison, *The Mirror of the Artist: Northern Renaissance Art in Its Historical Context* (Upper Saddle River, NJ: Prentice Hall 1995), 33.

4. William Dyrness, *Reformed Theology and Visual Culture: The Protestant Imagination from Calvin to Edwards* (Cambridge: Cambridge University Press, 2004), 6.

5. See Mariët Westermann, *A Worldly Art: The Dutch Republic, 1585–1718* (New York: Harry N. Abrams, 1996), and Michael North, *Art and Commerce in the Dutch Golden Age* (New Haven, CT: Yale University Press, 1997).

6. Two contemporary critiques of art in the Golden Age are important sources for the study of art in this period, with one written at the beginning of the century, and the other toward the end. Karl van Mander, *Schilderboeck* (Haarlem: Passchier van Wesbusch, 1603–1604; *Book of Painting*, 1604), and Samuel van Hoogstraten, *Inleyding tot de Hooge Schoole der Schilderkonst* (*Introduction to the Art of Painting*, Rotterdam, 1678). The "Essential Vermeer" Web site is an excellent resource for both Vermeer and many other Golden Age Dutch artists. See http://www.essen tialvermeer.com/index.html.

7. See Simon Schama, *Rembrandt's Eyes* (New York: Alfred A. Knopf, 1999).

8. It was still the accepted wisdom from the Greco-Roman tradition that the four humors, black bile, yellow bile, phlegm, and blood, caused melancholy.

9. Hanneke Grootenboer, *The Rhetoric of Perspective: Realism and illusion in Seventeenth-Century Dutch Still-Life Painting* (Chicago: University of Chicago Press, 2005), 4. "These deceptive images demonstrate that realism in painting can be surpassed only by a form hyper-realism that takes us by surprise. The *trompe l'oeil* is a practical joke that mines our reliance on our perceptions. The moment we are snared by the *trompe l'oeil's* lure, we enter a realm of illusion that forces itself upon us as a truth, whose artificiality we detect belatedly."

10. See Gerard de Lairesse, *Grondlegginge der Teekenkonst* (*Foundations of Drawing*, 1701), and *Het Groot Schilderboeck* (*Great Book of Painting*, 1710).

11. Kathleen Powers Erikson, *At Eternity's Gate: The Spiritual Vision of Vincent van Gogh* (Grand Rapids, MI: Eerdmans, 1998), 74. See also Chapter 2: "Pilgrims and Strangers."

12. Van Gogh remained in Saint Remy until May 8, 1889, when he desired to be taken to the Saint Paul de Mausole Psychiatric Hospital in Saint-Rémy, but after finding no relief there, he left the institution to settle in Auvers-sur-Oise, which was much closer to his brother, Theo, in Paris. He committed suicide in Auvers-sur-Oise on July 27, 1890.

13. The full title of the journal is *De Stijl: Maandblad Voor Nieuwe Kunst, Wetenschap en Kultur* (*The Style: Monthly Journal for Art, Science, and Culture*).

# Selected Bibliography

Arblaster, Paul. *A History of the Low Countries*. New York: Palgrave Macmillan, 2006.

Andeweg, Rudy B. and Galen A. Irwin. *Governance and Politics of the Netherlands*. New York: Palgrave Macmillan, 2002.

Blom, J.C.H. and E. Lamberts, eds. *History of the Low Countries*. James C. Kennedy, trans. New York and Oxford: Berghahn Books, 1999.

Brandt, George W., ed. *German and Dutch Theatre, 1600–1848*. Cambridge: Cambridge University Press, 1993.

Cook, Harold J. *Matters of Exchange: Commerce, Medicine, and Science in the Dutch Golden Age*. New Haven, CT: Yale University Press, 2007.

Deursen, A.Th. van. *Plain Lives in a Golden Age: Popular Culture, Religion and Society in Seventeenth-Century Holland*, Maarten Ultee, trans. Cambridge: Cambridge University Press, 1991.

Duke, Alastair. *Reformation and Revolt in Low Countries*. London: Hambledon Press, 2003 [1990].

Gelderen, Martin van. *The Political Thought of the Dutch Revolt, 1555–1590*. Cambridge: Cambridge University Press, 1992.

Geyl, Pieter. *History of the Dutch-Speaking Peoples, 1555–1648*. London: Phoenix Press, 1961 [1932].

Hart, Marjolein C. 't, Joost Jonker, and Jan Luiten van Zanden, eds. *A Financial History of the Netherlands*. Cambridge: Cambridge University Press, 1997.

Israel, Jonathan I. *The Dutch Republic: Its Rise, Greatness, and Fall, 1477–1806*. Oxford: Clarendon Press, 1995.

Jacob, Margaret C., and Wijnand W. Mijnhardt, eds. *The Dutch Republic in the Eighteenth Century: Decline, Enlightenment, and Revolution.* Ithaca, NY: Cornell University Press, 1992.

Kossmann, E.H. *The Low Countries, 1780–1940.* Oxford: Oxford University Press, 1978.

Lijphart, Arend. *The Politics of Accommodation: Pluralism and Democracy in the Netherlands.* Berkeley: University of California Press, 1968.

Meijer, Reinder P. *Literature of the Low Countries: A Short History of Dutch Literature in the Netherlands and Belgium.* Leiden: Stichting dbnl, 2006.

Nienhuis, P. H. *Environmental History of the Rhine-Meuse Delta: An Ecological Story on Evolving Human-environmental Relations Coping with Climate Change and Sea-level Rise.* New York: Springer, 2008.

Nordholt, Jan Willem. *The Dutch Republic and American Independence.* Chapel Hill, NC: University of North Carolina Press, 1982.

Po-chia Hsia R., and Henk van Nierop, eds. *Calvinism and Religious Toleration in the Dutch Golden Age.* Cambridge: Cambridge University Press, 2002.

Prak, Maarten. *The Dutch Republic in the Seventeenth Century: The Golden Age.* Diane Webb, trans. Cambridge: Cambridge University Press, 2005.

Rosenberg, Jakob, Seymour Slive, and E.H. Ter Kuile. *Dutch Art and Architecture, 1600–1800.* New Haven, CT: Yale University Press, 1993 [1966].

Schama, Simon. *The Embarrassment of Riches: An Interpretation of Dutch Culture in the Golden Age.* Berkeley: University of California Press, 1988.

Shetter, William Z. *The Netherlands in Perspective: The Dutch Way of Organizing a Society and its Setting.* Utrecht: Nederlands Centrum Buitenlanders, 1997.

Vries, Jan de, and Ad van der Woude. *The First Modern Economy: Success, Failure, and Perseverance of the Dutch Economy, 1500–1815.* Cambridge: Cambridge University Press, 1997.

Westermann, Mariët. *A Worldy Art: The Dutch Republic 1585–1718.* New York: Harry M. Abrams, 1996.

Wintle, Michael J. *An Economic and Social History of the Netherlands, 1800–1920: Demographic, Economic and Social Transition.* Cambridge: Cambridge University Press, 2007.

Wintle, Michael J. *Pillars of Piety: Religion in the Netherlands in the Nineteenth Century, 1813–1901.* Hull, UK: Hull University Press, 1987.

Zumthor, Paul. *Daily Life in Rembrandt's Holland.* Simon Watson Taylor, trans. Palo Alto, CA: Stanford University Press, 1994.

# Index

## About the Author

JOHN B. RONEY is a scholar of European history and a professor in the Department of History at Sacred Heart University, Fairfield, Connecticut. His areas of research focus on the small states in Europe that have managed to remain independent since the Renaissance, including the Netherlands, Belgium, Luxembourg, Switzerland, and Ireland. The place of religion in society has been of particular interest, as well as the study of how historians have written about history. He regularly teaches in these areas, as well encompassing broader fields ranging from the medieval era to modern France.